BEACH BOYS ARCHIVES
VOLUME 2

FOREWORD

The 1960s marketing machine was working hard to keep the Beach Boys in the spotlight before and after the introduction of the Beatles in America.

Their massive amount of musical output was to the band's benefit. Few other groups enjoyed the creative output that the Beach Boys had in the beginning of their career. And that doesn't even include the outside projects Brian had, producing a variety of records for other artists and occasionally tossing off things like a half finished number one song for Jan & Dean.

Teens were clearly the target market with the cash to spend and the willingness to buy Beach Boys product, which accounts for the massive frequency their photos appeared in the teen magazines of the time. Sometimes the publications used stock promo photos, but much of the time they featured custom photography of the boys in concert, posing with animals, cars (of course) and other candid shots.

And even while the interviews seem quite contrived as publicists worked hard to maintain their image as wholesome, clean-cut group of guys, reality squeezed itself in from all sides. Carl's conscienscious objector status placed him in the spotlight as did Dennis' rather unfortunate choice of friends. Their failed tour with the Maharishi didn't help, either. And as music scene had changed, so had Brian and the designation of troubled genius seemed to brand him. Which set the whole band up for the Brian's Back campaign of 1976, whether or not there was any real truth in it.

But all of it gave fans a wealth of reading material, and for you, the ability to look back on it all with an historical perspective. knowing what was still to come. So enjoy!

ISBN 978-1-941028-99-5
Copyright 2014 White Lightning Publications

All reprinted materials believed to be in the public domain, copyright abandoned as the publishing companies have folded or we have received permission to reprint these materials within. If you believe we are in error, please contact us with proof of ownership and copyright status so that the pieces can be removed from subsequent printings. We've worked hard to find good, reproduction-quality originals and did our best to clean up the digital scans for reproduction.

I GET AROUND 45 AD

THE BEACH BOYS

Portrait of the Industry's most consistent Hit-Makers.
They've just made a new one (both sides, as usual).

I GET AROUND b/w DON'T WORRY BABY
5174

SUMMER DAYS (AND SUMMER NIGHTS) LP AD

GOD ONLY KNOWS 45 AD

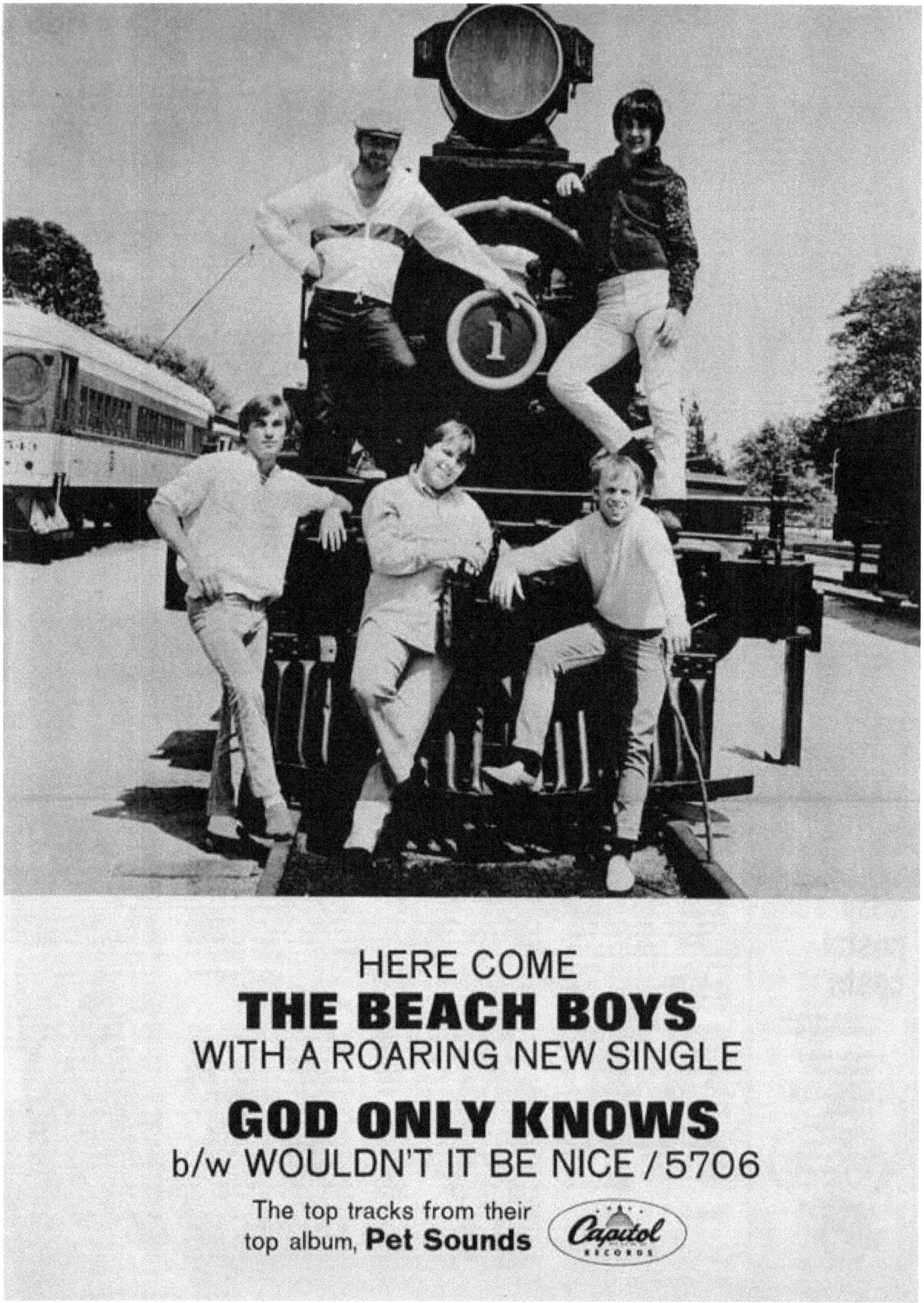

HERE COME
THE BEACH BOYS
WITH A ROARING NEW SINGLE

GOD ONLY KNOWS
b/w WOULDN'T IT BE NICE / 5706

The top tracks from their top album, **Pet Sounds**

BEACH BOYS - LEAD GUITAR MUSIC

409/SURFIN' SAFARI JUKE BOX STRIP SHEET

CAPITOL 4777

"409" ☆ THE BEACH BOYS ☆ **"SURFIN' SAFARI"** CAPITOL 4777	**"409"** ☆ THE BEACH BOYS ☆ **"SURFIN' SAFARI"** CAPITOL 4777
"409" ☆ THE BEACH BOYS ☆ **"SURFIN' SAFARI"** CAPITOL 4777	**"409"** ☆ THE BEACH BOYS ☆ **"SURFIN' SAFARI"** CAPITOL 4777
"409" ☆ THE BEACH BOYS ☆ **"SURFIN' SAFARI"** CAPITOL 4777	**"409"** ☆ THE BEACH BOYS ☆ **"SURFIN' SAFARI"** CAPITOL 4777
"409" ☆ THE BEACH BOYS ☆ **"SURFIN' SAFARI"** CAPITOL 4777	**"409"** ☆ THE BEACH BOYS ☆ **"SURFIN' SAFARI"** CAPITOL 4777
"409" ☆ THE BEACH BOYS ☆ **"SURFIN' SAFARI"** ☆ THE BEACH BOYS ☆	**"409"** ☆ THE BEACH BOYS ☆

★ STAR TITLE STRIP CO., INC.
842 Western Avenue   Pittsburgh 33, Pa.
Copyright 1957   Printed in U.S.A.

BEACH BOYS INTERNATIONAL FAN CLUB INC.

BASIC FACTS

NAME :
  BRIAN DOUGLAS WILSON
BIRTHDATE:
  June 20, 1942
MARITAL STATUS
  Married: Daughter-Carnie
ASTROLOGICAL SIGNS:
  Sun: Gemini
  Moon: Virgo

NAME
  CARL DEAN WILSON
BIRTHDATE:
  Dec. 21, 1946
MARITAL STATUS
  Married - Son - Jonah
ASTROLOGICAL SIGNS
  Sun - Sagittarius
  Moon - Sagittarius

NAME
  BRUCE ARTHUR JOHNSTON
BIRTHDATE :
  June 27, 1942
MARITAL STATUS:
  SINGLE
ASTROLOGICAL SIGNS:
  Sun - Cancer
  Moon - Taurus

NAME
  ALAN CHARLES JARDINE
BIRTHDATE:
  Sept. 3, 1942
MARITAL STATUS
  Married - Son - Matthew
ASTROLOGICAL SIGNS:
  Sun - Virgo
  Moon - Gemini

NAME:
  MICHAEL EDWARD LOVE
BIRTHDATE:
  March 15, 1941
MARITAL STATUS: (In Process of Divorce)
  2 Children - Hayleigh and christian
ASTROLOGICAL SIGNS:
  Sun - Pisces
  Moon - Libra

NAME:
  DENNIS CARL WILSON
BIRTHDATE:
  Dec. 4, 1944
MARITAL STATUS:
  Divorced / Two Children
         Scott and Jennifer
ASTROLOGICAL SIGNS:
  Sun: Sagittarius
  Moon: Leo

BEACH BOYS FAN CLUB 1960s

ATTENTION!   ALL BEACH BOYS FANS

Each and every fan of The Beach Boys will want to own this beautiful pictorial calendar -- in beautiful color -- with a different photo of the boys on each page. The calendar opens to 10"x16" in size. It sells for $1.00 and every fan will want to own one. How else could you have the Beach Boys with you.....every day of the year?
Get your order in now!

FOR THE FIRST TIME ANYWHERE IN BEAUTIFUL COLOR

YOUR Beach Boys PICTORIAL CALENDAR FOR 1968

For immediate attention write CALENDAR on envelope.

Please cut along dotted lines and return coupon with payment of $1.00 to:

CALENDAR
P. O. Box 1057
Beverly Hills, Calif.

PLEASE PRINT

Name _____
Address _____
City _____
State _____ Zip Code _____

◀ BEACH BOYS CALENDAR ▶

BEACH BOYS FAN CLUB 1960s

BEACH BOYS FAN CLUB 1960s

January

s	m	t	w	t	f	s
						1
2	3	4	5	6	7	8
9	10	11	12	13	14	15
16	17	18	19	20	21	22
23/30	24/31	25	26	27	28	29

February

s	m	t	w	t	f	s
		1	2	3	4	5
6	7	8	9	10	11	12
13	14	15	16	17	18	19
20	21	22	23	24	25	26
27	28					

BEACH BOYS FAN CLUB 1960s

March

s	m	t	w	t	f	s
		1	2	3	4	5
6	7	8	9	10	11	12
13	14	15	16	17	18	19
20	21	22	23	24	25	26
27	28	29	30	31		

April

s	m	t	w	t	f	s
					1	2
3	4	5	6	7	8	9
10	11	12	13	14	15	16
17	18	19	20	21	22	23
24	25	26	27	28	29	30

BEACH BOYS FAN CLUB 1960s

May

s	m	t	w	t	f	s
1	2	3	4	5	6	7
8	9	10	11	12	13	14
15	16	17	18	19	20	21
22	23	24	25	26	27	28
29	30	31				

June

s	m	t	w	t	f	s
			1	2	3	4
5	6	7	8	9	10	11
12	13	14	15	16	17	18
19	20	21	22	23	24	25
26	27	28	29	30		

BEACH BOYS FAN CLUB 1960s

July

s	m	t	w	t	f	s
					1	2
3	4	5	6	7	8	9
10	11	12	13	14	15	16
17	18	19	20	21	22	23
24/31	25	26	27	28	29	30

August

s	m	t	w	t	f	s
	1	2	3	4	5	6
7	8	9	10	11	12	13
14	15	16	17	18	19	20
21	22	23	24	25	26	27
28	29	30	31			

BEACH BOYS FAN CLUB 1960s

September

s	m	t	w	t	f	s
				1	2	3
4	5	6	7	8	9	10
11	12	13	14	15	16	17
18	19	20	21	22	23	24
25	26	27	28	29	30	

October

s	m	t	w	t	f	s
						1
2	3	4	5	6	7	8
9	10	11	12	13	14	15
16	17	18	19	20	21	22
23/30	24/31	25	26	27	28	29

BEACH BOYS FAN CLUB 1960s

		November								December				
s	m	t	w	t	f	s		s	m	t	w	t	f	s
		1	2	3	4	5						1	2	3
6	7	8	9	10	11	12		4	5	6	7	8	9	10
13	14	15	16	17	18	19		11	12	13	14	15	16	17
20	21	22	23	24	25	26		18	19	20	21	22	23	24
27	28	29	30					25	26	27	28	29	30	31

SURFSIDE '64 AUSTRALIAN TOUR

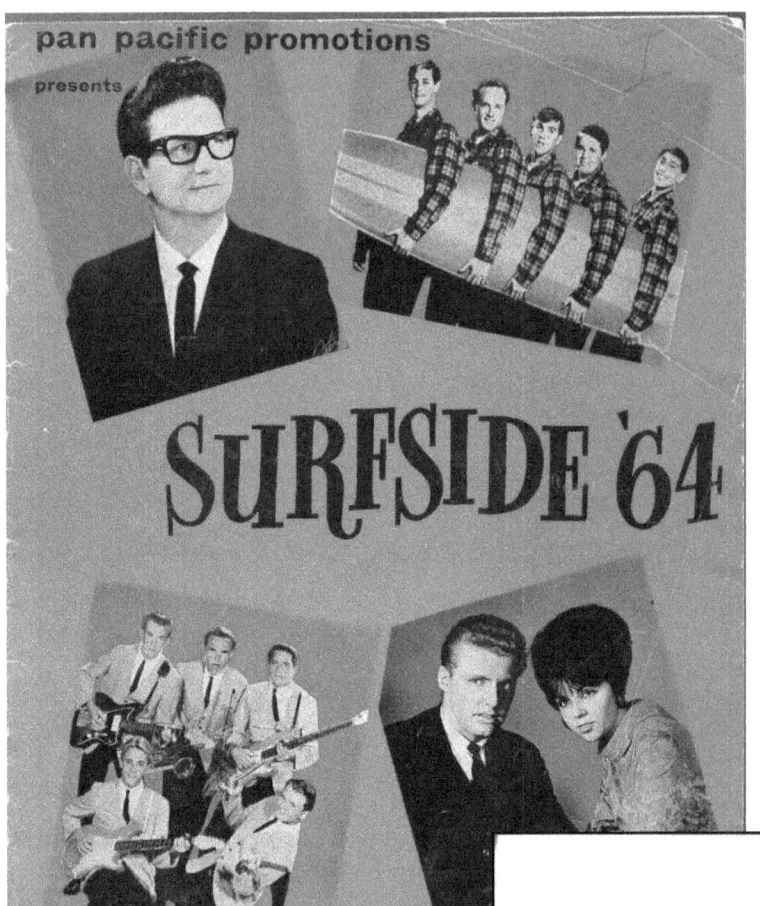

TERRIFIC DISCS
BY "THE BIG O", THE BEACH BOYS AND THE SURFARIS!

ROY ORBISON

12" Long Play		7" Single Play	
Lonely and Blue	HAA.2342	Only The Lonely/Here Comes That Song Again	HL.1671
Crying	HAA.7691	Running Scared/Love Hurts	HL.1811
Roy Orbison's Greatest Hits	HAA.7710	Crying/Candy Man	HL.1853
In Dreams	HAA.7737	Dream Baby/The Actress	HL.1932
		The Crowd/Mama	HL.1966
7" Extended Play		Evergreen/Lone Star	HL.1990
Only The Lonely	EZA.7560	Working For The Man/Leah	HL.2011
In Dreams	EZA.7564	In Dreams/Shahdaroba	HL.2069
Roy Orbison	EZA.7576	Falling/Distant Drums	HL.2111
		Blue Bayou/Mean Woman Blues	HL.2137
		Pretty Paper/Beautiful Dreamer	HL.2160

THE BEACH BOYS

12" Long Play		7" Single Play	
Little Deuce Coupe	T.1998	Surfin' Safari/409	CP.1484
Surfin' Safari	T.1808	Ten Little Indians/County Fair	CP.1503
Surfin' U.S.A.	T.1890	Surfin' U.S.A./Shut Down	CP.1517
Surfer Girl	T.1981	Surfer Girl/Little Deuce Coupe	CP.1533
7" Extended Play		Be True To Your School/In My Room	CP.1545
Surfin' Safari	EAP.1-20529		
Surfer Girl	EAP.1-20548		

THE SURFARIS

12" LONG PLAY — Wipe Out	HAA.7735
7" EXTENDED PLAY — Surf's Up	EZA.7570
7" SINGLE PLAY — Wipe Out/Surfer Joe	HL.2112

 the greatest recording organisation in the world.

SURFSIDE '64 AUSTRALIAN TOUR

Foreword

In filling the entertainment needs of Australia in all its varied forms — jazz, variety and the pops — the needs of the swinging younger set could easily be overlooked. That is one mistake that my partner Denis Wong and I do not intend to make.

And just to prove our point, we are setting the entertainment scene alight for 1964 with one of the most talent-filled packages of stars ever imported to this country.

No fewer than 16 topline American stars are represented in the "Surfside '64" show. Each is hand-picked to suit the tastes of the young Australian which have been reflected in record sales and the hit charts. Each artist is currently a big name in the hit parades of the world. Not youngsters who might be a big name in the future. Not veterans who were big once. But a whole troupe of stars who are right now riding high everywhere their music is heard.

You need no assurance from us that Roy Orbison, the Beach Boys, the Surfaris, and Paul and Paula are all at the top of the tree. Your enthusiasm for them, and your record purchases, have helped to put them there.

And if this treat seems too good to be true, please remember that this is only the beginning. We plan to keep right up with every new trend in the record business. As stars are born and hit records are cut, we will have your taste in mind. In the future, as now, we will bring you the best the world of entertainment has to offer.

We wish you much happiness and good fortune in this new year.

Sincerely,

Harry M. Miller

PAN PACIFIC PROMOTIONS wish to thank ...
E.M.I. Records, Philips Records, Travel Lodge (Sydney & Hobart), S...
American Airways, Ansett ANA, Chequers Nightclub, Sydney, Stadi...
friends in Radio, Newspapers and TV who have helped us so much...
PAN PACIFIC PROMOTIONS PTY. LTD., Box 60, Haymarket, Sydney. Printed by...

The Beach Boys

SURFSIDE '64 AUSTRALIAN TOUR

About the fabulous...
BEACH BOYS

When a group of sun-tanned young Americans recorded a song about their favourite sport, they had no idea that the tune was destined to ride a wave of popularity that would rival the sport itself.

But the song, "Surfin' U.S.A." became an overnight sensation and the group, calling themselves "The Beach Boys", found themselves recording stars. Their sequel, "Surfin' Safari", was as big a hit as their first.

The group is comprised mainly of Wilsons — from Hawthorne, California. There is Brian, Dennis, Carl and their father, Murray, a song-writer who acts as manager of the outfit. Then there is the boys' talented cousin, Mike Love, composer of "Surfin' U.S.A.". The remaining member is young David Marks, a neighbour of the Wilsons, who plays a driving rhythm guitar.

Brian, oldest of the Wilson boys, is the group's leader and vocal arranger. Carl is the accomplished lead guitarist, while brother Dennis sings as well as playing drums. None has had any formal training, but they all grew up in an atmosphere where music was an integral part of their lives. Everyone of them possesses tremendous natural ability, and each has a fine singing voice, too.

Their remarkable success, including further hits like "Be True To Your School" and "In My Room", has led to TV guest appearances, spots in network radio shows and now this tour of Australia and New Zealand. And, despite their busy life as entertainers, they still manage to squeeze time for their favourite sport of surfing.

PAN PACIFIC PROMOTIONS PRESENTS, DIRECT FROM AMERICA

SURFSIDE '64

Itinerary: BRISBANE — JAN 15th; SYDNEY — JAN. 17th & 18th; ADELAIDE — JAN. 20th; MELBOURNE — JAN 21st & 22nd; HOBART — JAN 23rd.

★ ★ ★ PROGRAMME ★ ★ ★

The Sensational Incomparable
ROY ORBISON
A Selection from
Only the Lonely; Blue Bayou; Crying; Runnin' Scared; Working For The Man; Pretty Paper; Mean Woman Blues; Uptown; I'm Hurtin'; Beautiful Dreamer.

DYNAMIC —
THE BEACH BOYS
A Selection from
Surfin' U.S.A.; Honky Tonk; Misirlou; Lana; Surfin' Safari; Surf Jam; Be True To Your School; Shut Down; Surfer Girl

FANTASTICS —
THE SURFARIS
A Selection from
Wipeout; Point Panic; Teen Beat; Green Onions; Memphis; Surfer Joe; Wild Weekend; Tequila; Wiggle Wobble.

WONDERFUL —
PAUL & PAULA
A Selection from
Hey Paula; Flipped Over You; You Send Me; So Fine; First Day Back At School; Love Comes Once; Oh What Love; We Go Together.

THE JOYBOYS

SURFSIDE '64 NEW ZEALAND TOUR

HARRY M. MILLER presents:

SURFSIDE '64

Starring:
**ROY ORBISON
THE BEACH BOYS
THE SURFARIS
PAUL & PAULA**
THE JOYBOYS

NEW ZEALAND TOUR

Foreword...

In filling the entertainment needs of New Zealand in all its varied forms — jazz, variety, concert attractions and the pops — the needs of younger theatre-goers could easily be overlooked. That is one mistake I do not intend to make.

In recent years I have been proud to present for you top American recording stars right at the peak of their careers. There have been Chubby Checker, King of the Twist, Bobby Rydell, Del Shannon, the Everly Brothers, Bobby Vee, Linda Scott, Connie Francis, the Kingston Trio, Gene Pitney... That by no means completes the list. But you will remember them all, because you helped to fill the halls. And it was your support and enthusiasm which made each successive show possible.

So it is only fair that 1964 should open with a really big treat for those young people who have supported me so well in the past — the biggest entertainment treat, in fact, ever presented in this country.

"Surfside '64" presents 22 overseas stars, 16 of them from the United States, and each one of them currently a big name in the hit parades of the world. Not artists who have been a big success in the past. Not entertainers who might be big in the future. A whole talent-filled troupe of stars who are right now riding high everywhere their music is heard.

You need no assurance from me that Roy Orbison, Paul and Paula, the Surfaris, the Beach Boys and the Joy Boys are all at the top of the tree. All that remains now is for you to relax and enjoy them.

Sincerely,

Harry M. Miller

WATCH FOR
PETER, PAUL & MARY
IN PERSON!

SURFSIDE '64 NEW ZEALAND TOUR

The Beach Boys

About the fabulous...
BEACH BOYS

When a group of sun-tanned young Americans recorded a song about their favourite sport, they had no idea that the tune was destined to ride a wave of popularity that would rival the sport itself.

But the song, "Surfin' U.S.A." became an overnight sensation and the group, calling themselves "The Beach Boys", found themselves recording stars. Their sequel, "Surfin' Safari", was as big a hit as their first.

The group is comprised mainly of Wilsons — from Hawthorne, California. There is Brian, Dennis, Carl and their father, Murray, a song writer who acts as manager of the outfit. Then there is the boys' talented cousin, Mike Love, composer of "Surfin' U.S.A.". The remaining member is young David Marks, a neighbour of the Wilsons, who plays a driving rhythm guitar.

Brian, oldest of the Wilson boys, is the group's leader and vocal arranger. Carl is the accomplished lead guitarist, while brother Dennis sings as well as playing drums. None has had any formal training, but they all grew up in an atmosphere where music was an integral part of their lives. Everyone of them possesses tremendous natural ability, and each has a fine singing voice, too.

Their remarkable success, including further hits like "Be True To Your School" and "In My Room" has led to TV guest appearances, spots in network radio shows and now this tour of Australia and New Zealand. And despite their busy life as topline entertainers, they still manage to squeeze in some time for their favourite sport of surfing.

SURFSIDE '64 NEW ZEALAND TOUR

HARRY M. MILLER PRESENTS, DIRECT FROM AMERICA

SURFSIDE '64
NEW ZEALAND TOUR

PROGRAMME

The Sensational Incomparable
ROY ORBISON
A Selection from
Only the Lonely; Blue Bayou; Crying; Runnin' Scared; Working For The Man; Pretty Paper; Mean Woman Blues; Uptown; I'm Hurtin'; Beautiful Dreamer.

DYNAMIC—
THE BEACH BOYS
A Selection from
Surfin' U.S.A.; Honky Tonk; Misirlou; Lana; Surfin' Safari; Surf Jam; Be True To Your School; Shut Down; Surfer Girl.

FANTASTIC—
THE SURFARIS
A Selection from
Wipeout; Point Panic; Teen Beat; Green Onions; Memphis; Surfer Joe; Wild Weekend; Tequila; Wiggle Wobble.

WONDERFUL—
PAUL & PAULA
A Selection from
Hey Paula; Flipped Over You; You Send Me; So Fine; First Day Back At School; Love Comes Once; Oh What Love; We Go Together.

THE JOYBOYS

RECORDINGS BY ROY ORBISON; THE BEACH BOYS & THE SURFARIS

12" LP HAM-U 6364 — Roy Orbison "In Dreams".
Numbers include: In Dreams, Shahdaroba, Sunset, Dream, All I have to do is Dream, My Prayer.

12" LP HAM 6164 — Roy Orbison sings: "Lonely and Blue".
Numbers include: Only the Lonely, Bye-Bye, Love, I Can't Stop Loving You, Raindrops, I'm Hurtin', I'll say it's my fault.

12" LP HAM-U 6215 — Roy Orbison "Crying".
Numbers include: Crying, Love Hurts, Wedding Day, Lana, Loneliness, Running Scared.

12" LP HAM-U 6236 — "Roy Orbison's Greatest Hits."
Numbers include: Only the Lonely, Crying, Running Scared, Dream Baby, The Crowd, Blue Angel, I'm Hurtin'.

45 EP Recording REM-U 6020 — "In Dreams" Roy Orbison.
Numbers: In Dreams, Shahdaroba, Falling, Distant Drums.

45 RPM Singles:
NZL-U873 "Mean Woman Blues" B/W Blue Bayou.
NZL-U 839 "In Dreams" B/W Shahdaroba.
NZL-U 857 "Falling" B/W "Distant Drums".

12" LP HAM-O 6259 — "Wipe Out" The Surfaris.
Numbers include: Wipe Out, Torquay, You Can't Sit Down, Green Onions, Wild Weekend, Teen Beat, Surfer Joe, Walk, Don't Run.

Coming Soon . . . .
45 EP Recording — "Wipe Out", The Surfaris.
Watch for it at Record Bars.

4 5RPM Recording:
NZL 863 "Surfer Joe" B/W Wipe Out.

12" LP T 1808 — Surfin' Safari — The Beach Boys.
Numbers include: Surfin' Safari, Ten Little Indians, Little Miss America, Surfin', Cuckoo Clock, The Shift.

Coming . . . to be released soon!

12" LP "Surfer Girl" The Beach Boys.
Numbers include: Surfer Girl, Catch A Wave, The Rocking Surfer, In My Room, Our Car Club, Boogie Woodie.

And 45 EP Recording: Surfin' U.S.A. — The Beach Boys.
Numbers: Surfin' U.S.A., Shut Down, Surfer Girl, Surfin' Safari.

45 RPM Singles:
F4932 "Surfin' U.S.A." B/W "Shut Down".
F5009 "Surfer Girl" B/W "Little Deuce Coupe".

1254

Products of
HIS MASTERS VOICE (N.Z.) LTD.
P.O. BOX 296, WELLINGTON

STEEL PIER, ATLANTIC CITY NJ PROGRAM 1960s

KFRC BLASTOFF

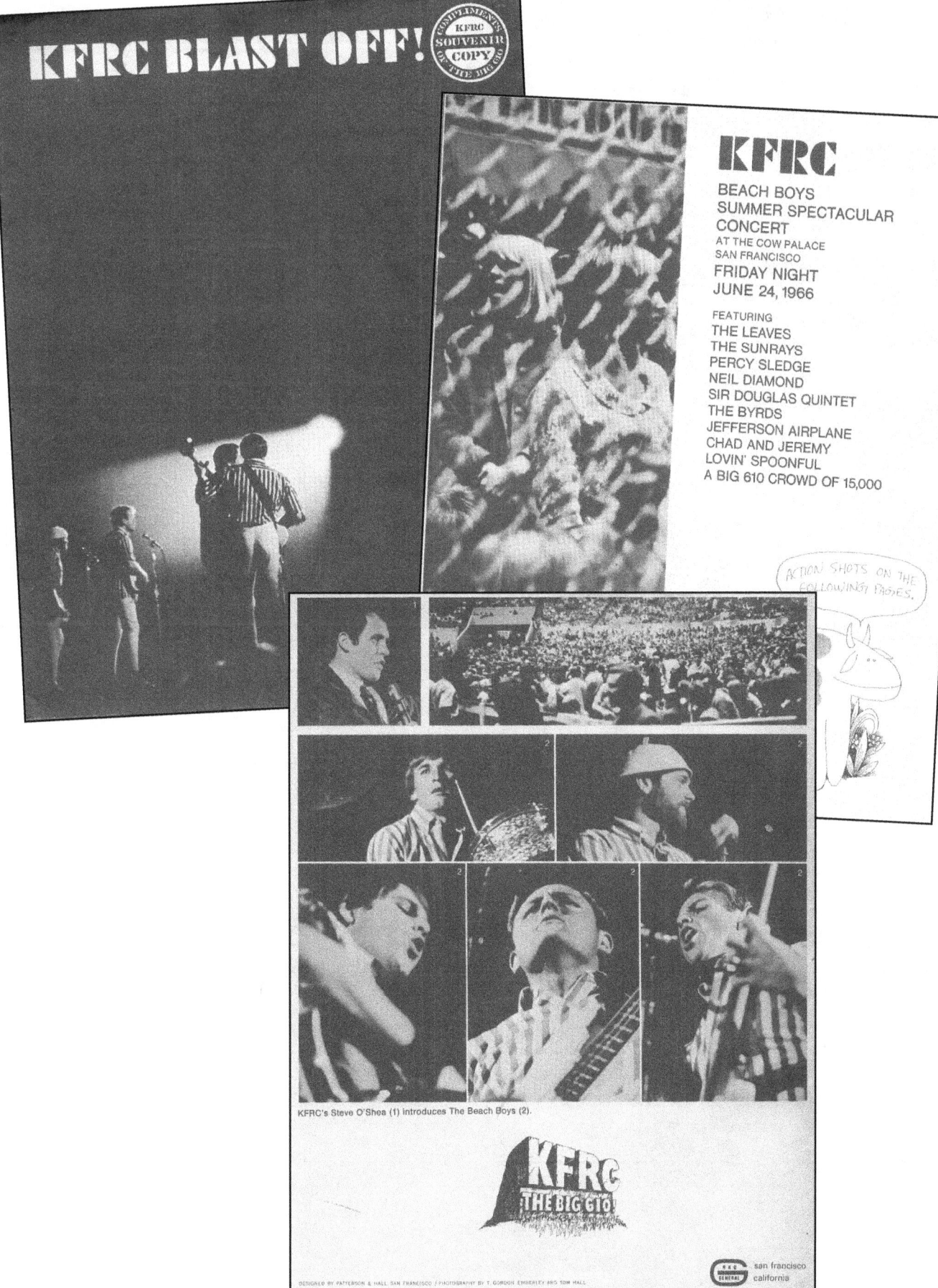

DULUTH ARENA AUDITORIUM 1966

The Beach Boys in the Arena Saturday, August 13.

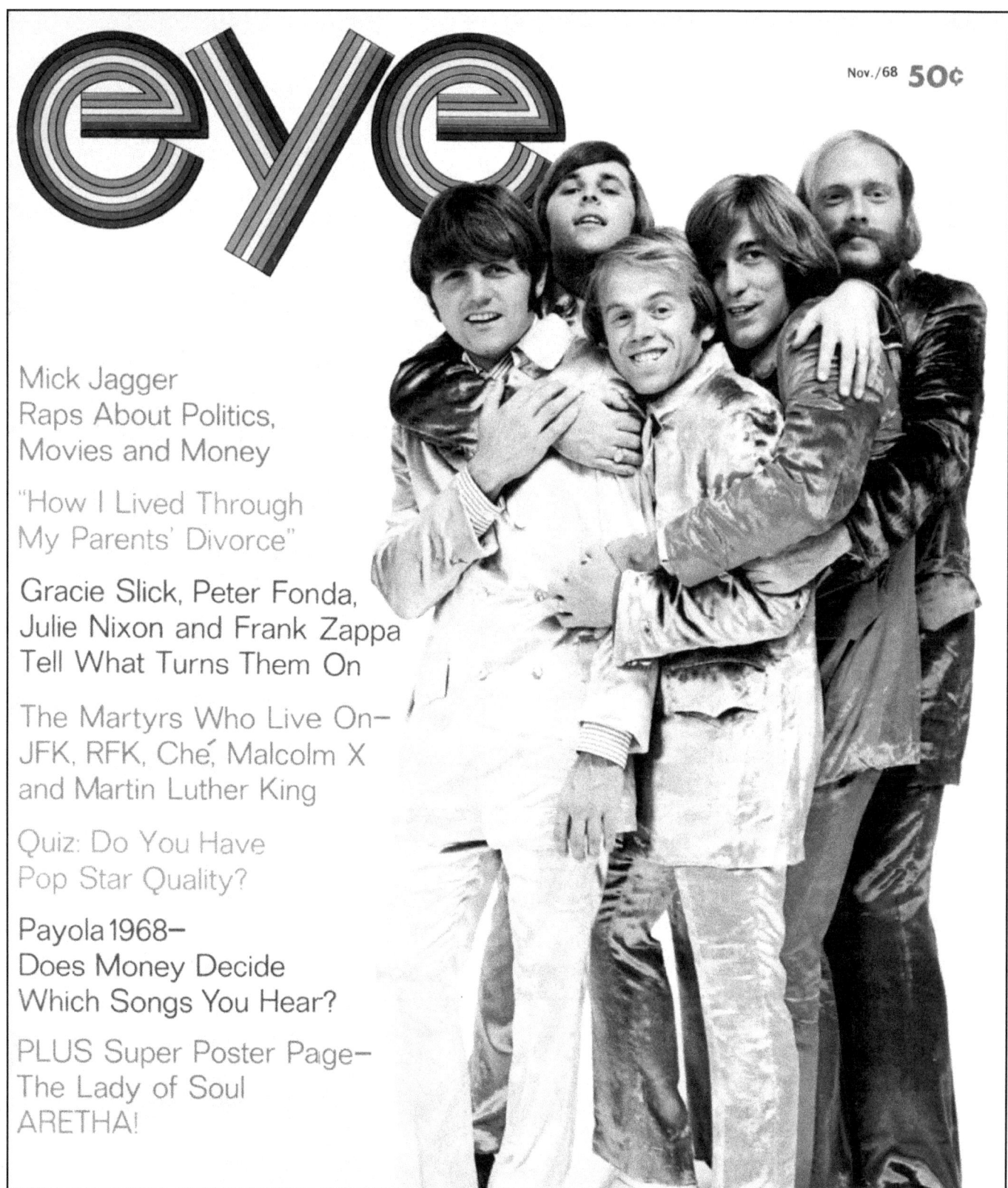

EYE

THE BEACH BOYS

PHOTOGRAPH BY J. BARRY O'ROURKE

Though it seems like ancient history, it was only five years ago that a wave of surf music broke upon the rock world. Riding the crest were the Beach Boys. Born of sand and foam, nurtured by the relentless beat of the surf, their music chronicled and proclaimed the quest for monster waves and golden tans. In wholesome harmony the boys sang "Surfin' USA," "Surfer Girl," "Catch a Wave," "California Girls," and America loved them. The surf music craze washed out to sea, but by that time the Beach Boys were already caught in more complex musical currents. In fact, "Good Vibrations," a kind of pop symphony, and one of the most remarkable singles ever released, was musically so demanding that Brian Wilson had to give up touring with the group to produce it. Now Brian concentrates on preparing Beach Boys albums while the rest of the group tours. They have concerts in Europe at the end of this month and visit the Orient next spring to do five benefits for UNICEF. It was at a UNICEF concert in Paris last December that the group met the Maharishi; they remain his disciples. On tour the Beach Boys are (left to right) Bruce Johnston, Mike Love, Dennis Wilson and Carl Wilson (Brian's younger brothers) and Alan Jardine.

PR PHOTO

PR PHOTO

THE BEACH BOYS (LEFT TO RIGHT) MIKE LOVE, AL JARDINE, BRIAN WILSON, CARL WILSON, DENNIS WILSON

AT LAST WE MEET THE

HULLABALOO got word that the Beach Boys were coming to town. Since we have been in business, the Beach Boys have never been in the New York area, so here was our opportunity finally to meet one of the biggest, if not *the* biggest, powers in American pop music.

We asked HULLABALOO photographer Glen Craig to follow the boys around and get this exclusive layout for us. First we went out to the Commack Arena on Long Island on a Wednesday night where the Beach Boys played to 8,000 fans. After a minor hassle with their road manager, Dick Duryea (Dan's son), we were able to get these great action shots on stage. From there we went to Newark on the following Saturday afternoon to Symphony Hall where they played to another 6,000 loyal fans. Here we were able to have an intimate conversation with the boys and capture their many moods on film, as you can see in these exclusive candids of Mike, Dennis, Al, Bruce, and Carl.

DENNIS WILSON: This 22-year-old Beach Boy drummer, sex-symbol, and singer is an untameable individualist who belongs to womankind, for there has never been a more complete ladies' man...

CARL WILSON: Brother of Dennis and Brian, 20-year-old lead guitarist Carl is possessed of an inordinate modesty which causes him to say that without the Beach Boys, he'd be nothing. They wouldn't care to be without him...

AL JARDINE: 24-year-old, blonde, blue-eyed Al was born in Lima, Ohio. Watch Alan's 5' 5", 135-lb. frame on stage. He is a very pulled-together man. Neat, tidy, deft. He dresses well and drives carefully. He has never had an accident. He has inner strength and it shows...

  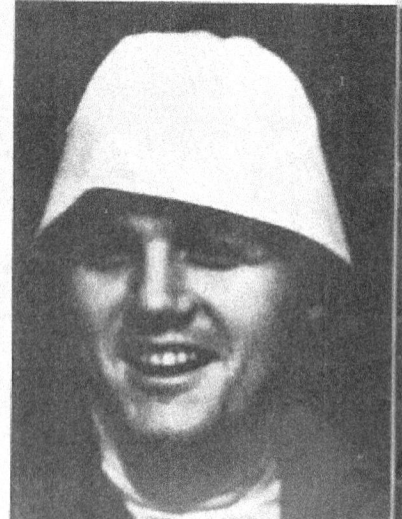

BEACH BOYS

MIKE LOVE: Non-conformist, individualist, 26-year-old Mike Love is blissfully happy and artistically fulfilled as the hugely popular stage-leader and MC of the Beach Boys. With his red beard or without, this lean, rangy figure prowls the stage hugging a microphone and whipping the group and audience into mutual excitement...

BRUCE JOHNSTON: He is 23-years-old, born in Chicago, has brown hair and blue eyes. Bruce Johnston is very clever, very healthy, very ambitious, and, potentially, very rich. His wealth, derived from drug stores and canning, is in a trust fund. He hopes that he may one day be trusted with the fund. For the present, he earns his own living, diligently and hard. His ambition is to win an Oscar for songwriting by the time he is thirty...

Fotos: Glen Craig

ALBUM AD

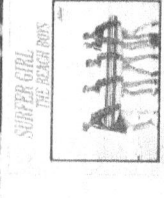

MUSIC BUSINESS
AUGUST 15, 1964

The Beach Boys ride the trends

Songs about surfing, hot rods and motor scooters have made them the symbol of California youth and helped them sell millions of records

They even do their own repair work

One of the most exciting new sounds in the record business, created and started by American artists and producers, is the West Coast pop sound. It has taken its place as one of the powerful forces in the industry, sparked by a flock of young, male artists on the West Coast like The Beach Boys, Jan & Dean, The Rip Chords, The Chantays, The Marketts, The Surfaris, and Dick Dale.

The West Coast pop sound has been identified as the "surf," the "hot rod," the "motor scooter," or in general, the outdoor sound, a sound loosely tied in with various favorite outdoor sports practiced by youthful cultists in the California sunshine.

Basically, the West Coast approach breaks down into two catagories: the vocal style, as exemplified by the Beach Boys, Jan & Dean and the Rip Chords, and the instrumental music, proponents of which are Dick Dale, The Chantays and the Marketts.

The Beach Boys, one of the hottest acts on record today, started their hit string with a surfing record on Capitol, and claim to have sired the original surf music movement.

The Surfing Sound

Says Beach Boys leader, Brian Wilson: "All the kids were interested in surfing and I remember one day when my brother Dennis came home from high school telling me about his friends who thought I should write a song about surfing. I was always playing around with

CONTINUED ON NEXT PAGE

songs anyway, hoping maybe I could get into the business some day, so I took a crack at it right away. We called it "Surfin'," and my two brothers and a couple of friends and I recorded it on our own. My brother Carl, who was 14, was the only one who could play an instrument, the guitar, and he played it on the record. That was in September of '61 and we got the record out on a small label.

"Then, a few months later, my father, Murry Wilson, got excited about our possibilities and took one of our masters to Capitol Records where he saw Ken Nelson. Mr. Nelson referred him to Nick Venet who finally saw him after a five-week wait and flipped over the record."

Capitol's a. & r. vice president, Voyle Gilmore, says that when Venet played him the tapes, he (Gilmore) said "Don't let that man get away. We want to sign these boys up." And that's what happened.

The two sides, "Surfin' Safari" and "409," were released right away. "We thought the 'Surfin'' side would hit on the West Coast and that '409' (which was about a Chevrolet) might hit in the East. But 'Surfin',' broke in Detroit and we figured we had something," said Gilmore.

It was one of the first major so-called "surf" hits. At nearly the same time the Marketts, one of the beach-based instrumental groups, came out with "Surfer's Stomp," and "Balboa Blue," examples of another wing of the evolving West Coast sound.

"After that one hit," said Wilson, a good looking young Californian, who prefers to sit in his office and think and work to cavorting on the beach, "We all took up instruments. We learned how to play in a very few months. Now I play bass and we have two guitars and drums. We've evolved about 800 percent since we started and that's in just two years. What happened was that I learned the art of production. In fact, now, I think we've evolved away from the strictly West Coast feeling. I've brought some eastern production values into our records, because you can't stand still in this business.

Riding the trend

"We rode the surfing trend while it was hot. There was a good identification there. You know, like the outdoor image and that scene. But I saw a chance to maybe broaden the appeal without really changing the style at all. You know how kids are with the cars. Well, I just started writing different types of lyrics with the same musical sound, and right away we had another something going for us."

Capitol and the Beach Boys actually contrived to break the new hot-rod trend while holding the surf beach-head at the same time. That happened with the single which coupled "Surfin' U.S.A." and "Shutdown." It's the only single in recent memory that ever spawned two separate hit albums, each one bearing the title of each individual hit single side.

It also gave birth to a rash of hot rod albums from a rash of West Coast labels, just as it happened at first with the surf

CONTINUED ON NEXT PAGE

Lads have built a solid campus following

"I Get Around" Hits Million

The Beach Boys celebrated their first million seller last week. Record Industry Association auditors qualified "I Get Around," as a gold record winner. An earlier hit, "Surfin' U.S.A.," is also nudging the million mark, although out considerably longer. Beyond all this, the boys' first five albums have sold a total of well over a million.

The group has had an unusually hot summer, from the box office standpoint, on an extended tour through the midwest and west. For approximately the first 20 dates (through July 28), they played to 98,000 (average gate of 5,000) and drew a total gross of $206,000 (for an average of $8,900). Their gross at a Sacramento concert last Saturday (1), where they were to do a live album recording, was $25,000, of which the group received 70 percent.

Ready for rehearsals at UCLA campus

scene. Typically, the albums were profusely illustrated with magnificent four-color photos of action surf scenes, and of the many kinds of favorite hot rods in vogue with the drag-minded set.

"A lot of those albums were sold," Wilson observed, "and for several reasons. Partly it was the material, but it was also the pictures and the information and the tables of words used by this group or that group. They were playing on the two great loves of young kids, their music, and their fads."

The Honda scene

"But now you don't see so many of the surfing and the hot rod albums. Surfing, in fact is strictly passe. And hot rods have hit their peak too. Now it's the Honda scene. You've got to be on the motor scooter kick now to be really 'in'.

"**We have a song** about 'Little Honda,' in our new album and it's getting played like it was a single. That is the new kick. I don't know what will be next. Some of the younger people are trying sidewalk surfing now, where you get a board and put some wheels under it and stand up on it going down a hill just like you were going down a wave. But I don't think that will catch on.

"As far as the Beach Boys are concerned, we just want to keep on identifying with what the young people like to do and like to think about. It doesn't have to be specifically about surfing or cars or scooters. Our new single will be called 'When I Grow Up (To Be a Man).' That certainly touches what every guy is thinking about.

"**I'm a little afraid** of limiting our subject matter too much. In fact, I want us to just keep building as a good vocal group with a well-developed sound. Some people say some of our harmonies sound like the Four Freshmen. That's no accident. The Freshmen have been the greatest for years. Their arranger, Dick Reynolds, is practically a god to me. What he does has been a great influence on me and the group.

"I just want to keep developing that sound. I don't know where we'll be five years from now. I can't look that far ahead. One year is enough and we'll be here, I hope, singing better than ever. But there's no sense in moving too fast.

"**There's a lot of work** in this but I like working. The other guys can have the fun, and they do. Dennis is the only real surfer we've got and he still does it. He also has an XKE and a Sting Ray. Carl drives around in a Grand Prix. But I'm usually in the office thinking and writing stuff. I don't go out of my way to write a lot for others but I did write 'Surf City,' 'Drag City' and 'New Girl in School' for Jan and Dean. Once in awhile I get out long enough to play some tennis. I played football in school and I like the competitive sports, but I like record hits too."

Career vs. marriage

One of the boys in the group is already married, and Brian Wilson is thinking of it too. He has a girl friend, Marilyn Rovell, who sings with her sister, Diane, and a cousin, Ginger Blake, in a group known as the Honeys. The Honeys had perhaps the first and one of the few girl surfer records.

"I'd like to get married," Wilson continued, "But there's a hang-up there for the image. I don't think it would be good right now. With the Beatles, it's different. John Lennon was married before they made it. It's accepted. But to get married after you're in the public eye could shatter the illusion."

Why haven't girl artists made it with the West Coast sound? Wilson has an answer. "In all this music, there's an association of the outdoors and sports. This is a masculine identity. The girls are sort of spectators. Besides, there's been so much female influence in the last couple of years with all the eastern girl groups, I think it's kind of a reaction.

"**When I said** I thought surfing was passe, I meant not as a sport, but that other things are making more excitement on records, like the Hondas and the other scooters. Other sounds are too, like the Beatles; they are as "in" as any sound could ever be. They've done a number of interesting things, I think.

"For one thing they really broke things wide open for vocal groups. They're a new concept too, because every one of their guys is a known personality in his own right, separate from the group image. That has really never happened before. The Beatles also glorified the drummer. Drums will be even bigger in group work from now on.

"I admire the Beatles. They have a lot of creative ability and they present their music well. It's a synthetic sound in a way, combining Chuck Berry, the Everly Brothers, Buddy Holly and others. But they do it very well."

Watching the field

Wilson watches carefully what other people are doing in records and will readily offer thumbnail opinions . . . on, for example, who is making the big impact and why . . . like Burt Bacharach. "He fascinates me. He has incorporated good music with the teen stuff and it just knocks me out to think about it.

"And Phil Spector. Some say he's cold now but there's no such thing as a cold great talent and in any era he would be a great talent. He did so much for the production world, bringing in drums and saxes like nobody else had done. And Tamla Motown. Well with them it's so obvious . . . like saying the sky is blue.

"**And Chuck Berry**. It's hard to really state how much his revival has meant. It's just tremendous. You hear that 'Memphis' beat in dozens of the new records. Johnny Rivers had a hit with it but the beat is everywhere. If there's a soul of rock and roll, Chuck Berry has to be it."

As for the Beach Boys, Wilson wants to "expand our style and versatility. I hope we can ramify our basic feel into just one of the best vocal groups. There isn't any pat formula but it helps to know what the others are doing in the business. We've never been to the east but we'll be there in September to do some concerts, and then in October, we hope, off to England, where our first hit 'I Get Around' is just breaking now."

REN GREVATT

Eastern concerts and England are next for the boys

BARBARA ANN/BEACH BOYS PARTY AD 1965

BRIAN WILSON

'More and more kids are thinking love and peace and friendship'

PEACE
Relative peace must be nice in New York.

FEAR
Not knowing what to expect is the only reason for fear.

DRUNK
I don't know anyone who gets drunk. In fact, I haven't been drunk myself for three years. There's no point in it. It isn't really fun. Why bother?

HONESTY
It's great and groovy and kicks all rolled into one big mind-blower. No one should be without it.

SUICIDE
It only makes things worse. You can't solve anything by killing yourself. I mean, things can always get better, but if you're dead, they may not.

WATTS
It's only four miles from my original home, where my mother still lives. We didn't panic — she just didn't go outside the house.

CRIME
Very consistent.

POLICE
They're nice men, I think.

KOREA
I was about 11 years old and primarily concerned with baseball.

JUVENILE DELINQUENCY
There seems to be a trend toward non-violence today. More and more kids are thinking love and peace and friendship, instead of hate and spite.

SCHOOL
I wonder how much longer school will be compulsory? Very soon, I think, education will not only be free-form, but free for the taking or leaving.

TIME
Time is fine when it's in cadence.

STEREO
I can't enjoy stereo much. I'm deaf in one ear.

EAR
The right one.

DRUGS
An underground train.

PATRIOTISM
Beer and brass bands.

HYMN
I think I can write one someday.

ORGAN
My dad gave me a pipeorgan for my birthday—that's what I'll write the hymn on. Or at.

DOOR
The door has been opened to a whole universe of experience for me.

NEWSPAPER
I don't read the newspapers too much because they depress me.

SWIMMING POOL
I have just rediscovered the delights of swimming. I'm completely turned on to swimming pools again. For a while, they bored me. Now I take a swim once a day and I'm completely healthy.

ALBUM
Our next album will be better than "Pet Sounds". It will be as much an improvement over "Sounds" as that was over "Summer Days".

RECORDING STUDIO
My recording studio has become a castle, with a wing for everyone.

TELEVISION
Someday I want to make commercials for TV —with a new twist.

DRUMS
Someday I want to write a symphony for drums.

HOLLYWOOD BOWL
The sound men at the Bowl are not rock 'n' roll sound men. I would advise people who want to play there and sound good, to change their plans or plan their changes.

SURFING
It's a very challenging sport. I've never been able to meet the challenge.

LYRICS
Let's make them all free form, so we don't get hung up on making rhymes.

DRUG SONGS
There are myriad drug songs on the pop music market today. I don't know which they are.

MIRROR
Have you tried the mirror technique of the subconscious? I'm reading a book about it—I'm fascinated by the mind and hypnosis and things like that.

CAR
One day everyone will sit up in his car and fall out to the groovy sounds of cartridge tapes. Do I sound like a commercial?

SUCCESS
Came very easily to me, professionally speaking.

GLASSES
I would recommend that everyone who gets eye strain when they read go to an optometrist and get reading glasses so that they can read more and longer. This is what I did, and I really do think everyone should do it.

RAIN
It's purifying. It cleanses the earth and help things grow. It's spiritual, too.

AUTOGRAPHS
I would suggest to every girl who collects autographs that she has them analysed. Amazing revelations.

THE MOON
Funny you should mention that—I've been reading a book about how the moon affects women's personalities. Fascinating.

PUBLICISTS
Professional wordsmen.

SMILE LP AD

THE BEACH

44

SMILE LP AD

BOYS GOOD VIBRATIONS

NUMBER 1 IN THE USA
NUMBER 1 IN ENGLAND

Coming—With the Good Vibrations Sound!

DT 2580

Billboard • 1967 International Record Talent Directory

Discover the Beach Boys' Groovy New Sounds!

**HEROES AND VILLAINS • GETTIN' HUNGRY • LITTLE PAD • WONDERFUL • WITH ME TONIGHT • VEGETABLES
WHISTLE IN • SHE'S GOIN' BALD • FALL BREAKS AND BACK TO WINTER • WIND CHIMES • GOOD VIBRATIONS**

CONTEMPORARY MUSIC FANS like you have been waiting for more than a year for an all-new album by the Beach Boys. You've heard their first million-selling single, *Good Vibrations*, and the smash follow-ups *Heroes and Villains* and *Gettin' Hungry*. You've wondered what they'll come up with next. Now here's your answer in "Smiley Smile."

New Sounds

All this time, Brian and the boys have been working on their new record, "Smiley Smile." The result is one of the most outstanding albums of the era. You were introduced to the new sound of the Beach Boys on "Pet Sounds," and "Smiley Smile" is a unique extension of that sound with many instrumental and vocal innovations.

Composer-singer Brian Wilson teamed up with pianist Van Dyke Parks to write new songs for the album. Two more songs were written with fellow Beach Boy Mike Love. You'll also hear novel sound effects such as the vocal imitation of *Wind Chimes* by the talented quartet.

Fall Breaks and Back to Winter reminds you of the instrumental work on "Pet Sounds," which Rex Reed in *Hi-Fi/Stereo Review* termed "spine-tingling" and praised as "The most exciting...modern music I've heard lately."

Thickly-textured Combinations

The Beach Boys' "sound" can be described as close group harmony which backs an exciting vocal solo by one of the members. The varied instrumental backgrounds are comprised of thickly-textured combinations of organ, guitars, strings, and more exotic instruments. Taken together, the result is a sound like no other, one uniquely "right" for the group – and one you're sure to like!

In a recent interview, Brian was asked the secret of his production, to which he replied, "I'm trying to be as harmonic and as melodic as I can, and at the same time, dynamic. I'm trying to use dynamics more effectively...I want to *grow*." His growth, and that of the group, is evident on "Smiley Smile."

Hits and New Songs

Good Vibrations alone took more than three months to record. *Heroes and Villains* is called "a three-minute musical comedy." For part of *Heroes*, Brian sang from the bottom of his empty swimming pool! Was this just a gimmick? Why not listen and judge for yourself.

Other songs featured on the album include the romantic *With Me Tonight* and *Wonderful*; the humourous *Vegetables* and *She's Goin' Bald*; the unusual *Whistle In*; and the parody of their earlier surfing hits, *Little Pad*.

Always Leaders

In 1961, the Beach Boys were locally successful in their home town of Hawthorne, California. Almost single-handedly, they started the surfing music craze with their first record. Their steady stream of successes and their standing as one of the most popular and influential groups in the business culminates with this album. It has been a long way from "Surfin' Safari" to "Smiley Smile," and the Beach Boys continue to win new fans without losing the continued support of all the people who made them so popular. Always pace-setters, the Beach Boys can be expected to pave the way for even more appealing new sounds.

YOUNG SWINGERS SELECTION OF THE MONTH

SMILEY SMILE, the Young Swingers selection of the month, will be sent automatically to all members of this division, unless the Advice Card on the back cover is returned. Other members may also enjoy the album by indicating one of the numbers below. Remember, there's no extra charge for spectacular stereo sound! Specify S9001 for stereo, M9001 for mono. Either version is yours for only $4.98. Brother.

Discover the Beach Boys' Groovy New Sound!

CONTEMPORARY MUSIC FANS like you have been waiting for more than a year for an all-new album by the Beach Boys. You've heard their first million-selling single, *Good Vibrations*, and the smash follow-ups *Heroes and Villains* and *Gettin' Hungry*. You've wondered what they'll come up with next. Now here's your answer in "Smiley Smile."

New Sounds

All this time, Brian and the boys have been working on their new record, "Smiley Smile." The result is one of the most outstanding albums of the era. You were introduced to the new sound of the Beach Boys on "Pet Sounds," and "Smiley Smile" is a unique extension of that sound with many instrumental and vocal innovations.

Composer-singer Brian Wilson teamed up with pianist Van Dyke Parks to write new songs for the album. Two more songs were written with fellow Beach Boy Mike Love. You'll also hear novel sound effects such as the vocal imitation of *Wind Chimes* by the talented quartet.

Fall Breaks and Back to Winter reminds you of the instrumental work on "Pet Sounds," which Rex Reed in *Hi-Fi/Stereo Review* termed "spinetingling" and praised as "The most exciting...modern music I've heard lately."

Thickly-textured Combinations

The Beach Boys' "sound" can be described as close group harmony which backs an exciting vocal solo by one of the members. The varied instrumental backgrounds are comprised of thickly-textured combinations of organ, guitars, strings, and more exotic instruments. Taken together, the result is a sound like no other, one uniquely "right" for the group — and one you're sure to like!

In a recent interview, Brian was asked the secret of his production, to which he replied, "I'm trying to be as harmonic and as melodic as I can, and at the same time, dynamic. I'm trying to use dynamics more effectively... I want to *grow*." His growth, and that of the group, is evident on "Smiley Smile."

Hits and New Songs

Good Vibrations alone took more than three months to record. *Heroes and Villains* is called "a three-minute musical comedy." For part of *Heroes*, Brian sang from the bottom of his empty swimming pool! Was this just a gimmick? Why not listen and judge for yourself.

Other songs featured on the album include the romantic *With Me Tonight* and *Wonderful*; the humorous *Vegetables* and *She's Goin' Bald*; the unusual *Whistle In*; and the parody of their earlier surfing hits, *Little Pad*.

Always Leaders

In 1961, the Beach Boys were locally successful in their home town of Hawthorne, California. Almost single-handedly, they started the surfing music craze with their first record. Their steady stream of successes and their standing as one of the most popular and influential groups in the business culminates with this album. It has been a long way from "Surfin' Safari" to "Smiley Smile," and the Beach Boys continue to win new fans without losing the continued support of all the people who made them so popular. Always pace-setters, the Beach Boys can be expected to pave the way for even more appealing new sounds.

 **YOUNG SWINGERS SELECTION OF THE MONTH**

SMILEY SMILE, the Young Swingers selection of the month, will be sent automatically to all members of this division, unless the Selection Notice on the back cover is returned. Other members may also enjoy the album by indicating one of the numbers below. Remember, there's no extra charge for spectacular stereo sound! Specify S9001 for stereo, M9001 for mono. Either version is yours for only $4.98. Brother.

HEROES AND VILLAINS
featuring Brian

VEGETABLES
featuring the Group

FALL BREAKS AND BACK TO WINTER
(W. Woodpecker Symphony)
Instrumental

SHE'S GOIN' BALD
featuring the Group

LITTLE PAD
featuring Carl

GOOD VIBRATIONS
featuring Carl

WITH ME TONIGHT
featuring Carl

WIND CHIMES
featuring the Group

GETTIN' HUNGRY
featuring Brian and Mike

WONDERFUL
featuring Carl

WHISTLE IN
featuring Carl

DENNIS (BEACH BOY)

"LIFE IS KIND!"

"BUT SOMETIMES I WORRY"

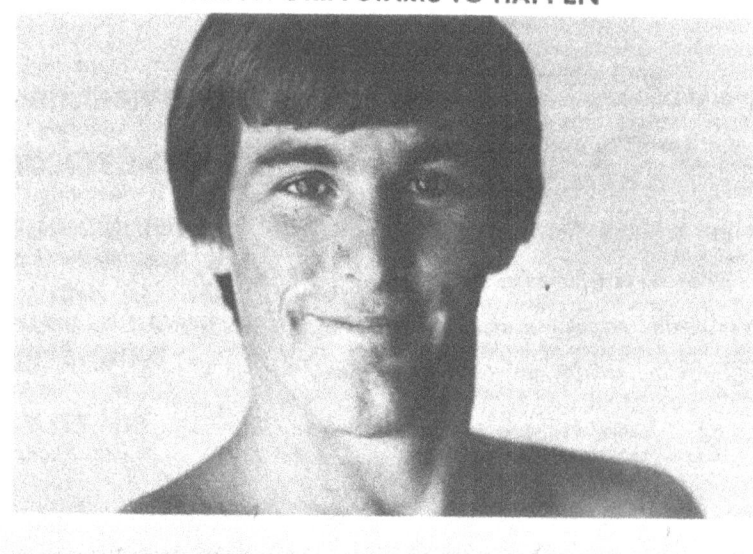
"THEN A GRIN STARTS TO HAPPEN"

WILSON FLIPS OUT!

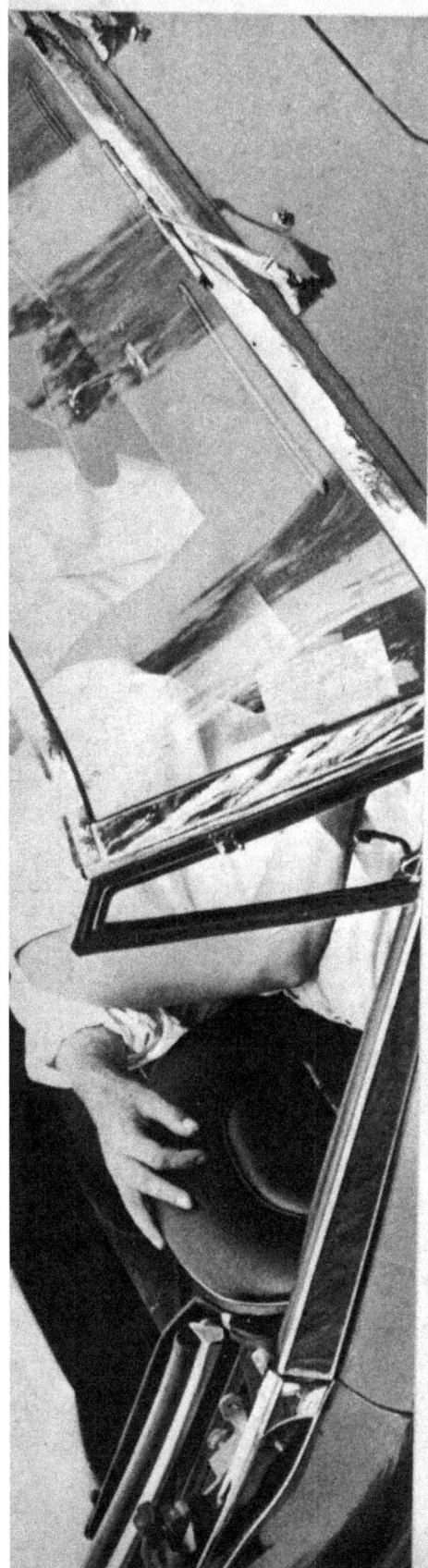

"IT GETS BIGGER..."

"...AND BIGGER!"   "UNTIL I CAN'T CONTROL IT!"

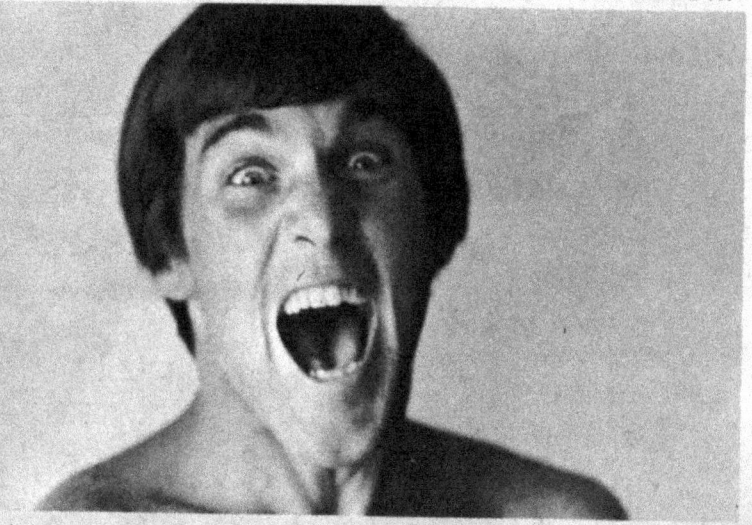

BEACH BOYS NEWS CLIPS

FEBRUARY 1967

I rang up Beach Boy **AL JARDINE** and got his charming wife Linda who said, "Oh, he's in the monkey cage!" I did a double-take (which is difficult over the phone) then she explained that he was just cleaning out their monkey's cage (taking care of the animal is his hobby, along with astronomy). Linda had to pass up traveling with Al on the BB's European tour—"Our baby was due just a few weeks afterwards, so I just trusted him to return with loads of toys," Al definitely earned the trust—he came back needing only a pot belly, white beard and red suit to look like Santa Claus!

FEBRUARY 1967

BRIAN WINS AWARD

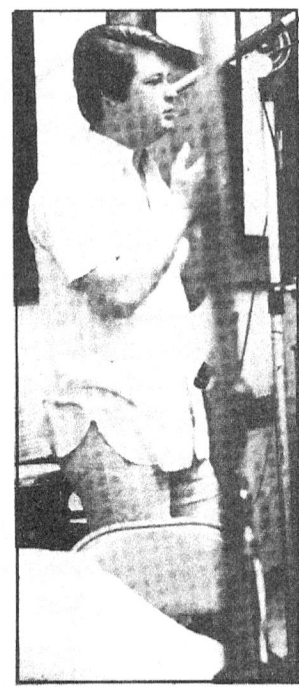

Brian Wilson of the Beach Boys has just become the first American winner of Denmark's 1966 **Ekstrabladet's Beat Pris**, the musical award that is given yearly to the producer of the Best Foreign Recording.

Brian, leader of the Beach Boys, received the award for his recording of "Good Vibrations," which was also the group's first million-selling single. Brian was also composer of "Vibrations."

The **Ekstrabladet** award, which is presented by (and named after) Denmark's leading newspaper, is given on the basis of a popular vote conducted by the publication throughout the country.

SONG HITS FOLIO 2

THE BEACH BOYS
SONG HITS FOLIO NUMBER 2

SPECIAL BONUS EDITION

HELP ME, RHONDA • DO YOU WANNA DANCE? • DON'T WORRY, BABY • I GET AROUND
LITTLE HONDA • PLEASE LET ME WONDER • WENDY • DANCE, DANCE, DANCE • and others

SONG HITS FOLIO 2

FROM THE PUBLISHER

We are very proud to make up this second Song Hit Folio containing nation wide hits by the fabulously talented Beach Boys. This group of fine young lads have not only amazed us, but the entire record industry with the way they have continued to make not only single record hits in the United States, but also each and every album they have recorded has made the charmed circle of top ten album charts, and their album sales as well as their single 45 RPM records continue to soar.

This is no accident—as you all know, Brian, Dennis and Carl Wilson are brothers and Mike Love is their cousin. Al Jardine went to the same high school at Hawthorne, California with Brian and Dennis and even played fullback on the varsity football team with Brian. Besides having Brian Wilson, who writes about 94% of all their material, who makes their vocal arrangements, who teaches the other fellows their harmony parts, he also now produces their hit sounds by writing out the band arrangements and even tells the Mixing Engineer in the recording studio exactly what he wants on the "mix" of both their vocal and instrumental tracks. On occasion, his father, Murry Wilson, who mixed their vocal recording sessions for the first two years, is asked to come in and lend a hand at a session, and who, by the way, was their manager for the first two years of their careers.

I guess you could say that because the construction of the vocal chords of four fifths of The Beach Boys are very similar, and because Al Jardine's voice blends readily to theirs, that this unique situation has made it easy for the fellows to sound so fantastic on their ballads. Secondly, on the faster type "rockin" songs, like "I Get Around" which sold over a million copies, their voices in the harmony background again blend so well that it is easy on the ears of the teeners. Thirdly, the Beach Boys copy no one in their style and every record they put out is different because Brian is so full of surprises in his unique song writing approach. Many rock and roll song writers are studying his songs and listening to The Beach Boys' recordings so much that they are using melodic phrases and gimmicks as well as their singing style in order to try to make song hits for themselves and other recording companies.

It is absolutely true that The Beach Boys have had as many as three songs on the single top 100 hit charts and four albums way up on the top 100 album chart at the __very same time__. Their employer, Capitol Records is delighted to have The Beach Boys as __artists__ because they were voted the Number One group in both singles and albums in 1963. In 1964 they were again voted the Number One vocal group in singles. Not only have The Beach Boys had more songs on the top charts in singles and albums than any other American artist at Capitol Records but they have had more hits on these same charts of all Capitol's American Artists put together over the last three years period, and this is a fantastic achievement for being a self-taught group both vocally and instrumentally and being in the business only three years.

To show our thanks to all of you loyal Beach Boy fans and to the Beach Boys themselves, we have really gone all out on this second song hit folio with bonus cut out pictures in color as well as color shots of their recent European tour, some shots of the Australian tour and miscellaneous pictures we thought you might like to see. The Beach Boys asked us to thank every one who might read this preface "that they __do thank everyone__ for the wonderful loyalties rendered to them and for the great success their fans have given them." Dennis asked us to say, "all of the guys will always try to wail on stage at their big concerts and we love every minute of the screams and cheers because it makes us feel we are doing a good job."

One thing you can be sure is that their great success has not made them get the big head and they do take time out every time they can to stop and talk to fans and sign autographs whenever they are permitted. Sometimes the crowds are so great that special guards are instructed to whisk them away so they will not get crushed, and you all can well understand this.

The Publisher,

SEA OF TUNES PUBLISHING COMPANY

SONG HITS FOLIO 2

Also Available...

Contents

BALLAD OF OLD BETSY, THE

BE TRUE TO YOUR SCHOOL

FARMER'S DAUGHTER, THE

"409"

FUN, FUN, FUN

HAWAII

IN MY ROOM

LITTLE DEUCE COUPE

LITTLE ST. NICK

LONELY SEA, THE

NO-GO SHOWBOAT

SHUT DOWN

SURFIN'

Price $2.00 in U.S.A.

SEA OF TUNES PUBLISHING COMPANY
3701 W. 119th St., HAWTHORNE, CALIFORNIA
Sales & Shipping: Suite 611, 1841 Broadway, New York 23, N.Y.

PROMO PHOTO

PROMO PHOTO

Carl Wilson   Dennis Wilson   Mike Love   Al Jardine   Brian Wilson

PROMO PHOTO

THE BEACH BOYS

PROMO PHOTO

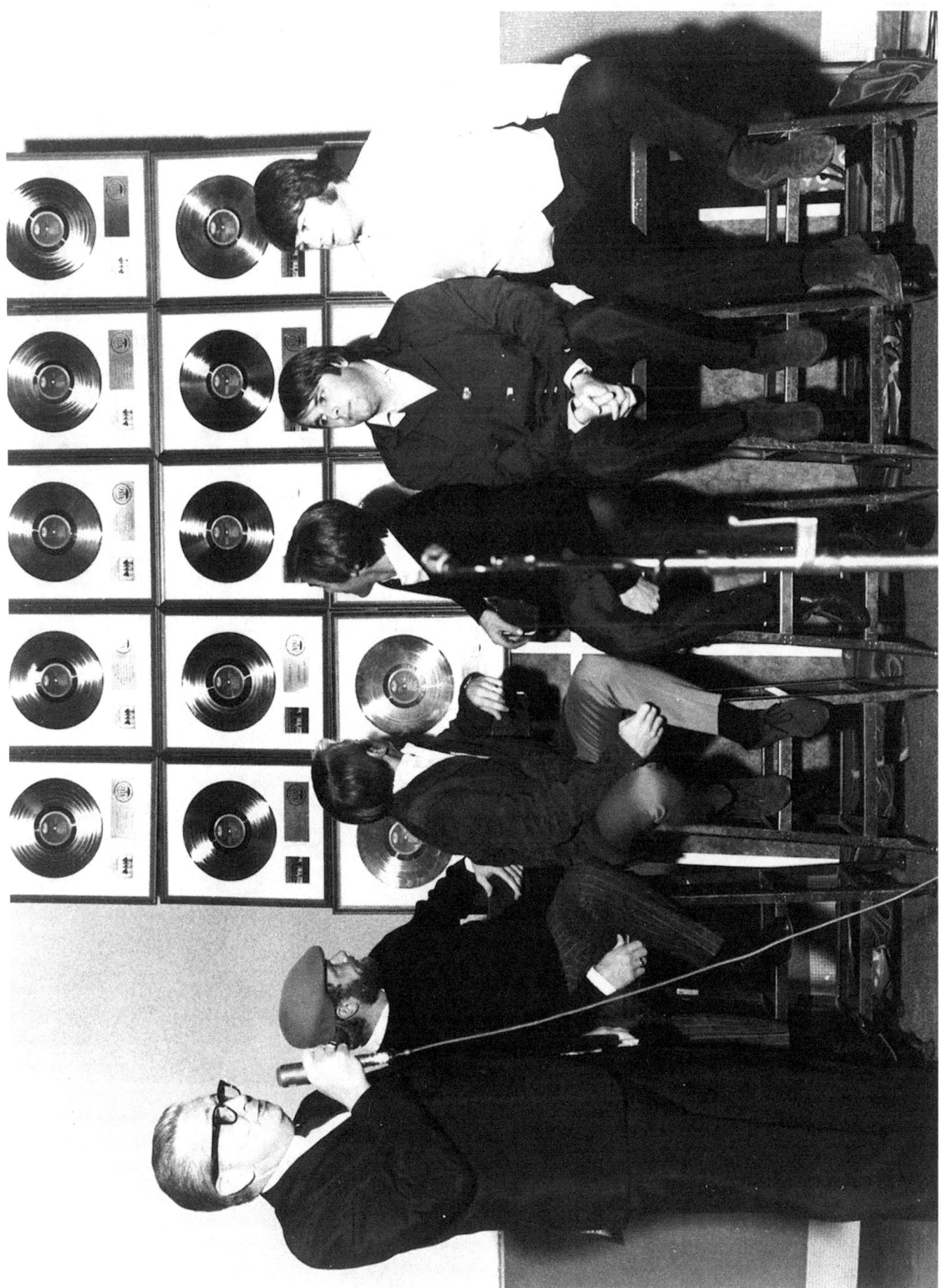

KRLA NEWS ITEMS

DECEMBER 17, 1966

Beach Boys Latest To Earn Goldie

The Beach Boys were greeted with some nice news when they made their triumphant return from England this weekend. Their latest single, "Good Vibrations," has surpassed the 925,000 mark in sales and has thus become the biggest-selling single in Beach Boy history.

"Good Vibrations" has now outsold such big Beach Boy hits as "Help Me, Rhonda," "I Get Around" and "Sloop John B.," all of which were in the 900,000 category. If "Vibrations" continues its sales pace it will become the first million-selling single for the group.

SEPTEMBER 24, 1966

BEACH BOYS enjoy that pause that refreshes before taking off for a rather short tour of England. It will be their first British tour and the Beach Boys will hit Finsbury Park Astoria, Totting Granada, Leicester de Montfort, Leeds Odeon, Manchester Odeon, Cardiff Capitol and Birmingham Theatre. Other European stop-offs for the Beach Boys will be in France, Germany, Austria, Denmark, Sweden and Holland.

Another Smash Hit For Beach Boys

MAY 26, 1965

THE FABULOUS BEACH BOYS have done it again! They have a new smash record, "HELP ME, RHONDA," and a top-selling album, "The Beach Boys Today." They earned nearly a million dollars last year in less than 80 concerts, and the Southern California stars should do even better this year.

KRLA NEWS CLIPS

APRIL 22, 1967

Beach Boys Wind Up Tour

HOUSTON—The Beach Boys wound up a ten-city tour of one night stands here. Their gross earnings for the performances promoted by Irving Granz totaled over $198,000.

Stops en route included Fort Worth, Texas; Dallas, Texas (where top earnings of more than $40,000 were taken at the gate); Austin, Texas; Memphis, Tenn.; Tulsa, Okla.; St. Louis, Mo.; Kansas City, Mo.; Davenport, Iowa and McCool, Ill.

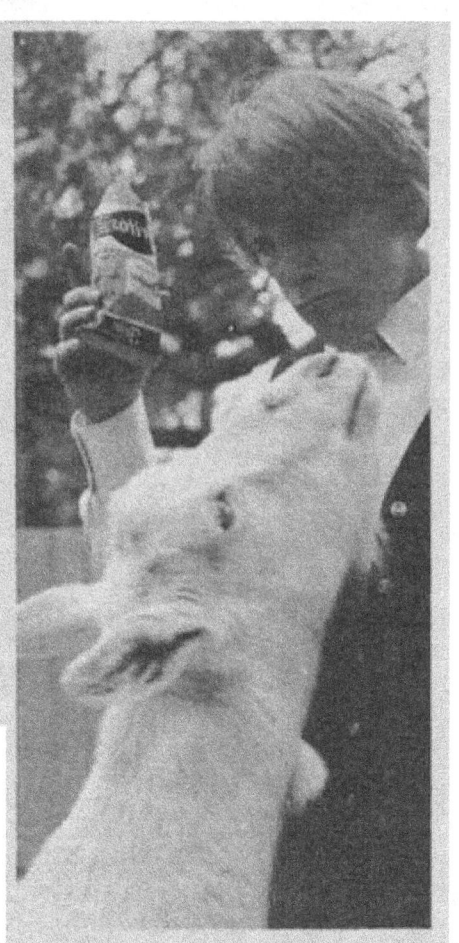

JANUARY 14, 1965

Backstage at the TAMI show, Bobby Dale talks to one of the Beachboys. The TAMI show pictures are the pics that most of you requested, especially after seeing the groovy show. KRLA made it possible for 3000 of you to not only see the filming of the show, but to actually be in the movie itself!

FEBRUARY 22, 1965

In case you're wondering where Dick got all those groovy scoops on the Beach Boys, now you know . . . right from the source! The Beach Boys recently finished a tour of England and said that it was a gas.

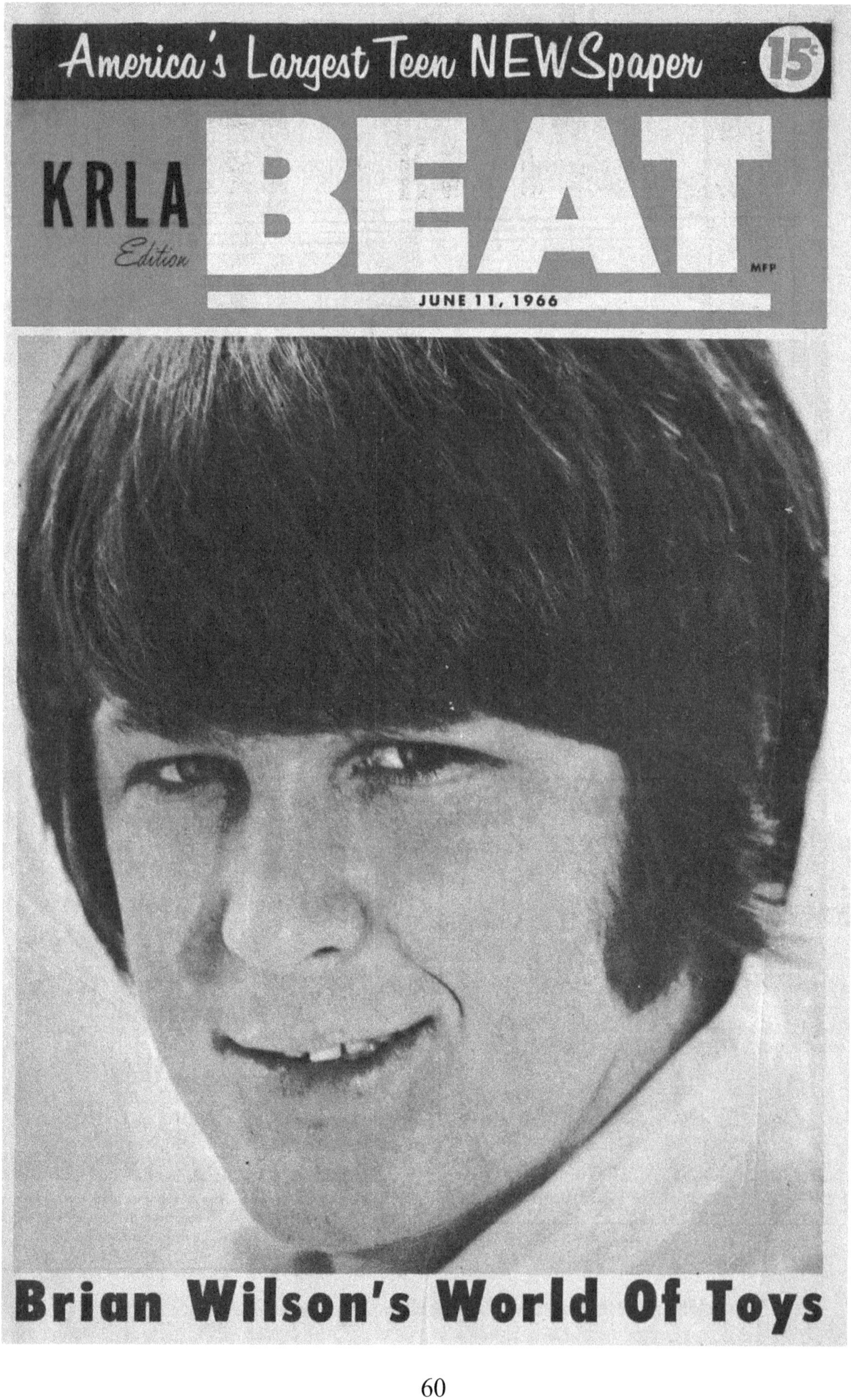

KRLA BEAT JUNE 11, 1966

America's Largest Teen NEWSpaper — 15¢

KRLA Edition BEAT
JUNE 11, 1966

Brian Wilson's World Of Toys

Brian Wilson: 'Toys Are Gonna Happen!'

By Jamie McCluskey III

Well, Brian Wilson has discovered the wonderful world of toys. Yep—he has discovered a whole new world of things to get into and you probably wouldn't believe it, but come along anyway as Brian lets us take a peek at some of the latest additions to his toy chest.

Brian explains that he first met a young toy salesman in a Hollywood toy shop about six or seven months ago who promptly mistook him for a weird hippy-type who just flipped out over toys.

Went Along

With his usual amount of straight-faced humor, ultra-cool Brian went along with the joke and became friends with the young man—allowing him to demonstrate all of his latest and weirdest toys which had come into the shop.

Brian explained to us that the salesman "thought I was some sort of pseudo-hippy getting some sort of pseudo-kick from all of it. I went along with it, but actually I think there was some sort of deeper meaning to it.

"Actually, I think that buying these toys represents some fantasy of childhood that we are trying to relive."

Brian purchased, among other things, some silly putty—which can be pressed against a comic strip in the newspaper and will exactly reporduce the print.

Then there is the "cop car" which Brian was delighted with—until the battery fell out! When I asked the Chief Beach Boy just why he had purchased a police car, he explained that he felt that it was protecting him in some way. "I'll never have to worry about being protected by the police because I'll have my own police car!"

But Brian laughs as he describes the noises which his little "cop car" makes when it is turned on: "It gives very uncool, very square police calls! One of them says, 'you are completely surrounded by the police. Come out and you will not be harmed!' And a siren plays in the background."

Brian also has a monster robot which is capable of saying four wonderful things, one of which is: "I am a mighty man and I have one million volts of electricity stored up inside of me. I'm bullet proof too!!" (Then it begins to laugh ... Ha, Ha, Ha!)"

Toy Boat

One of the toys which Brian recently acquired was a little boat, complete with two outboard motors on it which is run by batteries. The night after he purchased it, he was all set to journey over to brother Carl's house in order to sail it in his pool, however it never quite worked out. Oh well—there's always the bath tub!

In closing, Brian just gathered all of his brand new toys around him, and looking up very solemnly (well, as solemnly as anyone could look if one happened to be a Beach Boy!) prophetically procailmed for all *BEAT* ears: "Toys Are Gonna Happen!"

... BRIAN AND HIS DOG.

... BRIAN ON STAGE

KRLA To Host Bowl Concert

KRLA, the first station to offer all-request radio along with dedications in Los Angeles, is now adding another first to their long list—the first all-request concert.

The concert will be held June 25 in the Hollywood Bowl, the site of many top pop concerts by the likes of the Beatles, Sonny and Cher and this summer, the Rolling Stones.

Featured will be the artists and songs that have shown up repeatedly in requests phoned into KRLA.

Headlining will be the Beach Boys doing their latest hits, "Sloop John B" and "Caroline, No." This concert will also mark one of Brian Wilson's rare appearances with the group. He has stopped traveling with the group so he can devote his time to writing and producing their records; however, there is a definite possibility that he will appear at this date.

Also appearing will be the Byrds with "Eight Miles High," the Lovin' Spoonful with "Did You Ever Have to Make Up Your Mind?" the Outsiders with "Time Won't Let Me," the Leaves and "Hey, Joe," the Sir Douglas Quintet and "Rain," Percy Sledge and "When A Man Loves A Woman," the Love with "In My Little Red Book," and Captain Beefheart and his Magic Band with their first hit, "Diddy Wah Diddy."

For ticket information contact the Hollywood Bowl.

See you there.

...THE BEACH BOYS

CARL WILSON: 'Weird Sounds Don't Blow My Mind'

By Eden

There are three Wilson brothers, a cousin, and a friend. Brian, Carl, Dennis, Mike and Al. Collectively, they are The Beach Boys. There are five of them, but they are seldom "collected" into the same place at the same time unless they are on tour, or performing.

You will find them dropping in on one another at home, or racing their cars, or riding their motorcycles, or writing a new song, or re-recording a track until it "feels" just right, or just "getting away from it all" down by the beach.

Unusual Trio

The Wilsons Three are a most unusual trio of brothers. Brian and Carl are the two most alike; apart from the obvious physical resemblance, Brian—the eldest—and Carl—the "baby" of the family—think and speak and even act very much along the same lines. They are very much interested in thinking; in the various thought processes, in the spiritual and emotional concepts of the mind, and with the various powers—both *known* and as yet undiscovered,

which are possessed by the mind. Dennis — the middle Wilson brother—is the "nature boy" as brother Brian describes him. He is the young man so sensitive that he can communicate with the creatures and creations of nature. He loves all things concerned with the outdoors, and is an avid enthusiast of nearly all outdoor sports.

Racer

He is also the driving expert in the family, and is well-known for his expert racing.

As human beings, the Wilsons are all warm and generous people. They have a talent for more-or-less "adopting" you and making *you* feel like a member of the family. Which might, at times, be easier than it sounds, for it quickly seems as though the *whole world* is a part of the Wilson family! There are a vast number of cousins and other assorted Wilson-type relatives to be found in the near vicinity of any one of the Beach Boys.

All five of the Beach Boys (except Bruce Johnson) are married now, but this has in no way hurt their popularity. Perhaps that is because their fans are able to pick up the warm family-vibrations from the group, and can feel somehow included in that family.

Carl is the most recent departee from the bachelor ranks, and his beautiful bride is the sister of Billy Hinsche, of Dino, Desi, and Billy.

I stopped in to visit Carl and Annie in their beautiful Beverly Hills home and was immediately greeted with the usual warmth and hospitality which is so characteristic of the Wilsons.

Carl studied guitar briefly for about three months once when he took lessons from a studio. Then, a friend—John Maus, of the successful Walker Brothers—taught him a great deal about the guitar.

Harmony

This was the only formal musical education which Carl has had, yet he is a member of a group whose music has had a very widespread affect on the very structure of popular music. Like his talented brother, Carl is very much interested in harmony—always one of the most important factors in the unique Beach Boys' sounds, and for a moment he considered the possible meanings of harmony.

He called it a "love vibration" —a really strong emotion or feeling. And "vibrations" are very important to both Carl and Brian. Each record must have exactly the "right sound," the "right feeling." It must give very good vibrations before they will release it.

Emotions

He explained that, "I don't think people would be as emotional listening to a one-note solo instead of a beautiful harmony passage. Harmony carries a vibration that, I think a single note just doesn't have."

Carl feels that "vibrations" are important to everyone, though everyone is not consciously aware of them. Trying to relate his concept of these vibrations to others, Carl tried to sum his ideas up by explaining that "Vibrations are just another plane, or plateau of sensitivity. It's just another *feeling*; you *feel* vibrations."

Carl has a fine appreciation of good music—music which is well-written and well-executed. And though he enjoys different and interesting instrumentations; he doesn't necessarily go for the ultra-weird. "Weird sounds don't blow my mind—*great* ones do!"

He hasn't yet begun to involve himself in the writing and producing area of record production, but agrees that he would be interested in someday giving it a try. He greatly admires the work and talents of Brian, but feels that he hasn't yet become interested enough in these things to be able to work in this area. Philosophically, he concludes that, "If it will come—it will come."

New Album

Motion pictures hold a very strong attraction for Carl, and he hopes to be able to become involved in that medium of entertainment as soon as possible. The immediate future holds the creation of a new album—an LP which is very important to all of the Beach Boys—and a European tour in October.

As for the future after that . . . well, it is undoubtedly full of very good vibrations for the Beach Boys.

BEAT Exclusive

Vibrations—Brian Wilson Style

KRLA BEAT DECEMBER 17, 1966

(EDITOR'S NOTE: Every so often we turn The BEAT typewriters over to the entertainers themselves. This time around, Brian Wilson has written an exclusive story for us. What's it all about? Only Brian knows for sure!)

By Brian Wilson

PART I

It was a sunny day outside, but Brian Gemini was unable to appreciate the beauty of nature as he stumbled through the Vegetable Forest, choking with ill health.

Suddenly, in the midst of a violent nasal attack, Brian fell into a giant tomato, and tumbled down, down, *down*, to the very seedy bottom. There were large bagpipes under Brian's eyes, but even those didn't prevent him from seeing many grotesque and frightening seeds on his way down through the tomato.

He landed at the bottom — *SPLAT!* — and looking back up to the top, he saw a carrot floating down toward him. Grasping firmly onto the carrot, Brian ate it quickly, and, *lo and behold!*—it gave him some very out-of-sight vision, of a very out-of-sight world.

Now, Brian Gemini was a very quick-witted sort of soul, and he perceived instantly that he would need a great deal of out-of-sight energy to be able to cope with this brand new out-of-sight world which he had just seen with his new-found out-of-sight vision.

Shortly after this enlightening perception, a large glob of very green spinach quite fortuitously splatted down upon Brian's knee. What luck! But then, the glob of spinach—who's given name was Michael—began to speak: "Now, I'm *really* mad," he said, said he. "There is a Roving Radish reporter who wants to change my name to Sidney Spinach. I will not bend to the wishes of the teen-oriented Reporter Establishment," Michael Spinach-Glob globbled firmly.

"Hmmmph!" retorted Brian Gemini. "Why don't you let yourself get eaten up, just once?"

"Well," hesitated the Green Glob, "if I don't have to be called *Sidney*, I will if you will call me Michael."

Brian Gemini agreed immediately and enthusiastically ate the spinach, which gave him instant energy. Just then, Brian saw the Jolly Jewish Carrot (who had escaped from the Chicken Soup) floating down toward him. Watching the Carrot's descent, Brian G. said loud enough for everyone to hear: "That carrot is much too big to eat."

At that precise moment in tomato history, the Carrot landed and introduced himself: "I'm the Jolly Jewish Carrot, and I've just escaped from the Chicken Soup. Hello! I've just come down from Carrot Heaven to help you see just *Where It's At*, and tell you that the world is really *Out-Of-Sight!*" Thus spake the Jolly Jewish Carrot.

Pulling himself up to his full carrot-top height, Jolly J. continued: "I see you've just devoured Spinach, and with that energy — you are now going to explore the out-of-sight world."

Inspired by J.J.'s pep talk, Brian Gemini, filled with new-found vegetable vigor, jumped to his feet and was red as a beet and then said with great emotion: "David Carrot — we'll soon be in the pink!"

"That's what *you* think," poetically retorted the carrot, with somewhat less emotion than Brian.

Just then Brian exclaimed: "Oh! Here comes the celery now!"

"Ouch!" he added emphatically as he was smashed upon the heady by a stringy stalk of impertinent celery that didn't seem to know just whose head it had smashed.

Well . . . Brian blew his cool and chucked it as far as he could. To which David Carrot immediately reproached: "That's not very nice Brian! Don't be so up-tight. You've got to use the strength that the spinach gave you for *good things*," he instructed

(Turn to Page 14)

MIKE "SPINACH," DAVID "CARROT," BRIAN "GEMINI" AND BRIAN'S COUSIN, BARRY. YOU MAY BELIEVE IT IF YOU WANT TO!

KRLA BEAT DECEMBER 17, 1966

'VIBRATIONS'

(Continued from Page 6)

Immediately seeing the error of his youthful ways, Brian G. agreed and said: "C'mon David Carrot, let's go find that celery!" And suddenly from deep within, Michael Spinach encouraged: "Hurry up, man—find that celery and eat it. I'm *lonely* in here!"

Brian burped compassionately and exclaimed: "We've got to get *out* of this tomato!"

PART II

Brian uttered, "Ooops—I just fell into your swimming pool, and the fact that I have on a Super Face Mask and a pair of Pro Swim Fins is merely *happenstance!*"

Just then, Hal Blaine vigorously beat a blue-eyed path to the swimming pool and pointing doggedly at Brian Gemini screamed: "*Get out* of my Chicken Soup before I get sore and call the cops!"

So, watching the nice looking young man (whose hair was always combed neatly in place) Brian thoughtfully went like this: "OK — let's hear that one more time, but a little bit *louder* this time. And, hold it *right there* while I call Guy Webster!"

PART III.

— THE END —

JULY 30, 1966

Customized by George Barris, of Hollywood, this candy-striped Austin MINI-SURFER comes with a Yamaha Campus 60 strapped to the back, a custom surfboard by Kon of California cresting the top, a Borg-Warner 8-track stereo tape player, and two giant portable speakers with a half-block of cord!

DECEMBER 31, 1966

Beach Boys Rate Riots On Their English Tour

The way English crowds were reacting, you'd think the year was 1965 and the Beatles were in the vicinity.

But it's almost 1967, the Beatles have probably forgotten each other's names, and the world—England, at least—appears to have a new set of heroes.

Those heroes are America's Beach Boys—and they're receiving as riotous a welcome in England as the Beatles ever witnessed. Sources in London say the six Californians have all but replaced the Beatles as England's favorite group.

The Beach Boys, even without the presence of Brian Wilson, were assured of a sell-out tour before they left America.

Beach Boy Defies Draft
Would Rather Go To Jail

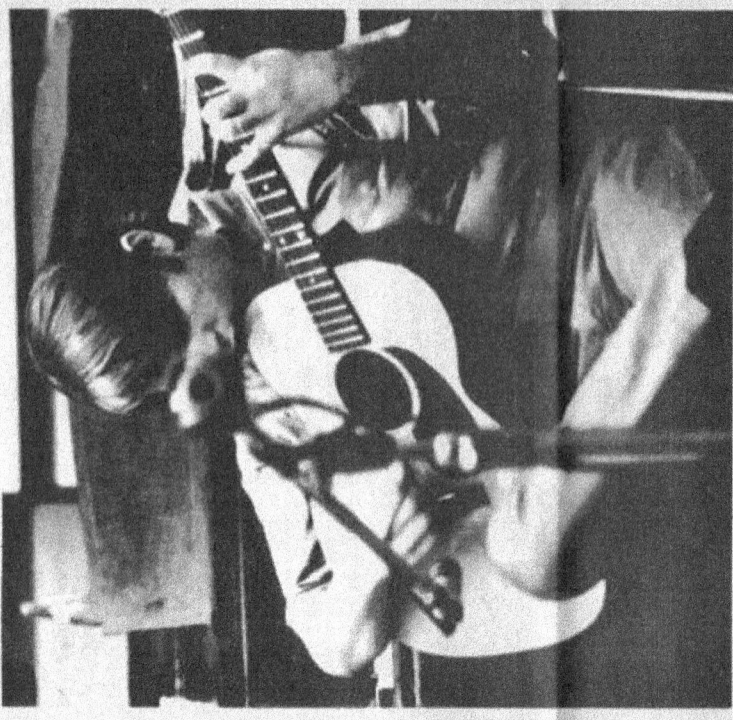

CARL WILSON WILL GO TO JAIL RATHER THAN SERVE IN THE ARMY.

Carl Wilson of the Beach Boys has decided to risk jail rather than report for induction into the Army.

Under a federal indictment charging him with violation of the Selective Service Act, Wilson plans to fight the case through the courts as a conscientious objector.

He faces the same charges as Heavyweight Champion Cassius Clay, although Clay has not yet been formally indicted.

Wilson was ordered to report for induction in Los Angeles on January 3. Like Clay, he refused to step forward to be sworn in.

He was indicted by a federal grand jury in Los Angeles on April 5 and later surrendered to the FBI in New York, where he was allowed to post bond.

Surprise

Carl's decision to fight the draft apparently came as a surprise to most of his friends—and perhaps even to his family.

The singer's father, Murray Wilson, cut short a European trip and returned home immediately after learning of his son's arrest.

"He never mentioned it to me," one close friend told The BEAT. "I don't ever remember hearing him even talk about being drafted, or how he felt about the draft in general."

Appearing before a Federal Judge in Los Angeles, Carl Wilson pleaded innocent to draft evasion charges.

He received permission to join the Beach Boys in England for a previously scheduled European tour. However, he was ordered to return June 20 for a trial on the charges.

Permission to travel abroad for the tour was granted only after he posted a $25,000 bond.

U.S. District Judge A. Andrew Hauk also ordered the singer to report periodically by telephone to Howard Smith, general attorney for the Beach Boys.

At the hearing, Attorney J.B. Tietz solemnly told the court his client "objects to all wars."

Although the arraignment will be June 2, Carl will probably remain free for a long time, even if he should ultimately lose the case.

A source in the U.S. Attorney's office privately estimated that he could remain free on bond for "at least a couple of years" if the attorneys use every legal recourse available.

Carl is scheduled for arraignment in Los Angeles on June 2. He faces a possible $10,000 fine and five years in jail if convicted.

Lawyer Optimistic

But his lawyer is optimistic about Carl's chances of winning the case, possibly on appeal. When asked if Wilson will go to jail rather than submit to induction, Tietz replied, "Oh yes, sure. But I don't think he'll have to."

Wilson Acquitted Of Draft Dodging

LOS ANGELES—Beach Boy Carl Wilson has been acquitted by a U.S. District Court for draft dodging. Carl had appealed his induction notice on the basis that he was a conscientious objector.

Wilson's acquittal, however, was based on a technicality. Judge A. Andrew Hauk, who handed down the ruling, said Carl's local Gardena (Calif.) draft board had acted "irregularly" by ordering the induction from one panel of his board and having the induction papers signed by a member of another panel of the same board.

Not Guilty

"I am not going to find a man guilty of a felony when the board does a thing like this," the judge said.

Anthony Glassman, the assistant U.S. attorney for the case, argued heatedly that any board member or even the board's clerk can sign an induction order. He claimed the board's clerk signed the original induction ordering Carl to report August 9, 1966.

The attorney said that the panel that classified Wilson 1-A allowed induction postponement until Sept. 6, 1966, and the panel member in question merely signed the postponement in his administrative capacity.

Carl's attorney, J.B. Tietz, argued the order signed by the panel member was illegal, and that Wilson was denied due process because he wasn't allowed to personally appear before the board to discuss his situation again.

When the judge asked Carl if he would consent to a non-combatant job, like working in a hospital, the Beach boy replied, "Most definitely—I just want to do something good."

During the trial, Wilson testified, "We were put here to live—killing is very evil and destructive and results in human suffering. I love my country very much, but I won't take part in the destruction of people."

In March, 1965, when Carl submitted his classification questionaire, he didn't fill out the conscientious objector part. Little more than a year later he did file a conscientious objector application, but it was denied.

Carl was supposed to report for induction last January 3, but when he didn't, he was indicted by a federal grand jury.

Re-Inducted

Since he was acquitted on a technicality, Carl could be re-inducted legally this time. Glassman told *The BEAT* the case was now out of the hands of the federal government. "It's up to the Gardena draft board, now" the attorney said.

The Gardena draft board in turn said that any information about Wilson's case is confidential. A spokesman did reveal to *The BEAT* that Carl was still classified 1-A, so he could be subject to immediate induction.

AUGUST 26, 1967

BEACH BOYS FORM OWN RECORD CO.

LOS ANGELES — Capitol Records has agreed to produce any new Beach Boy's albums under their own label called Brothers Records. This new label will also produce records made by other artists.

This agreement indicates that the Beach Boys' contract with Capitol Records, which was not due to expire for a few years, has been changed to allow the Beach Boys more freedom.

The first record to be released under this new label is the Beach Boys' "Heroes and Villains."

AUGUST 27, 1966

Single For Beach Boys

Early sales figures indicate that the Beach Boys' new single, "God Only Knows," might be one of the biggest sellers ever taken from any Beach Boy album.

The single, taken from the group's "Pet Sounds" album, and released just last week by Capitol Records, picked up more than 250,000 orders for advance copies.

"God Only Knows" is the fourth single in a row to be taken from a Beach Boy album following the LP's release. Prior to this one, the group met success with "Barbara Ann," "California Girls," and "Help Me Rhonda," all from previous albums.

All of the three previous singles were in the Top 10 nationally and "Help Me Rhonda" hit the number one spot on every major survey. The four songs were all written by Beach Boy leader, Brian Wilson.

NOVEMBER 4, 1967

Beach Boys Tape Stint

HONOLULU — The Beach Boys' "Summer Spectacular" shows in Honolulu have been recorded for later release on their own label, Brother Records.

NOVEMBER 27, 1965

Beach Boys Good Judges of Talent

The Beach Boys are not only talented performers in their own right, they are also good judges of talent.

Carl Wilson met three guys at the Hollywood Professional School and was impressed by their sound. He introduced them to his father, Murray Wilson, who manages the Beach Boys.

His father was also impressed. He arranged for the three guys and two others in their group to cut their first record which is reported to have gone "absolutely nowhere."

But they didn't give up and now the Sunrays, discovered by the Beach Boys, have a best seller in their second release, "I Live For the Sun."

DECEMBER 31, 1966

... THE BEACH BOYS CAME BACK — WITH WIVES

You voted... and then you waited for the results... and now, here they are... the winners... in the FIRST ANNUAL KRLA BEAT AWARD!

FIRST PLACE:

the group that contributed the most this year to teenagers and popular music is:

The Beatles

with 657 votes

SECOND PLACE:

The Rolling Stones

with 656 votes

THIRD PLACE:

The Beach Boys

with 477 votes

FOURTH PLACE:

The Dave Clark Five

with 296 votes

FIFTH PLACE:

The Four Seasons

with 145 votes

AND... IN ADDITION... THE KRLA BEAT HAS SELECTED THE TOP GROUPS IN THESE CATAGORIES:

FOR: *Best Ambassador to this country, best cooperation, and for making the best impression of any group to visit this country:*

GERRY AND THE PACEMAKERS

FOR: *Dedication to the type of music they perform, and musical sincerity:*

THE ROLLING STONES

FOR: *Best new female group on today's pop scene:*

THE SUPREMES

FOR: *Best new male group of 1964:*

THE RIGHTEOUS BROTHERS

KRLA BEAT OCTOBER 22, 1966

like the Beat said...
the Beach Boys have wives

The BEAT has been saying it for months and the Beach Boys have been denying it for months but when too many people found out about it, they were forced to admit it. The Beach Boys are married. All except for Bruce Johnson, that is. The newest Beach Boy is still a bachelor but Brian, Dennis, Carl, Mike and Al are very much married.

Why the Beach Boys have denied their marital status as long as they have is anybody's guess. Several months ago, the then-married Brian Wilson stated: "Marriage has no bearing on a girl fan's adoration for an artist anymore. Two of our guys, Mike Love and Al Jardine, are already married." But what Brian forgot to mention—so was he!

...AL AND LINDA JARDINE

...CARL AND ANNIE WILSON

...MIKE AND SUZANNE LOVE

...DENNIS AND CAROL WILSON

...BRUCE JOHNSTON AND HIS MOTHER

KRLA BEAT APRIL 30, 1966

Some Producers' Hints From Beach Boy Brian

For the last few weeks, we have been speaking with various record producers exclusively in *The BEAT* in an effort to take *The BEAT*'s readers behind the radio dial to find out just how records are made.

In our concluding article of this series, we are speaking with Brian Wilson—a man who has succeeded in producing one of the most important sounds in pop music in the last five years.

Standing in the middle of today's contemporary music production and looking around us, we asked Brian to give us an idea of what was going on in production. "I think that record production has definitely improved. Several people have managed to raise the standards of the record business, and I feel that records are being made with much more care and there's much more *music* involved in the record industry.

"First of all, there's a consciousness of the value of a good bass line, and records are being made so that they sound as though they were thought out and the things in the records belong there for a reason; there aren't as many unnecessary elements in records."

No Traveling

Brian has produced the Beach Boys' many hit records with a great deal of care and skill for several years. Lately, he has discontinued his road traveling with the rest of the group in order to devote more and more time to his producing activities, experimenting with many new sounds of his own. "In record production, I'm trying to be as harmonic and as melodic as I can, and at the same time dynamic. I'm trying to use dynamics more effectively.

"I'm experimenting in sound combinations with combinations of instruments which aren't generally associated with the rock 'n' roll business.

"I think that the melody is a thought in itself, and it has body just like the words are in a good word-body. I think that a marriage of good lyrics and a good melody is a very powerful medium of expression.

"I try to be conscious of originality in melody. I think *harmonically*, to start with. Harmony inspires melody with me. I feel that there could definitely be more originality in melody writing in the business; melodically, I think this business is weak and there isn't enough emphasis placed on it."

As a record producer, Brian must constantly watch the rest of the record business, observing all new techniques which are being employed in producing as well as any elements which gain increased importance over a period of time.

"Other elements which have evolved are elements such as using voice a little more subtly—not quite as much of the stereotyped background sound. I think background music—especially in vocals—are using much more than just three notes now. I think that subtlety—thanks to Phil Spector—is in record making where you hear something as a total unit, and eventually discover things in the record, which is a beautiful contribution to the business. Also, subtlety in arrangement."

Brian has created, developed, and expanded his craft—and he has some very definite opinions about what is being done with it. "Popular music—in the form of Top 40—has to expand and has to gain much more widespread respect as a result of someone making an art out of that kind of music. There are enough elements to work with now.

"There is now an acceptance of certain instrumentations. There is a widespread acceptance of new and unlimited instrumentation in this business, that we have reached the spot now where there is an infinite amount of things you can do; now it's really just up to the creative people."

Inspiration

Brian explains some of his efforts in this way: "I think *any* artistic endeavor—if it's really inspired—is something that only the person that's inspired knows, and to make that manifest—it's generally very individualistic how a person goes about making manifest what he conceives.

"So, when I conceive of something, generally it's a conception of harmony-melody-arrangement-song . . . it's all more or less *one* conception. I usually develop the song and the arrangement simultaneously, and the production ideas I build. I usually go in very prepared—before I ever get to the studio I have a general idea of how it's going to come out. But a lot of things develop *in* the studio out of enthusiasm about what's happening at the time. Usually, the record comes out a *little* bit differently than I originally conceived it, but only different because it's more *expanded*.

"I don't mean that the original conception was buried with all kinds of ideas that were generated in the studio; the original conception always shines right through. Things happen in the studio that don't happen at home—there's an *atmosphere* working in a studio, and only there can certain things be generated."

Other Producers

About record producers in general, Brian theorizes that: "I think it is essential to a producer's ability to generate an enthusiasm toward a product which *he* has, to other people. It's a *controlled* enthusiasm to those you're working with—that is what is really important."

As for himself, when asked where *he is going* as a record producer, he replies: "I want to *grow*—and I think that the only way to say where I'm going is to listen to the new sounds I have produced in 'Pet Sounds.' I think that is the only good, accurate indication of where I'm going."

Thank you, Brian—and thank you to all of the producers who given their time and shared some of their knowledge of record production and what it takes to produce a good record with *The BEAT* over the last few weeks. We hope that it has been as interesting and informative for you as it has been for us.

ONE OF THE GREAT all-time name groups, THE BEACH BOYS will always be remembered for their overnight rise to fame and their fantastic holding power.

KRLA BEAT DECEMBER 31, 1966

Beach Boys Lift Beatles' World Crown

Indications of the approach of an entirely new era were revealed when the Beach Boys replaced the Beatles as the world's most outstanding group in an annual poll taken by an English magazine.

The Beach Boys' victory marked the first time in three years the Beatles have failed to win the top position — and furthered America's claim as the pop citadel of the world.

The Beach Boys drew 5,321 votes compared to the Beatles' 5,221. Despite losing their world crown, the Beatles drew an easy victory over the Rolling Stones for the most outstanding group in England.

The Beach Boys' victory wasn't entirely unexpected. The reaction they received on their recent tour of England was reminiscent of the furore caused by the Beatles several years ago.

But the Beatles haven't toured England for nearly a year and it has been months since their last release. The Beach Boys, meanwhile, sold more than 300,000 copies of "Good Vibrations" in England alone.

Had their emergence as the world's top group affected the six Californians? "The group was in good shape for what happened to them in England," said leader Brian Wilson, who didn't make the recent English tour.

It is very inspring," he added. "It's a great lift to the group."

Brian said the award would possibly affect the respect the group commands, but probably would not alter their recording and stage performances.

"But," Brian concluded, "the guys are getting stronger and stronger."

BEACH BOYS Mike Love and Carl Wilson meet the 4 Tops in London where both groups were on a smash tour

BEAT Photo: Philip Godop

SEPTEMBER 4, 1965

"CALIFORNIA GIRLS" DIG THE BEACH BOYS

NOVEMBER 8, 1967

BEACH BOYS SET THEIR EUROPEAN TOUR MINUS CHIEF BRIAN WILSON

The Beach Boys, minus Brian Wilson, will revisit Europe. In May they start a six-nation tour in Dublin, Ireland. Then they'll play Belfast in British Northern Ireland and hop over the Irish Sea on May 4 for their first London Concert. Following their British tour, the group will visit Norway, Holland, Germany and Sweden.

The group's latest single, "Heroes and Villains" is the first collaboration between Brian Wilson and Van Dyke Parks, who are also writing the new album, "Smile" to debut this spring. The album has a 12-page insert book of color photos of the group.

Brother Records, Inc., The Beach Boys' own recording company, has opened offices in Los Angeles. The group is currently developing a TV and films production operation at the same office.

Beach Boys Tops In English Polls

If English popularity pollsters have anything to do with it, the number one group in the world is right here in the United States.

An unexpected victory for America's Beach Boys came after English voters chose the Californians ahead of their own Beatles and Kinks.

World's Top

But while the British publication conducting the poll allowed its country doesn't at present possess the world's top group, it predicted the Beatles are well on their way to recapturing the position.

Still, vote tabulations indicated the Beatles have a good way to go before replacing the Beach Boys.

Behind the Beach Boys, Beatles and Kinks, the voters chose the following: the Small Faces, the Walker Brothers, Dusty Springfield, Cilla Black, Dave Dee, Dozy, Beaky, Mick and Tich, the Spencer Davis Group and the Troggs.

The poll, however, may not be as accurate as it appears. The Rolling Stones were listed only as the number 12 most popular group in their native land.

The poll proved two things: groups are still the most dominant force in pop music and the Beatles are still holding their own.

The poll, taken weekly and tabulated on a basis of 30 points awarded the No. one position, 29 points for the No. 2, and so on, down to one point for No. 30, rated the Beatles No. 24 at the end of June.

'Revolver'

The publication said the impact of the Beatles No. 1 hit, Revolver, was the dominant factor boosting the group's popularity.

In a rating taking in the United States, meanwhile, the Beatles have a massive lead over the Lovin' Spoonful. The Rolling Stones are third, followed by the Mama's and Papa's and Simon and Garfunkel.

Beach Boys: Instant Insanity

...BEACH BOYS — All six of them showed up for this picture. Or were they corralled by Kimmi Kobashigawa and auctioned off as interviewers?

By Kimmi Kobashigawa

It was a night like many other nights (where have we heard *that* before?), except for the fact that I was attending a Beach Boys recording session on this particular evening.

I was going to also do what is commonly referred to in "cool" circles as an *interview* ... but if anything, the BBV ended up interviewing *me*! Not to mention themselves, just about everything else in sight!

"That's a *splendid* example of the group's humor—it's inane, laugh-a-minute jocularity, carries us from the sands of Malibu, lolling on the beach by bikini-clad dolls, all the way to the mountains' heights where we filmed our classic tape to go along with one of our other million-selling hits ... 'Mickey's Monkey!'"

Bruce was lolling hysterically in the corner while Carl was reclined on the couch observing the whole scene.

cold weather. There's art to water fights these days!"

Then Chief Beach Boy, Brian Wilson, clad in his fashionable blue-and-green competition-stripe *whatever*, appeared from behind a machine, wearing a pair of someone else's sunglasses, which prompted Mike to ask him for an interview.

Full Consent

Brian graciously consented and ace reporter Mike Love conducted the following in-depth interview:

question!" His feathers slightly ruffled, Mike asked, "Oh! Am I to understand that you're being *derogatory?*"

"No," replied Brian sincerely. "It's just a shame." "Do you think *that* is!) of me to ask the question, or do you think that I am—as you would say—quote, 'straight'?"

Mike was interrupted here by a loud blast of music, being played back on a tape the boys had just completed recording, which imme-

We got off to a really marvelous start when I asked bearded, fur-capped Mike Love to describe the group's humor for us.

Good Humor

"I would like to talk to you about the group's humor," proclaimed Michael proudly, to which Bruce Johnston immediately added: "It's *good* humor . . . would you like a drumstick?!"

Michael groaned and continued:

Water Fights

I asked whether or not the boys played practical jokes on one another while on tour. In a bass voice extracted from somewhere deep within his cocoa-colored ski sweater, Mike informed me: "No—we just have water fights! Sometimes the water fights get a little rough!

"Sometimes we use toilet water, if we feel *nasty*—and if we feel *devilish*, a little *ice* water, or sometimes *scalding hot* water—if it's

"Have there been any changes in your music since 'Luau,' Brian?" "No," replied Brian, at length. Undaunted, Mike forged ahead. "There have been a lot of inquiries from the State Department, wondering if we'd do a tour on behalf of the 50th State, Hawaii, becoming involved in the States.

"You know, not *every* foreign nation actually knows that Hawaii is a *State* of the United States, and not just a domain or a territory, or a holding of the United States. So they were wondering if we'd do a tour of the Soviet satellites."

Way Too Big

"I'm *way* too big to even *consider* that," Brian explained Mike decided to follow that line of thought for a moment, and promptly tripped over the very next question! "Do you believe that the Beach Boys are too big, or yourself are too great, for involvement in national and international affairs?"

Brian gave this a degree of thought, and replied. "It's going to be a while before we find out where we're at ourselves." "Oh" exclaimed Mike, in surprise and great interest. "Well," he continued brightly, "is that popular among the singing groups of the day—finding out just *where they're at?*"

Brian replied: "Exactly!" Like a good reporter, Mike attempted to pin Brian down to a more specific answer. "Could you elaborate just a *little bit* and tell me exactly what is the connotation of the obvious parenthetical, "where it's at?"

Speaking more directly, Brian explained: "First of all, it's a shame that you had to ask that

diately caused Brian to throw a violent explosion of temper around him, and he severely chastized the engineer for having interfered with our interview! "You've just ruined it! You've ruined our tape!" he cried, pointing at our trusty *BEAT* tape recorder.

Tape Session

This caused Mike to suddenly turn a serious face to our microphone in order to inform us: "For those of you who don't know—these frantic interruptions are because we are right in the middle of a real-live Beach Boy tape-cutting session . . . which is quite different from a vocal session!"

BEAT Reporter-for-an-hour, Mike Love, queried: "Brian, I understand you used to be a dance instructor at Mae Murray's. Is that right?"

Brian replied that he used to tap dance . . . on his toes! but had to give it up. Mike sympathized with him, explaining for our benefit: "Yes, Brian broke his toes. You should *see* his toes!—they look like a Black Belt Karate expert, they're so all-broken up from dancing on them!"

In a fit of passion, Brian grabbed the microphone away from Mike and conducted a little interview of his own. Turning to Al (who had somehow managed to hide out quietly in the corner beneath a chair all this time), he said, "Al—tell me a little bit about your shoes." "They're great!" Al offered. "They've got 'sole'!" Bruce added. "Awwwwwwwww!!" groaned the remainder of the Beach Boys in unison.

Finding the whole thing a bit difficult to believe, I grabbed my tape recorder and headed for the nearest looking-glass back to sanity . . . *I think!*

BRIAN WILSON was reported to have uttered a loud "Mooo" after this photo session. Due, of course, to his genuine cowhide vest!!

KRLA BEAT NOVEMBER 6, 1965

HEAD BEACH BOY

Brian Wilson Turns Serious

By Jamie McCluskey III

A funny thing happened to me as I was sidewalk surfin' the other day. At the crucial moment, just when I was about to hang eight—Alas!—I slipped!! Well, actually, I sort of *slid*—right into a building which just happened to be conveniently standing nearby. Oh hevvins, what a coincidence *that* was, especially since Brian Wilson of the Beachboys also just *happened* to be there.

So, being ever ready with super fab ideas, I immediately trapped Brian with my trusty Secret Agent Kit and secured him to the edge of my giant, transistor-powered skateboard, whereupon we rapidly sped off to a nearby Cloud Nine in the skies, at which time I was fortunate enough to obtain the following exclusive interview for *The BEAT*. (Phewwww!!)

Somewhat puzzled by the many different "sounds" currently circulating the airwaves, I queried Brian as to the reasons behind the Beachboy sound, the British sound, and the type of music which he prefers to listen to.

His Voice Quality

"What is unique about our sound? Possibly the quality of my voice, the higher range of our total voices, the production techniques and arranging, and of course, in song writing.

"Personally I like a certain kind of orchestrated sound, like Nelson Riddle (Did we hear you right, Brian???), and contemporary popular music. Actually, I enjoy all kinds of music, but I enjoy creating in that popular vein of orchestration. I personally prefer to sing a group ballad kind of a number.

"I think the British influence in American production has been stimulating because a lot of the creative producers were eclipsed, and a lot of their artistic records lost their significance, and I think they tried that much harder to make a unique-sounding record that stuck out. For that reason alone I think the British influence —in the end—produced a good result. I think the Beatles' influence is so far-reaching that it's hard to say what their influence is to date. I think it'll show up even in the next five years.

Speaking of Dylan

Speaking of Bob Dylan, and of the current trends of folk and protest music, Brian confided to *The BEAT* microphones:

"Bob Dylan stands for such a large segment of the folk industry. He stands for the contemporary and liberated minds—I think—of today, and so many people are considered 'Dylan people,' but there are 'Byrd people,' and 'Stone people.' I think it's all really part of a movement of liberaion—of self-liberating feeling. And I think he's definitely the king—by his talents alone.

"The protest records are very direct—outside of Dylan—I think that Dylan is very implicit, and his lyrics have to be read into for quite a time. I think in that protest bag, most of the protest songs are very direct, and they can only mean one thing."

...BRIAN WILSON

Upbeat of the Week

KRLA BEAT NOVEMBER 6, 1965 and JANUARY 8, 1966

PORTMAN'S PLATTERPOOP

By Julian Portman

HOLLYWOOD... Sensational rumor hitting Sunset Blvd. THE ROLLING STONES have inked a Christmas and New Year date for "It's Boss" nitery. Pleeze make my reservation Mr. Raffles... Legendary Phil Spector, the man whose music created the RIGHTEOUS BROS. and the RONETTES, is opening a chain of Karate parlors in Los Angeles... Elke Sommer—does three songs on the Nov. 3 Jack Benny special. It's a first for the lovely doll.

Capitol records goes into the motion picture business. Their first epic will feature THE BEACH BOYS... Speaking about Louise's favorite boy singers, THE STONES, they kicked off their tour of the North American continent October 20 in Montreal, the home of my mother's relatives. Lots of excitement for this largest French speaking city in this part of the world. The "Gendarmes", if you're inclined towards the French, the "Bobbies" if you're inclined towards the British, the "Mounties", if you're just plain Canadian, had their hands full. The boys broke all attendance records. They hit Los

ley's new movie "Harum Scarum", was changed to "Harem Holiday" for European release. It'll not effect the title of his newest RCA album... The night before Christmas will find Sonny & Cher, Joey Heatherton, and Frankie Randall cavorting on the one-eyed TV monster... Era records has a good one in "Wait Till Spring" by Jimmy Lewis... Frankie Randall, the brightest young prospect on the Victor label, has been asked to do two more Dean Martin appearances. He'll introduce his latest record effort during one viewing.

Didja enjoy Zsa Zsa Gabor's singing of "High Heel Sneakers" on the Oct. 14 *Shindig*. It was hysterically funny!

Ian Whitcomb, the English lad that came to the American shores to make good before the British would accept him, was sensational in his Oct. 25th opener at "It's Boss." He was also snared for a Nov. 11 *Shindig* appearance... Lloyd Thaxton, the American-lad that made good in America, takes-off for a two week tour of England. Of course, he'll film English artists... The Dave Clark 5 have signed to

By Eden

Have you heard Barry McGuire's new single yet? It's filed under "Positively Out-of-Sight" at your local discery, and it comes complete with two great sides—"Upon A Painted Ocean," and flip-sider "Child of Our Times."

This one's a winner at twice the price! The Byrds are flying high and wide these days, and after hearing their new single—"Turn, Turn, Turn"—it's absolutely certain that these boys aren't about to have their wings clipped! And just for the record, the lyrics to this great new disc aren't just beautiful by accident. The words are taken from the *Book of Ecclesiastes*, and set to music and arranged by one Mr. Peter Seeger. This is one to watch, 'cause the Byrds are going to soar up the charts with this unusual record.

Passing quickly down the line of sounds 'n' singles this week,

Brian is a talented writer—of both songs and prose—as well as being an accomplished producer and Number One Beachboy-type. He is a very thoughtful and introspective boy, and he furrowed his brow very introspectively as he thoughtfully began to speak of his composing endeavors:

"Sometimes I just sit down at the piano and write, and before I even start writing I know that I'm not writing for commercial reasons, so I'll just write to explore some of my musical capacities. I'm always doodling at poetry and thoughts—mostly prose. I'll probably write a book on something; that's the only way you can really pass on what you know. Musically I'm still searching for a new thing, a new bag, a new field. I don't know what's coming, but I know what's here. The Dylan cult is now a realization, and other than that—things like the Phil Spector approach to production, and the Burt Bacharach style of writing.

Soon it was time to clamber

Beach Boys In Hassel Over Movie

Capitol Records made a lot of noise a while back by announcing that they were going into film making and were starring the Beach Boys in their first production.

Well, now it seems the whole thing has fallen through and there may not be any Beach Boys film at all, at least not from Capitol.

Steve Broidy, former president of Allied Pictures was hired by Capitol for the film, which Capitol had hoped would be the start of something great.

No Script

The disagreement between the Beach Boys and Broidy, which may mean the death of the whole deal, seems to center around the lack of a working script. The five California boys want script approval before filming and won't agree to anything until they see a script, which Broidy apparently doesn't have yet.

Everyone involved with the film has gotten a little angry over the delay and even the Beach Boys themselves have been reported to be arguing among themselves over it. There have even been reports that Brian Wilson has been offered other picture opportunities if the Capitol deal falls through completely.

But they are still negotiating over the thing. After all, the Beach Boys are Capitol's top selling American teen act, and Alan Livingston, president of the label, has frankly stated, "We want to make a picture."

KRLA BEAT APRIL 9, 1966 and JUNE 9, 1965

Eden had to ask Brian Wilson of the Beach Boys about something.

There we saw not only the Beach Boys, who were finishing up an album they're cutting, but a slew of other people as well.

We first saw Bobby Hatfield of the Righteous Brothers, with a new and very short hair cut. Bobby and Bill Righteous were cutting something with this huge mass of people they casually refer to as a band (it's actually more the size of an orchestra.)

CARL WILSON — Thanks for the very delicious steak dinners.

BOBBY HATFIELD — Short hair and an extremely large band.

Danny Hutton and one of the "Hollywood A Go-Go" dancers wandered in for a short time.

After what seemed like hours Eden found out whatever it was she wanted from Brian and I clued her in that I was going to collapse from pure unadulterated hunger any minute.

Well, Eden's not too bright at times either and she ignored me. However, Beach Boy Carl Wilson finally took pity on me and took both unsympathetic Eden and starving me out to dinner (never let it be said that these Wilsons aren't generous people — that was one of the best steaks I've ever tasted.)

After bidding farewell to Carl, my faithful companion and I trooped over to a local folk type night club where Eden had to set up an interview with Eddie Brown, of Joe and Eddie.

After a brief talk with Eddie we fled the scene and dashed over to another recording studio where I had an interview with The Astronauts while they were recording.

There was only one minor problem — the studio that The Astronauts were supposed to be using is the one that The Rolling Stones do the majority of their recording in. And guess who just happened to be in town and had just happened to decide to record that night?

Would you believe The Beatles? No, well, how about The Stones — OK?

Anyway, The Astronauts got moved to another studio, but that wasn't the problem — it was a small matter of the fans camped outside the door and one uniformed guard (well, actually there were more

They're Still Tops

THE BEACH BOYS REMAIN AMERICA'S MOST CONSISTENT HIT-MAKERS. 'HELP ME RHONDA' IS STILL ONE OF THE TOP SONGS ACROSS THE COUNTRY.

KRLA BEAT MARCH 9, 1968

The Beach Boys Haul In $60,000 For Four Days!

LOS ANGELES—Probably the most often repeated question asked concerning the field of pop music is "how much money does a successful group make doing personal appearances?"

The net amount is almost impossible to determine but for a successful group such as the Beach Boys the gross for a five performance "short" tour is $60,000.

Take, for example, the Beach Boys' recent swing through the Northwest. Their opening date at Everett Community College broke all existing records for the small institution and grossed $8,050 from a sell-out house scaled from $2.00-$5.00.

Their date at the Seattle Sports Arena (also scaled $2.00-$5.00) grossed a nice $18,885 despite the area's snow storms. Vancouver's Agradrome (with tickets scaled from $3.00-$5.00) was another complete sell-out, grossing $10,000.

An afternoon date at the Portland Coliseum was the top money, grossing $18,918 with the tickets scaled from $2.50 to $4.50. The Beach Boys final date was at St. Martin's College in Olympia, Washington. The concert (with tickets scaled from $2.50 to $5.00) grossed $8,000.

So there you have it. If you're as popular as the Beach Boys you can gross $60,000 for four days of work. Needless to say, not many pop groups are as popular as the Beach Boys . . . But, then again, if you're as popular as the Beatles, $60,000 is peanuts.

MIKE QUIGLEY INTERVIEW 1969

MIKE QUIGLEY interviews the Beach Boys
Al Jardine, Bruce Johnston, Carl Wilson & Mike Love
at the Vancouver Airport on January 15, 1969.

Mike's description: It was recorded on January 15, 1969 after the Beach Boys deplaned from a champagne flight before embarking on a three-concert tour of Vancouver, Victoria and Seattle. This interview was previously published in Vancouver's underground newspaper, The Georgia Strait, in the July 30-August 3, 1971 issue.

Mike Quigley: I was wondering what it is that has influenced your vocal style -- for example, on Little Deuce Coupe, there's an awful lot of really thick stuff, you know -- vocally ... like in the one about James Dean -- "A Young Man's Gone". I was wondering how did you get the style? Was it ... what groups influenced you mainly for that?

Al Jardine: Mainly the Four Freshmen.

MQ: Who actually works on it? Is it ... does Brian do your arranging?

AJ: Uh, yeah.

MQ: And...

AJ: Brian arranges our vocals.

MQ: Yeah. And you just do it ... is it the five? Do you just stick with five or do you do any double-tracking or anything like that?

AJ: Yeah, we overdub -- you get a more thicker sound, a more vibrant sound. We like to overdub as much as we can, which means putting on our voices twice, or sometimes for kicks, maybe three times.

Jim Allan: You've used your voices on some of The Monkees' stuff too, haven't you?

[I can still see myself here rolling my eyes thinking "Oh, Jesus..."]

AJ: I beg your pardon?

JA: On some of the other groups, you have done some vocal work as well, some of the people in the group? I heard a rumour that some of the high parts on The Monkees' songs were done by some of The Beach Boys.

AJ: No...

MQ: It's not speeded up when you do high stuff, is it?

AJ: No...

MQ: What about the low notes? Does Mike do those mainly?

AJ: Yeah, Mike is our low note man. Sometimes I popped in for a low note. Once Mike was sick or something, so I did a thing, but Mike ... you know, just for kicks. It's fun sometimes switching parts, like singing out of your own range. It's fun to try something else. Like, you know we always make little cracks at each other about, you know ... "heavy low note man", you know, so you try to do somebody else's part in the group just to show him that he's not the only guy in the group that could do it, but it's a lot of fun, just...

MQ: I notice that from some of your ... you cut out things and throw them in the album at the last minute or something. You don't intend to put The Beatles on in your next album, do you? This "Back in the USSR" ... what do you think about that?

AJ: No, I have no plans for that at all.

MQ: Do you think they're spoofing you in that album?

AJ: Yeah, I think it's a very poor imitation.

MQ: Yeah, I would say so too. It doesn't sound like you.

MIKE QUIGLEY INTERVIEW 1969

AJ: I think as The Beatles, they sound fine. I don't know...

[Interruption of some kind.]

MQ: Yeah, I was wondering...

AJ: I'm sure they're not serious.

MQ: I was wondering ... your image has sort of switched. First you had surf music and then you went into hot rods, and then ... I really can't say ... Pet Sounds sort of stuff. Are you doing this to attract new fans or is it mainly an appeal to the older fans? You have ... like you've been going for seven years as you say, you have many old fans, as The Beatles have too. Who are you considering when you think of your image now? Is it both the old fans and the new fans that you're trying to appeal to?

AJ: Yeah. Also trying to get ... to stay current with the young people ... young fans, too. Like we're doing a song now ... it's very much like a surfing song. It's a lot of fun to sing, it's a lot of fun to listen to, it's got a good solid four-four beat to it, and it's got castanets in it and everything. It's gonna be a real happy song -- it might be our next single.

JA: You're pushing for a happy...

AJ: Yeah, happy-go-lucky, simple lyrics, nothing heavy, just fun, and I think that may be our next single.

MQ: One of my friends from England said when he was over here that what he thought was The Beach Boys' real contribution was a sort of positive music. You've never considered going on a negative trip like The Doors or something like that, have you?

AJ: No, that's terrible ... that's a downer.

MQ: Happy stuff is what you really dig?

AJ: Yeah.

MQ: I see.

JA: What about your tour with the Maharishi? It bombed in some places ... do you have any idea why?

AJ: I don't know. Nobody was ready for it.

JA: Are you still affiliated with him in some way?

AJ: Yeah.

JA: I see one of your songs from your released LP has got "Transcendental"... uh ...

AJ: "Meditation".

[Interruption.]

AJ: Yup, that's for a fact.

JA: Are you going to be doing any.

AJ: It's a song. It's done... I like it very much.

JA: I was meaning more or less not the song itself, but the thought behind the song. The Beatles have put the Maharishi down and I was wondering whether you people...

AJ: Well, that's The Beatles again. That's their interpretation. We... It's in the eyes of the beholder, you know, I think, more or less. We have our opinion about things, and we don't associate with them in the least respect, musically or philosophically or ideologically. That's ... you know...

JA: Yeah.

MQ: Most of your songs seem to be about two minutes long, and you seem to have established pretty well the two-minute song as an art form. Like on The Beatles' new album, there's a lot of really short cuts as opposed to the long stuff. Have you ever thought of making a long album, long album in quotes. You know, like Sergeant Pepper has a lot of really long cuts, and people like The Doors are going into things for twelve, thirteen, fourteen minutes. Do you think you'll be doing this in the future?

AJ: Uh-uh... What I mean is, I couldn't answer that question 'cause I don't know. Whatever you feel at the time is what you do. It's a very now business ... it's right now. If you feel like doing fifty thousand minutes and so on, you do the ten-album folio and do it -- one song, if you want to. I don't think we'll do that much, of course, but we might. Whatever happens, happens.

JA: Do all of you decide together, or is one person spokesman for the group and says: "I think we should go here now. Like Brian does the arranging and producing -- does he have a lot...

AJ: Well, it's from one area to another. It just depends who has a good idea, you know. Bruce ... it could be myself or Brian ... it just floats, it happens ... it could go into action immediately.

JA: Why did Brian leave the group?

AJ: Did he leave?

JA: Well, is he still doing anything. Like I saw that promo thing...

AJ: No, that's an appearance group.

[Interruption by waiter.]

AJ: Salmon? Did you say salmon? Sounds groovy. It's my third dinner tonight. They keep feeding us, you know. Can't seem to turn it down. I love salmon. I'm a Northwesterner, and I'm sure it'll be great. Anyway...

JA: Does Brian appear on stage with you?

AJ: No, he hasn't for the last six years. I don't recall that ever being very much of a question.

JA: Well, I've never heard your show live. I just heard the LP.

AJ: Oh, you never saw ... well, I see. He never has appeared with us for the last five or six years.

JA: How long has Bruce been in the group?

AJ: Ah, going on four, I think. Glen Campbell was with us for a while.

JA: Why isn't the picture of Bruce on the LP covers then?

AJ: That's just a transition ... photo catalogue transition.

MQ: I think he was on Friends, wasn't it?

AJ: Yeah, but it's hard to keep photographs up to date. We had lots of catalogued photographs with Brian in them, and without Bruce. Sometimes Capitol Records will do something without thinking, and not being demeaning to Capitol, of course, they would just do something like they take the best picture in the catalogue. Once, I wasn't even on a cover ... and it just happened to be the best shot.

MQ: That was California Girls, wasn't it?

AJ: Yeah. I mean, those things happen.

MQ: You sort of put yourself on at times, you know, like on Shutdown, Volume 2, you have this little "Cassius" Love versus "Sonny" Wilson, or something. Do you ever consider any of your songs as put-ons? Like "Be True To Your School," for example. A lot of my friends don't really think you could be serious when you're recording that.

AJ: Yeah, well, it's ... that was a long time ago. That's more of a musical endeavour anyway. I don't know.

MQ: You mean you were concerned with harmonic stuff rather than the words.

AJ: Yeah, I mean that's a very important marriage. I think ... I didn't write that song, and so I don't know.

MQ: Well, in "Heroes and Villains," you get that effect really good -- you're not worried about the words any more. I think there's been several articles, one in the Evergreen Review about a couple of months ago. The guy said you're concerned just with the song now rather than the words.

AJ: No, that's not true either, but I guess some of the stuff you can do now, you know, you can ... it's just how you want to interpret it and how you write it. We might write in one context one moment and in another it might be in another context, but if it goes down and close to music and seems to make some kind of sense, then that's good.

JA: Do you think Bruce will get any writing with the group at all?

AJ: Yeah, Bruce wrote a tune on our last album -- "Near Far Away Places" it's called. It's an instrumental and it's really beautiful. Bruce, did you write more than one tune on the album?

Bruce Johnston: One. One very straight, maybe bordering on square, but it really fits. It's really just kinda nice. There's always room for nice -- I mean there's a lotta nice very forward, radical, groovy, funky things, you know. This just fits. This wouldn't turn any nose up, you know. That would be digging only very heavy things that are big contributions. It's really groovy. It's a nice melody, the thing that I wrote. It's not important, you see. It's just something nice that'll sound groovy to you -- it's naive to me. I wrote all the arrangements, but the arrangements are naive, but they sound groovy. You know, if I wrote the arrangements two years from now, they would probably be a lot slicker. Nevertheless, I'm not putting my song and my arrangement down. I just know where I'm at. But it'll sound nice anyway with the stereo of our albums...

MQ: Are you actually ... I was reading in Eye Magazine that Brian, because of an ear impediment, can't produce in real stereo. Has that been fixed? Is his ear okay?

BJ: He can produce in stereo in our engineer's advice, you know. He just never had to produce in stereo. This isn't for the radio, is it?

[Interruption by waiter.]

BJ: Records ... a record just shouldn't be that important. I mean it shouldn't hang you up emotionally if your record fails. You shouldn't get into it that way. It's just nice if it all happens. I wonder if someone might read that and think, "Well, this guy's connected with a group that probably has enough investments or something to say that. It's not important because he has that security, but it really isn't."

MQ: Were you part of making Smiley Smile?

BJ: I've been part of everything since...

MQ: Since when? You've been singing with the group. Does Brian sing with the group?

BJ: Yeah, we all sing. Sometimes one of us might be missing because we might be away or something, but there's always four or five. I've been with the group since 1965. I will be beginning my fifth year on April ninth this year. I don't even know what you asked me. You didn't ask me anything. What am I talking about?

MQ: Oh, Al said something and he threw it over to you.

BJ: Oh.

MQ: Do you think The Beach Boys has the potential of becoming rather camp? You know -- people will not look upon you for The Beach Boys today, but it's a process -- you have to wait several years and then look back, which is what I do now, and why I really dig some of your early stuff.

BJ: Oh, yeah. Of course The Beach Boys will be camp. That's what's really kinda fun. It's funny -- we're kind of a ... now this is gonna sound ... you're probably gonna disagree ... we're really kind of an underground group that's way above ground because of some of the things that we try. Those people who associate our old big groovy hits with...

MQ: "Surfin' U.S.A."...

BJ: Yeah, plus "Good Vibrations." We try some really interesting things besides being outright commercial.

MQ: Which album would you recommend to listen to for these new sonic developments?

BJ: Maybe then they were, but now they're just kinda ... for a lot of them together, I'd say

MIKE QUIGLEY INTERVIEW 1969

Smiley Smile, but more than that I'd say Pet Sounds.

MQ: Yeah, I think that's a really terrific album.

BJ: I think that's the best Beach Boy album.

MQ: It sorta sums up... I think if you'd quit right there, you'd have a perfect set, because it's almost the Sergeant Pepper of The Beach Boys.

BJ: I thought so too, yeah. We aren't competing with anyone, really, racing any other group to be innovators. We just do what we do. Some of our things come out just eucchh, but other things come out really groovy just doing it. We're just not in any kind of race...

MQ: Well, when you recorded "Heroes and Villains," how did you get all this fantastic harmonic texture. Did you keep playing the tapes and re-recording over top of them and this sort of stuff, or did you actually have it planned out in advance?

BJ: Oh, all these things are planned out in advance. You talk about our re-recording over the tapes, well, if you kept re-recording voices over the tapes, you...

[Interruption.]

BJ: Do you remember Les Paul and Mary Ford? Well, they recorded over their voices and made a lot of harmonics. We've recorded over our voices once and double the harmonies, make them thick. The Four Freshmen do that.

MQ: The Byrds do it a lot.

BJ: For their background. Yeah, I saw The Byrds ... one of my friends, Terry Melcher, used to produce The Byrds. Before I joined The Beach Boys, I was working at Columbia Records as a producer, and saw The Byrds come in and do their first overdub before Terry even met them. They were really groovy then. I really dig The Byrds. I think they are the most underrated -- in their original form -- pop group. I really do.

MQ: What's next? Al was telling us about this happy surfing song. Are you going back to surfing or something? Perhaps have a sort of Beach Boys revival and sing "Surfin'" again?

BJ: No, that's not where it's at. There's room for one record. There's a lot hipper and sophisticated and subtler ways of survival, if you're gonna get into that. We are a business, and you do a little of what you think's right, pay your bills, and attract ... a single record attracts attention to your concerts and your albums. For us ... you know, we're not The Beatles. We're The Beach Boys and I think we're not such a phenomena the way The Beatles are. We're just kinda surviving at a very comfortable level. Maybe someday there'll be a really forward good vibrations popping out of it. We're not trying to top ourselves with each record, obviously. Otherwise you wouldn't hear songs like "Bluebirds Over the Mountains" which isn't doing well, or "Do It Again", which did a million and a half world wide.

MQ: To switch to another track completely ... what do you think about these people who don't dig The Beach Boys (now I know that's going to put you in a certain frame). I mean they don't dig The Beach Boys because you're only considering the happy stuff. Frank Zappa, for example, puts you on in a couple of spots. Of course, he doesn't take into consideration the happy stuff, he just takes the negative side. Do you think there's a happy medium you can strike in music between negativism like The Doors, which is in a way healthy, because it helps you see the opposite, and the happiness which The Beach Boys have? Do you think that a happy medium can be realized between them?

BJ: Well, a lot of our concerts do okay, and I know we still get royalty checks which still isn't that important, but again, I have to just say that we're making our records. We're just doing our thing and why should everybody dig us? Everybody can dig The Beatles, but why should everybody dig us? You know, The Beach Boys' image is kinda like a group Doris Day, you know what I mean? A lot of people stopped digging The Beach Boys, you know, and in their

MIKE QUIGLEY INTERVIEW 1969

minds that image is probably still that Doris Day image and I think a lot of kids are going away from all that "clean" thing because that's where their parents are at, and they're trying to get into another thing and they don't like groups that represent that "clean" thing as much as other groups, which is OK because it's just another form of growing up.

MQ: Who's Roger Christian?

BJ: Roger Christian is a disk jockey that at the time his words were sufficient for some of Brian's melodies, but now I'm sure that some of those groovy melodies ... I'm sure that "Don't Worry, Baby" could be rewritten. The words are so trite now, but that was where it was at for about five minutes.

MQ: What about this "Frosty the Snowman" that's on your volume three of your Greatest Hits?

BJ: That's in a Christmas album.

MQ: Is it sold out or something now?

BJ: I don't know. Oh sure, it is ... every Christmas I see The Beach Boys Christmas Album.

MQ: There was one fellow in the group on the first three or four records, and then he left...

BJ: David Marks.

MQ: David Marks? Who was he?

BJ: He's ... Al Jardine was the orig... Al, Carl, Dennis ... wait. Carl, Dennis and Brian are brothers, and Mike Love's a cousin. And Al Jardine was also one of the original members. After the first hit, or two, he left the group to go back to school because he wasn't sure and I don't blame him that a group's gonna have a successful business-like affair making surfing records. You know, they're all young. Then Dave was the next-door neighbour to Dennis and Carl and Brian, and he came in the group for a while. Then Brian stopped touring. The group started getting bigger and bigger, so Al started replacing Brian on the road, and then finally there was a big flare-up with Dave Marks and he left the group. Brian came back in on the road and Al stayed, but Al's the original member of the group. You know, Glen Campbell sang with the group right before I joined the group.

MQ: Is he on any of the records?

BJ: No, no, he's not. Let's see ... Brian didn't tour for a while so we replaced him with Glen Campbell and then they replaced me ... I mean they replaced Brian with me because Glen was starting on his own thing, and then ... Glen's played a lot of guitar on our records, and Glen ... Brian produced Glen Campbell on a song called "Guess I'm Dumb" -- really good. It should have been in Pet Sounds. You know, I'm sure you probably wouldn't be able to get it, but it's so heavy, so far ahead ... wow ... you know, Glen's a good singer and he had trouble singing this song. That was put out three years ago and it was a bomb. It was a lovely, lovely record.

MQ: I was just asking Al ... uh ... what the hell was it now ... oh, yeah, the songs ... do you think that any of your songs are put-ons. For example, "Be True To My School". I mean, when my friends hear it, they say, "Aw, they couldn't be serious when they were singing it."

BJ: That was five years ago. That was ... a lot of people ... that's where they were at. That was a year ahead ... and a year and a half before it all started changing, you know. People started, luckily, getting freer. I really dig the scene that's happening now, I really do, because there might be a lot of bad things going on, but if out of all of those bad things ten per cent of the groovy part of it stays, wow ... you can't beat that.

[Pause in taping.]

BJ: And really ... don't record this...

MQ: OK.

[Pause in taping.]

MQ: That little bit you said about the taunts...

MIKE QUIGLEY INTERVIEW 1969

BJ: Oh, yeah. The taunts that kids might give a group like us ... maybe even The Association ... you know ... they're pretty clean.

MQ: Yeah, but I don't really dig them -- they don't seem to have any group personality.

BJ: No, they don't, but they make groovy records. But, you know again, getting back to what a group like ours might represent -- the cleanliness thing. A lot of kids are always rebelling against their parents and I'm sure, connecting us to that "clean" thing they might want to put us down. You know ... like "Hendrix ... wow ... heavy!" and he is heavy, very heavy, and so are a lot of the other groups. I never could get into The Chambers Brothers. They make good records, but I never could get behind it.

[Pause in taping.]

MQ: Carl? My name is Mike Quigley, and I'm writing an article on the cultural significance of The Beach Boys for the University of B.C. paper which has about twenty thousand readers, and in working on this thing, I was wondering what about the influences for your group. Al said The Four Freshmen. Are there any other groups at all?

Carl Wilson: What?

MQ: One of the originals...

CW: Oh, yeah, you know ... well, I ... what do you mean ... original what?

MQ: You know, one of the original brothers.

CW: The original...

MQ: A couple of guys have dropped out so far, haven't they?

CW: Yeah, yeah ... oh, oh, no ... everybody's cool.

Mike Love: It's shit, though.

CW: It's the same group that always was, except for Bruce who takes ... well, of course, you see ... Bruce has been recording also, so I guess you could say he's in the group also.

MQ: What about the influences except The Four Freshmen. Any other groups?

CW: No. No other groups. No. I was influenced personally by Chuck Berry, you know ... his guitar .. boogie-woogie.

ML: We were all influenced by Chuck Berry's sentence for being ... you know ... crossing the state line with an underage chick. It influenced us a lot too.

MQ: I see.

ML: Good. Mostly ... not culturally. However, in other ways...

MQ: Yeah, like "Surfin' U.S.A." is a Berry hit.

ML: What's your name?

MQ: Mike Quigley. I'm from the University of British Columbia.

ML: Hi, there. I'm Mike.

MQ: Mike Love.

ML: Yeah.

CW: Yeah, anyway ... so that's our main influence. I guess we're influenced by life, you know, and just everything as far as the music goes. You get inspiration from anything ... there've been inspirations just from cans and bottles and jars, and just everything ... people. Those are the influences for songs.

MQ: So what's in store for you now after Friends? Have you got another album coming out soon?

CW: Yeah, we have an album called 20/20 coming out, and it'll be out any second. [Reaching into the air] Ah, here it is. No, it'll be out... like next week. Will it be out next week, Mike?

ML: Well, I would say that if it isn't out by next week, it'll either be out earlier than next week or in the very near future, but not wishing to seem ambiguous, I would give it a date somewhere between the ... whatever it is now and about the first of February.

CW: Yeah, I would say that.

MIKE QUIGLEY INTERVIEW 1969

ML: Thought I'd take a little of the suspense out of it. Did I hear you say something about the cultural significance.

CW: Yeah, I...

MQ: Yeah, believe it or not.

ML: Aren't you trying to read something into this whole thing?

MQ: I don't know ... do you think I am?

ML: Probably.

MQ: You mean you don't consider yourself that seriously? Considering all the guys that are listening to you now. You've been here for seven years or so, haven't you?

ML: We consider ourselves very seriously, but I think that the erstwhile critics get into it a little too much for their own good. I think they overdo it a little bit. Like in finding hidden meanings...

MQ: No, I don't mean that. I don't mean your song content. I mean, just the fact that you've existed and influenced all these kids, like the last seven years you've been around. The Beatles have been around for five years, isn't it? And Elvis Presley's been around for God knows how many years. There's very few groups that seem to last and have this continuing influence. The Beach Boys is one of them.

ML: I guess it's greed.

MQ: Yeah.

ML: No.

CW: No, really, I guess our influence was just the good-time music, that's all. You know ... having fun, wouldn't you say?

ML: Yes ... we've never really been that much of a ... what do you call it ... a protest ...

MQ: Negative ... like The Doors and that...

ML: Yeah, well, not that, but we have mostly concentrated on the more fun-type elements that you can work with. You can do one or the other, or go both ways, but we always, more or less...

MQ: Do you think any of your songs are put-ons? "Be True To Your School", for example?

ML: Yeah, well maybe it would be a put-on if we did it now.

MQ: But back then it was real?

ML: It was ... it was reminiscingly real. We were maybe a couple of years removed from that actual feeling, but ... writing in that sort of...

MQ: Yeah, well, if you did it today it would be like Frank Zappa or something ... putting people down. I think he's already put you on ... on what the hell was it? He was doing "Louie Louie" like you did the duh-duh-duh.

ML: Yeah, well, Richard Berry did that before we did it, and Richard Berry wrote it. Frank Zappa's a very hep cat and everything ... what would you call him? But he's clever...

CW: I would say Frank ... he is...

ML: Heavy.

CW: Heavy? Well, I don't know. He's funny.

MQ: Do you get along with him?

CW: I don't know him.

ML: I'll tell you something, though. If Frank and The Beach Boys got together and did a Super Session album, it would be a gas.

MQ: I hear his new album's called Ruben and the Jets.

CW: Yeah, Cruising with Ruben and the Jets. I think that's really out of sight, man.

ML: If he keep comin' up with titles like that, he's gonna have friends for life from The Beach Boy organization.

CW: You know, we think those type of things are humorous. Ruben and the Jets...

ML: They're somewhat esoteric, but Frank knows what they mean.

CW: That's out of sight, man.

MIKE QUIGLEY INTERVIEW 1969

MQ: I think he's doing another one called No Commercial Potential.

ML: He's got no commercial appeal, so you notice he keeps making albums. I think he sells several albums -- internationally, too. He's big in Poland.

CW: We all have a good time, don't we? That's the group thing... Like there's something for everybody.

MQ: If I want any information about you, the history of the group, should I get in touch with the fan club or something? Is there another address?

CW: Oh, ask me.

MQ: Ask you ... oh, hell ... I wouldn't ... just a sec, I've gotta flip this thing.

[Pause in taping while I struggled to remove the tape. Carl finally pointed out that I had to push the tape deck lever off, not just the remote control switch on the mike in order to flip the tape over.]

MQ: You must be quite busy going around the world and doing various tours all over the place. How many times have you been round the world? Got any idea?

CW: Oh, I'd say about ... travelling internationally ... four or five times, beside other side trips, you know ... as a group ... we've been around the States ... you know...

MQ: Quite a lot.

CW: Yeah.

MQ: I was asking Bruce, I think ... most of your songs seem to be about two minutes long. Do you ever intend doing anything long, like The Doors are doing pretty long stuff and The Cream ... I mean not doing it on stage, for example, but recording it. And putting it on an album.

CW: Yeah, sure. Like we're done things that've gone on a lot longer, for ten or fifteen minutes, you know, but like you have to cut 'em down. We've gone into three, four minute records, but not...

MQ: I think "Heroes and Villains" is your longest...

CW: Yeah. It was much longer, really ... it was about seven, eight minutes.

MQ: What about Pet Sounds? Was that a very complicated album to produce? And work out? It seems to me one of your best...

CW: Well, if flowed. It came right out ... it just came out. It was the most fun album to do, I'd say, and we worked the hardest on it.

MQ: Were you considering making that your last album?

CW: Uh ... I don't know ... why?

MQ: Well, I was just wondering, because if it was, if it had been your last album, it would've really finished up a terrific cycle. Do you have any plans...

CW: It was the end of a cycle...

MQ: Yeah, just like the Eye Magazine article said...

CW: What did it say?

MQ: They were talking about all the albums up to Pet Sounds ... they were one thing, and then you sort of switched ... and went into the good feeling, good vibrations stuff which is kinda cool.

CW: Yeah, well, we did what we could do, you know. That's all there was to it, really. Nothing else...

MQ: Were you one of the first groups to start actually surfin' music?

CW: Yeah?

MQ: You were the first?

CW: Yeah, I believe so...

MQ: There was nobody before you? Who came up with this idea?

MIKE QUIGLEY INTERVIEW 1969

CW: Uh ... we did.

MQ: You mean you were just sitting ... did you live around the beach or something?

CW: Yeah, right ... right next to the coast. Dennis I think had the ... I think Dennis was the one that said it.

MQ: Your father was working with you. What was he doing on the first albums? Producing or something? Managing?

CW: Yeah, he was our manager. He helped to mix ... studio sessions ... doing that.

MQ: Well, how did Brian become a producer? Did he ... had he just been fooling around in the studio or something? With the musicians and...

CW: Well, he always was the producer.

MQ: Well, the first three albums were produced by somebody else, weren't they?

CW: Well, they said they were produced by somebody else, but he just sat in the booth and said "OK ... Take one, take two, take three..." He didn't do shit except say that. Brian really produced records from the beginning.

MQ: Well, I think that's about enough...

CW: Oh, OK. Good.

WORLD COUNTDOWN

THE TRUTH ABOUT THE BEACH BOYS BY MARTY CERF

As a musician and song writer, I believe people who deserve credit should get it, and it just so happens that the Beach Boys have had a great influence on what today's record buying public considers underground. I can also tell you, honestly as an authority on music structure to some extent; I have heard many, many of the so called underground songs and groups imitating the exact same thing musically the Beach Boys were doing back in 1966, 3 years ago and even before; so I as a strong believer in originality, think they deserve some of the credit. To continue, their new album is one that could stand up to any of the current-underground albums such as the Doors, Creedence Clearwater, the Cream, and even the Beatles (USSR, the last album the Beatles did). It contains a phenomenal cut originally done by Phil Spectors' Ronnettes group titled "I Can Hear Music" and they do it so well you might even Phil was on the session! Any way the album is second to none that I have heard out recently. You owe it to yourself in all fairness to give a listen to it and see what the Beach Boys are up to now, I think you may find you enjoy the very same material that you may be disqualifying from your music library simply because you think it may be a collection of all surfing safari records, well it is not, and I guarantee you will enjoy every cut on the current 2020 album, if you would let yourself get into it.

I'd like to get into the individual personality of the boys here in my column. I've found it very interesting, and as in the case of Dennis Wilson, very intriguing to know what they are really like.

Brian Wilson, now at the age of 27 has been with the Beach Boys since the beginning. He has been the real musical backbone of the group. His music should go down in history as the young pop sound of the 60's. It has been recorded by many famous people and groups, even people like Hugo Montenegro who currently has a hit version of Good Vibrations on the charts (goes to show the versatility of his writings). Brian is pretty much a quiet person he likes to be alone a lot so he can communicate to himself and others musically through his talents. His musical works are so advanced in many of his songs that he has written that he refuses to record songs he has worked on for what some time is many months, simply because the public he feels is not prepared for his phenomenal transition in music yet. States Brian "When the time comes they'll all come out." Truly Brian is in a class where only Lennon-McCartney, Bacharach-David, and Dylan belong. Al Jardine sort of kicked off the Bach Boys through his, first recording session, where the rest of the Beach Boys were supposed to be hired to back up Al on a folk song. But that session evolved to the same session which has produced the biggest fave rave of this half of the century Surfin' on Candix Records. Allan is married to beautiful Linda, and they are both outdoors people, very down to earth. Sometimes they like just to go in the back of their home and crash in the quaint little tree house Allan has built ---- Freaky.

Dennis Wilson is probably the hippest member of the Beach Boys! A true human being, and a firm believer in the phrases "Love thy fellow man" and "Share alike." So much so that he never has permanent residence, at the moment living in an apartment at a friends house. At one time or another Dennis is known to have given most all of the possessions he's owned to people he truly believes needs the things more than he, strange but true. Dennis should be careful as their are a lot of people who would like to take advantage of his kind heart. Dennis is surprisingly the only member of the Beach Boys who can surf well and still does. A true athlete, Dennis is the master of many sports. He is probably the most popular member of the group among the girls, but not yet married. Watch out though, bet it won't be long, but she's going to have to be able to ride a horse and pack a sleeping bag, for when Dennis gets "itchy feet" you better move fast to keep up with him.

Mike Love, the bearded member of the group, is often seen around town on his fave 650 cc Triumph cycle. Mike is the lead singer of the group and has truly the most identifiable and pleasant voices I have ever heard. He is an authority on everything from East Indian philosophy to American History. He spends a lot of his time at the Beach Boys offices in Hollywood working with the management division. He likes to collect antiques and cars ranging from a 1938 Rolls Royce to a 1967 Jaguar sedan.

That's about all this time, be sure to pick up on the new 2002 lp, by the boys on Capitol. Truly a musical experience, by the most unique group to come along in many years and for a long time to come.

In England 1966

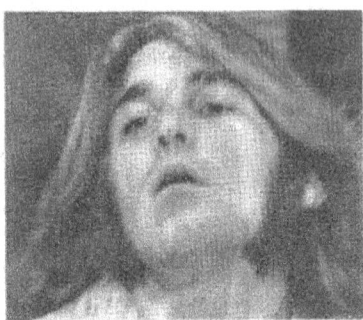

▲ Al Jardine
▶ Dennis Wilson
▼ Carl Wilson

THERE are two ways of seeing a band: the easy way (by jumping into a cab and nipping out to one of the city's clubs), or the difficult way, which is waiting until the band goes on the road and then following to the other end of the country. The latter was the method I chose to employ in order to see and hear the Beach Boys on their recent European concert tour.

The gig was at the Fiesta Club, Sheffield. How I got there with a new electric piano (belonging to Mandrake) in the van is a story in itself; suffice it to say that the journey had one or two exciting moments.

The Beach Boys themselves don't believe it, but it's true: all the numbers which were performed on stage, including *Good Vibrations*, *Cotton Fields*, *Sloop John B* and a fairly representative selection of their past hits were performed 'live' in such a way that they could well have been recordings. Considering all the hype we had about how much production went into *Good Vibrations* the live version was almost identical. I asked Dennis Wilson just how much work they had put into the perfection of their cabaret act.

'As you know we have only worked for a few weeks this year (1970), so we obviously had to do some heavy rehearsals. Even when we used to work hard we didn't do much very cabaret, but then I guess this place is an exception to most of the places we get asked to appear in. Even in Las Vegas we don't get dressing rooms like these. As Al said (on stage). "Man, this is the greatest club we have ever played!".'

Dennis is the latest member of the band to take the lead on vocals (he sang two in Sheffield). 'Put it this way, I sang more tonight than I have ever done on a Beach Boys' Show before. If you didn't quite understand the words on the second song, don't worry about it—I forgot them, and made some new ones up as I went along.'

Super-Sessionman-Dragon

At the end of December there was a 'Hit-Pick' on Radio Luxembourg by Dennis and Daryl Dragon. Was this yet another step towards the great slow-down of the group's act as the Beach Boys? 'No. We do have a great deal of free time, though, so we can do our own thing. Daryl plays with virtually any group; you name a top band and I guarantee he'll have played with them.' Daryl is, in fact, a dark horse as far as the present tour's hype programme is concerned; he sits at the back of the stage playing his piano—no showmanship, no gimmick—and yet he probably gives as much to the sound as any of the BB's themselves.

I asked Al Jardine about the musical direction the band were taking. 'At no point did we stop and decide to change. There is a lot of emphasis put on our argument with Capitol, but it wasn't all that bad; quite understandable really—from a pure business angle. They were on a good thing with surf/hot rod music and they were just reluctant to give it up. Then again, we were getting a bit frustrated because we wanted to do other things—that's when we got ourselves really hung-up for a while. When the contracts ended it was all up to us as to what we did, so we got Brother together and began making our own type of music again. OK, the close-harmony surf sound is what we are best known for, but I think what we are doing now is still very similar. Not so much the harmony bit, but by using harmonious instruments for the same effect. The kids who were on the sunshine trip with us have all grown older now so they want older music.

'I mean, look at the audience we had tonight; they were all in their twenties (or thirties).'

On the technical topic for which the band are most hyped at the moment, I asked for comments on the two tracks from *Sunflower* which were recorded in quadrophonic. 'People tend to treat it as a gimmick in this country,' said Al, 'because stereo has only just caught on here. At home, FM radio has been stereo for quite a while

now, and a few stations in the Bay Area are going "quad" now. The principal is so much better than stereo, because sound will come from all round and not from the front only, just like being in front of a bank of amplifiers at a concert.'

Dennis has a more basic approach. 'It might sound silly to you, coming from me, but *I* prefer mono. I love one speaker. It's so much more of a challenge to get good quality from one speaker, but when you get that quality there is much more punch. You listen to two cats talking, one'll say "come to my pad and listen to my stereo"; they don't say "come and listen to my records". How many albums do you hear nowadays which have phasing and effects for very little reason except to show how well Joe Doe's stereo works.'

Now that Dennis has started to record outside of the Beach Boys and Carl is spending so much time producing other bands (the one-time London based South African group Flame are members of his stable), what were the others doing as individuals? Mike Love answered for everyone. 'We fly. No, seriously, we have so much to do with the administration of our affairs (Brother)—and Brian has our studio to look after—that we don't really have all that much time to be bored.'

In addition to solo recording, Dennis spent a short time with James Taylor making a movie. 'We were just two ordinary guys in a film, completely separate from our musical pasts. There are lots of things you can read into the film—the generation gap, etc.—but, as a journalist I was talking to last week said, "that's the quality which can make or break a film".'

There are a couple of films already in the can here in London (made for the Beach Boys during their last European tour), which haven't yet come on release. I queried the reason, but Dennis would say nothing on the subject except that there were 'hassles' with the financial side of things. Al went so far as to admit that, although he had commissioned the film as a documentary of their tour, he had not yet seen the final product. Depending on his opinion, it could very well be released to TV or commercial cinemas in early spring.

In the States, Fender gear is used almost exclusively, so it seemed strange to me that on this European tour Orange amplifiers and speakers should be used; was there a special reason for this? Dennis replied, 'We sent our road manager over here first to buy some gear, we didn't care what make it was as long as it was good—for that matter I don't think we knew too many English makes of amplifiers. It was all left up to Manfred.'

Charity gigs

On their last visit to these shores the Beach Boys played a charity gig with Jimmy Saville in Leeds Infirmary, and on this occasion they repeated the gig. As very few groups of the same stature perform free of charge in this country; did society's illnesses, etc., mean a great deal? 'Man we made it, we got money,' answered Al, 'we're all healthy (well sort of), so it just seems right that we should do something for others, it makes me feel good. The bad thing is that once you say

▲ *Bruce Johnston*
▼ *Mike Love*

that you like charities, hundreds of letters come pouring in, asking us to play for free, or to give bread.'

While I had Al cornered, I asked him if there was any possibility that since McCartney had issued his writ against the other Beatles (and thus made the break absolute), was there any chance of the rumours which circulated a couple of years ago (about McCartney joining forces, for recordings or writing with the Beach Boys) proving true? 'I guess that's possible.' Al went on . . . 'anything's possible with him. I couldn't really see him doing anything other than writing, though. He's the sort of guy that I would expect to just find singing in a little English pub somewhere. I honestly don't know his plans.'

S.H.

33

AS THEY START THEIR BRITISH TOUR

IF THE Beach Boys are really in Britain to make some quick money and get themselves in the black again... they're certainly making sure they earn it!

At the sedate Hammersmith Odeon on Saturday the world's most popular active group turned an uncommonly apathetic first-house audience into rousing cheers with 50 non-stop minutes taking in no less than 18 hit songs.

The Beach Boys all looked happy, well-fed and affluent. On stage they are a strange mixture of personalities and temperaments. Bruce, as always, is the "crowd-conscious" Beach Boy, always anxious to tell the audience how great it is to be in England again, slipping in little news snippets on the progress of Carl's baby, or the current health of Brian Wilson. Bruce is also the versatile one, switching from organ to bass guitar frequently and with great agility.

Carl is still the leader and the voice, and either seriously or playfully (it's difficult to tell which) chooses to ignore all the "asides" from the others and keeps the music going. His voice still misses the high notes on the loud numbers, and he still becomes quite overwhelmed by the reaction to "God Only Knows." God only knows—he should by now—that this will go down in history as the group's finest-ever recording.

Mike Love has grown his beard, grown his hair (on those parts of his head where it still grows, that is!) and has acquired an incredible white tunic/smock/mini-habit.

The over-all effect is a cross between the Maharishi's younger brother and the original hermit from the hills.

All very incongruous, especially when he bursts into "Well, East coast girls are hip. I really dig those clothes they wear"!

Mike has always looked the misfit in the group, and gives the impression on stage that he doesn't really know what he's doing up there. His ad-libs with the audience are becoming more and more outspoken.

But Mike gets away with it, and other comments like "Here's a Beach Boys oldie but mouldie for sure which you'll remember, especially those elephants down there."

Al Jardine keeps himself to himself, looks worried when his amplification equipment apparently doesn't work—though you can't hear his guitar anyway. This time he's been given his first solo—"Cotton Fields" from the "20/20" LP.

And Dennis Wilson, maybe because he never says anything, and always looks so wild and unpredictable, gets the bulk of the fan screams.

Yes, there were screams, plenty of them, and it will be a sad day when they stop. Dennis chews gum perpetually, occasionally mouths a few words of a song that takes his fancy, rebukes the band-leader for playing the wrong rhythm, and generally looks as if he can't wait to get off stage.

So much for the five men—what of the music? There's very little new to say about the Beach

On stage —wonderful as ever

Beach Boys (Bruce Johnston, Carl Wilson, Al Jardine, Mike Love) during their unaccompanied number

Boys' music on stage. It's always good and with so many hits under their belt it's difficult to see how they can fail. Opening with "I Can Hear Music," which harmonically, left much to be desired, they swing into "Wouldn't It Be Nice," "California Girls" and "Darlin'."

Then came the first highlight—a medley of the old slow songs we all loved so much. Linked together as a ten-minute special we had "Warmth Of The Sun, Don't Worry Baby, Please Let Me Wander, Surfer Girl and In My Room"—great stuff.

One criticism of the Boys in concert is that they rarely delve right back into their nostalgic archives. This medley should more than satisfy those critics.

Then "I Get Around," followed by the only "surprise" item of the evening—an excellent version of Buffalo Springfield's "Rock-n-Roll Woman," possibly the first time the group has ever sung someone else's hit.

The other highlight was the unaccompanied song "Their Hearts Were Full Of Spring," and the only real chance to hear those fabulous Beach Boy harmonies, plus Mike Love's bass lines that seem to get lost in the backing band at all other times.

The rest was true to format—"Do It Again," "Barbara Ann," "God Only Knows," "Good Vibrations" and "Breakaway," followed by the quickest curtain I've ever seen!

The lucky second house audience got an impromptu Mrs Mills medley from Bruce Johnston on organ, and a raving "Johnny B. Goode" as encore. Perhaps if you clap loud enough you'll get them too!

CATCH UP WITH THE BEACH BOYS
Tomorrow (Friday) Birmingham Odeon; Liverpool Empire (Saturday), Manchester Free Trade Hall (Sunday) and Glasgow Odeon (Monday).

Beach Boys' biggest fan is a 'pirate!'

IT IS eight months since the Beach Boys last single and a year since their last LP. Surely no group with a second place rating in the world section of Disc's Poll can afford, either in terms of money or popularity, not to release records.

EMI should release a new single now, while Roger "Twiggy" Day, their greatest fan, is broadcasting on Radio North Sea. It would receive continual plugs and be a nationwide hit, probably more successful than their previous releases that had airplay from Radio 1. This is an opportunity for record promotion that should not be missed!—Jacqueline Roy, 49 Salford Road, Streatham Hill, London, S.W.2.

Beach Boy Al Jardine

DISC AND ECHO

SURF-IVAL

DISC AMERICAN SPECIAL — 2
The most loved and influential U.S. group talk about their future — Ray Coleman reports

Apart: but the Beach Boys will never split!

HOLLYWOOD.—Mid-afternoon on a sunny Sunday, and Dennis Wilson is playing with two Irish setters beside the piano-shaped swimming pool in Al Jardine's house. Dennis, the most mercurial Beach Boy, is in reflective mood, having just lost at chess to his girl-friend, Barbara. All the other Beach Boys, with the automatic absence of Brian Wilson, are there with their wives—standing around, smiling, talking, playing the piano and eating crisps.

But there has always been something about drummers that gives them an identity bewilderingly different from anyone else. And Dennis Wilson is a drummer, who also has a beard.

Madrigal and Largo, the Irish setters, liked him a lot, even when he threatened to chuck them into the pool. But Wilson's thoughts were a long way now from parties and dogs and chess and the delicious ginger cookies made by Linda Jardine.

"I am planning right now to leave the city here, or even the country," he suddenly announced. "I don't know where I'm going but I'm going to live somewhere else. I don't like America—the land is OK. It's the Government.

"I don't like seeing wealth used so that every 10 months they make the Beverly Hills roads wider for the drunks to drive their fast cars, while people are starving in the ghettoes. I don't have the power to control this, but I don't have to stay among it.

"Also, the smog in Los Angeles makes me sick. Maybe I'll go to live in Scotland. This isn't a cop-out. I'm a citizen of the world ..."

Three days earlier, Bruce Johnston and Mike Love had talked of their plans to buy houses in Britain. Bruce said: "I've been living on a tight budget for the last three years. Now I want to buy a farm just outside Brighton, on those Sussex Downs."

And so the seeds might seem sown for the Beach Boys—nine years old in December — to go their separate ways.

Carl Wilson is busy producing records by a promising group from South Africa, the Flame. Dennis Wilson plans to release a solo album of himself singing — and on paper at least, it looks like a repeat of the Beatles story, but without the friction.

Yet there is something indefinably child-like that will keep the Beach Boys together. To each of them, the group is still a favourite toy—and they are thrilled and proud that Princess Anne scheduled to see their show at Canberra during their current tour of New Zealand and Australia.

THE news from Beatledom was fresh and grave, and Al Jardine was considering all its implications with his cool logic. "We didn't get as rich as they did, and it didn't happen so quickly for us either," he observed.

"So our graph has not been so dramatically successful, but the peaks of the mountain can still be scaled. I don't think the things members of the Beach Boys are into now can be considered dangerous for the group's future.

"We don't have the same sort of scene that the Beatles had with John and his association with Yoko—I mean, it's difficult to see how that sort of individuality could be contained within a team.

"And if one goes from an entity, it can only serve to weaken that entity. It's a very difficult thing to be a team and grow up together as well."

Surfing is where the Beach Boys came in, with their first record called "Surfing Safari" and plenty more later which reflected the water. After going through a period of trying to forget the surf era and regarding it as beneath their dignity to recreate those songs on stage, the Beach Boys have come full circle.

Bruce and Dennis are the only ones who surf today to keep the old image intact. "It's been a stigma and we went through a period of trying to get away from it," said Al.

"We figured there were a million people on the planet who didn't know about 'Good Vibrations' and the 'Pet Sounds' album, but thought we just sang about surf boards. So we developed a real complex about it.

"Now we have convinced enough people we are on to other music as well, we can afford to go back and sing about surfing."

IT would be perfectly reasonable to assume that there is no such person as Brian Wilson.

The giant of the Beach Boys makes a full-time occupation of keeping himself aloof, shut in his luxury Spanish-style mansion in Bel-Air. Casual callers aren't welcome. He doesn't show up when he's expected.

"Oh, he exists all right," says brother Dennis. "Look around you. He's everywhere."

Recently he came out of hibernation and played seven concerts in the States with the Beach Boys, playing keyboards and singing the high parts. "And I think he'll come to England when we tour there in June or September," says manager Fred Vail.

Meanwhile, Brian is mainly at home putting the finishing touches to the group's next album, "Sunflower," out in the States in about a month. It is another example of the diversifying interests of the boys, for they have each contributed songs of different styles.

Brian and Mike wrote "Add Some Music To Your Day" and "When Girls Get Together," Al wrote "Susie Cincinatti" and "Take Load Off Your Feet, Pete," Dennis wrote "Falling In Love" and "Slip On Through," and there is a knockout track from Bruce called "Tears In The Morning."

But with the Beach Boys' label, Brother Records, still not lined up for British distribution—they are still trying to sort out the best deal from a British record company—British fans will have to be patient.

"We don't want to launch in England and then have it go wrong like a sour apple," said Bruce with searing innuendo.

"English fans are very important to us. You know sometimes when we get on stage there, I get tears in my eyes from the way we are welcomed. Maybe when I get to live in Sussex, I'll handle the label in Europe . . . "

Both Bruce and Dennis, the ones most gripped by wanderlust, emphasise that they will not quit the Boys. "We'll just commute. We can be anywhere in the world in a day from anywhere."

Dennis Wilson lazes in a deckchair, laughing away at the stories from Britain about the Beatles split. "They can never split. They'll be back."

Mike Love still meditates and sun-worships at his home in Manhattan Beach. He wears an orange scarf round his forehead and does not own a record player. He has plenty of records.

Brian Wilson sleeps by day, gets up by night, and listens to the radio. He is a Top 40 student.

They don't get together much —mainly for recording sessions and concerts — and that's probably their strength.

In Al Jardine's house in Brentwood, high up above Los Angeles, a load of framed gold discs hang on the wall. Dennis Wilson paused to look at them, and said: "Bits of metal. They don't mean much, you know."

It seemed a weird thing for a performer to say. But then, the Beach Boys are different from most.

Separate lives—the Beach Boys (back) Mike Love, Carl Wilson; (middle) Dennis Wilson, Al Jardine; (front) Bruce Johnston.

BRIAN WILSON: he'll probably visit Britain on the Beach Boys' tour.

JOHN SEBASTIAN: an original

BEACH BOYS CONCERTS HERE IN JUNE

BEACH BOYS will be back in Britain again in June—at their own request.

They will do three special shows. And provisional dates are: London, June 6; Birmingham (7); and Manchester (8).

These are the only live concert appearances they will make. A supporting bill is being set up; and there will be two shows at each venue.

The news was revealed exclusively to Disc by Bill Fowler, of the Arthur Howes office, which handled the Beach Boys' last UK tour last December.

He explained: "The Beach Boys asked to come over again —mainly because of the success of the last trip.

"They originally wanted to do all three concerts in London. But this wouldn't be possible. I gather they plan to spend about a week here after the shows."

Another reason for the early return is that the Beach Boys have been approached to make a full-length film in America later in the year and shooting might clash with plans for an autumn trip to Britain.

During the visit in June, Mike Love hopes to go into the studio with Dominic Grant, managed by Bill Fowler, to cut some Beach Boys songs. On the group's last tour they met Dominic and agreed to help his career.

Beach Boys' latest single "I Can Hear Music" entered the chart this week at No. 26.

Another gem from the Beach Boys...

BEACH BOYS—Tears In The Morning (Capitol-stereo). You may have read my ecstatic ramblings a few weeks back about "Sunflower." Well this is the first single from it, and what a gem. Not a song I originally would have selected as a single, but listening again it has hit written all over it! Bruce Johnston's first stab at writing and singing solo lead, produces a sentimental sound. Accordions, occasional gushing strings, staccato piano—and that Beach Boys harmony! Only complaint is that it ends rather oddly—sort of drifts offstage—where it could have been chopped short. Welcome back, Beach Boys, it's been worth the waiting.

Beach Boys nostalgia

I WAS down at the Whisky, which is something akin to torture no matter who's there. This time it was crowded; people sitting in the tiny spaces between tables that the waiters facetiously call aisles. Somebody said Paul McCartney was there, but I never saw him. The occasion for all this madness—the first Los Angeles appearance of the Beach Boys in four years.

The Beach Boys at the Whisky must be likened to the Rolling Stones at London's Speakeasy. A bit crowded.

I arrived early so I could sit at a table and not in an aisle, which meant I had to sit through the Flame. You all know about the Flame, right, the African group discovered by the Beach Boys on a trip to England? They must have played for two hours, a long set of unmitigated dullness.

They're good instrumentally, mediocre vocally, and visually unstimulating. They were introduced as the next great international sensation. Spare us.

The Beach Boys didn't play so long, but they covered a wide range of old and new songs. There were 15 people on that stage—five horns, two percussion, an extra bass and an extra keyboard, plus the much heralded appearance of Brian Wilson, who hasn't performed in years.

Brian looked slimmer and more handsome than the last time I saw him. He sat down at the electric piano near the Moog and didn't really seem to do a heck of a lot.

Carl still carries the group, with Mike and Al close by. Carl's voice and guitar are the mainstays, and he handles that role with enthusiasm, something which seemed to be lacking in the others. Dennis, traditionally the heartthrob, came out from behind his drums to sing one song, looking uncomfortable. He slouches, I never noticed that before.

The whole Beach Boys thing here is a combination of nostalgia (their early hits capture more feeling about being young in America in the early '60's than any other group) and the more recent cerebral appreciation of Brian's musical genius and the group's vocal expertise. Listening to the Beach Boys is an exercise in balancing intellect and emotions; when I hear their new stuff I feel like I'm listening to jazz—I know it's good, but it doesn't move me; when they play the oldies, I perk right up and feel like singing along.

They encored with "I Get Around," and for me it was the high spot. I almost wish that weren't true, because while the Beach Boys have evolved and progressed, most of their audiences want the earlier teenage stuff, which the group must have tired of playing about five years ago.

AT THE BIG SHOWS

Front line Beach Boys (left to right): Bruce Johnston, Al Jardine, Carl Wilson, Mike Love. Drummer Dennis Wilson got his share of the limelight, too. See review.

Beach Boys

DENNIS WILSON took his solo vocal spot for the first time at the Beach Boys opening concert at London's Hammersmith Odeon last week on "Forever," his own melodic and poignant song from "Sunflower" album. A credible voice he has, too, although his lack of front-line stardom showed in the way he constantly pulled up his trousers, scratched himself and generally looked like a five-year-old reciting for the first time at a Sunday school concert.

The theme of the Beach Boys show did seem a little looser this time—no stage suits and a general coming and going onstage—and a few new songs. With an impressive line-up of backing musicians they did most of their hits, but how can you criticise repeats of songs that really are the greatest, and sung so well?

The five-piece brass section was well utilised and should be commended for their discreet sounds.

During "Riot"—"a raving R-n-B number, however, wild though it was, did become rather chaotic.

Flame, the group the Beach Boys have such faith in, had a tough time at the second house, but I think the faith is justified.

The Flame forgot that although America has accepted them they still have to make it here and opening with an acoustic set was disastrous.

As soon as they went electric and into their single, "I See The Light," the talent was obvious.

To listen to them one does get whiffs of a Beatle sound, but it's sweet-smelling. They also have an oriental Beatle-like personality that comes ever.

In spite of electric shocks from the microphones they followed through—and although it was not one of the best pop group sets I've seen—I wouldn't knock them. It would be like the man who knocked a Beatles off-night on the eve of "Love Me Do" entering the chart.—GAVIN PETRIE

DISC AND ECHO

A GREAT GROUP WITH A NEW SERIES

HOLLYWOOD, Tuesday—On the eve of the Beach Boys' tour of Britain stay-at-home group leader Brian Wilson, who refuses to fly or go on tours, dropped the biggest bombshell in the group's seven-year topsy turvy success story. He revealed that the group's empire is crumbling and in deep financial trouble. It's got so bad that the Beach Boys are considering filing bankruptcy.

The beefy 27-year-old group boss told Disc: "We're pretty low on money. We owe everyone money and if we don't pick ourselves off our backsides and have a hit record soon we will be in worse trouble."

The stunning news that the Beach Boys are struggling to make ends meet comes as a tremendous shock on the American pop scene. Their sad story is strangely similar to the revelations John Lennon made about the Beatles' fortunes a short time ago. But unlike the Beatles the Beach Boys have not had any recent hits, nor has their record company had anything like the success of Apple.

The introspective, usually not very talkative elder Wilson, the acknowledged boss of the bunch declared: "Nick Grillo our business manager says if we don't start climbing out of this mess he will have to file bankruptcy in Los Angeles by the end of the year."

Brian Wilson who hasn't toured with the group since 1964 but prefers to stay at his luxurious Bel Air mansion and compose said he has already started economising. He has sold his Rolls-Royce—but still has a Mercedes, a Porsche car and two motor cycles, one of which is used by his ex-singer wife Marilyn.

The news of the Beach Boys plight is even more surprising as not so long ago they were all self proclaimed millionaires and riding high on the wave of international popularity.

What has caused the empire to fall apart?

"Things started deteriorating about 18 months ago," said Brian. "Thousands of dollars were being frittered away and thrown away on stupid things. We spent a heck of a lot of corporation money on Brothers Records, our own company, and in boosting other recording artists who just didn't make it, and didn't have a single hit.

"When our records started to bomb out we looked around desperately for something to save ourselves. We had one hit, "I Can Hear Music" but one isn't enough to pay for our tremendous overheads. Then recently Nick (Grillo) told us how bad things really were. It was a big shock for all of us, a really rough blow."

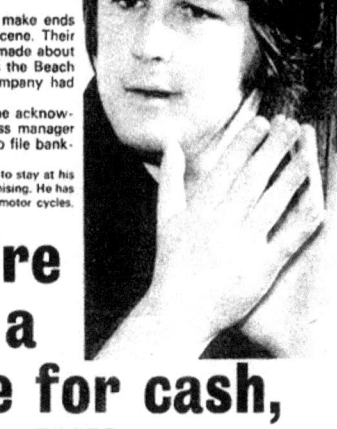

Why we're in such a struggle for cash, by Brian Wilson

Brian has written a new single, "Break Away", which he says can change the group's fiscal fortunes. "It's the kind of disc that will either be a smash or be a miserable flop—lay a stone dead egg. And the British tour will I hope help our waning popularity.

"I've always said be honest with your fans. I don't see why I should lie and say everything is rosy when it's not. Sure when we were making millions I said we were. Now the shoe is on the other foot."

Their overhead weekly costs are enormous. They have a huge headquarters in the heart of Hollywood. It's a long street block which from the outside is a nondescript pale green building. But inside the offices are plush, furnished in deep pile carpeting and with expensive modern furniture.

They also have a 15-member staff to run the affairs of the group and its offshoot activities which include real estate investments, a highly expensive sound system which they built for themselves and now rent out—not too successfully—to other groups.

They also bought a film studio in Hollywood which they never use and also rent out.

Wilson said other money was wasted on bad investments and besides poorly selling records their tours were playing to half-filled theatres.

"We all know that if we don't watch it and do something drastic inside a few months we won't have a penny in the bank."

On the non profitable tours they took along top heavy staff, much more than they needed, and ran up heavy expenses.

Explains Brian: "When we started earning good money it was the same old story all over again. A lot of guys started throwing their money around, buying cars, houses and other things and pretty soon the cash started dwindling."

Drummer Dennis Wilson, 24, now lives in a one-roomed cellar in the basement of a friend's Beverley Hills home. His car was smashed up in a traffic accident—he had loaned it to a friend—and he has never replaced it. His room has a bed and a piano and nothing else ... not even a bathroom.

Comfort

Said Dennis, always the wildest and most unpredictable member of the group: "It's comfortable for me. What more do I need? Material things are useless."

Carl Wilson, the third brother Beach Boy, is still living in comparative comfort with his wife and baby son but says Brian: "He is taking the brunt of everything on his young shoulders (Carl is now a beefy fifteen and a half stone and only 22) and the strain is beginning to show. He has a wife and family and plenty of responsibilities."

The other Beach Boys have their homes and possessions but their bank balances are not as fat as they once were.

Besides the bad investments, the flop records, Brian says whenever business manager Grillo wanted to invest money he had to check individually with every single member of the group. He got different answers from each one and adds Brian: "He was left hanging in the air because there was never a unanimous answer —we were all too busy doing something else."

"Nick has been with us for a long time. He hasn't done badly but the job has given him two ulcers and he's working on a third. The other day Mike Love had a battle of words with him and Nick said he wouldn't quit the group for anything. He is a member of our family as well as the other guys."

Today the Beach Boys no longer have a full time publicist and their rocky financial affairs is a well kept secret in pop music circles in America.

"It was simple," said Brian. "When we didn't have hits there just wasn't enough bread coming in to pay for the overheads and we started to feel the ship sinking."

The Wilson brothers, Mike Love, Al Jardine and Bruce Johnston are even talking about doing a soft drink commercial, something they have never done before, to beef up their bank balance. So it is with mixed feelings and fortunes that they embark on their tour of Britain knowing that it must be a success if the Beach Boys are to survive.

WHERE THEY'RE AT

THE FIVE Beach Boys, Paul Revere and the Raiders, featuring Mark Lindsay and newcomer Joe Hicks were all due to arrive at London Airport from Los Angeles early this morning (Thursday).

Says tour manager Ron King: "Seats have gone very well and this will definitely be a sell-out tour."

Their complete concert list is:—
- Friday (May 30) **BRIGHTON** Dome, 6.15 and 8.45 p.m.
- Saturday (May 31) **HAMMERSMITH** Odeon, 6.45 and 9.15 p.m.
- Friday (June 6) **BIRMINGHAM** Odeon, 6.30 and 9.00 p.m.
- Saturday (June 7) **LIVERPOOL** Empire, 6.10 and 8.40 p.m.
- Sunday (June 8) **MANCHESTER** Free Trade Hall, 6.00 and 8.30 p.m.
- Monday (June 9) **GLASGOW** Odeon, 6.15 and 8.45 p.m.

Nail biter's nails

keep away the males

Are you lonely — and wonder why? The truth is that no man is attracted by ugly, bitten down nails. You need Stop 'n Grow, the wonderful new nail biting deterrent. Stop 'n Grow is instant willpower at your fingertips. Just brush it on. Doesn't show, doesn't stain — goes on over nail polish. New Stop 'n Grow liquid stops nail biting immediately. 3 weeks later — hey presto! — 10 long, strong, naturally grown nails!

Chemists stock Stop 'n Grow at only 7/6d — if any difficulty obtain direct for 7/6d post free from — "Stop 'n Grow", Dept 168, 34 Fairlie Road, Slough, Bucks.

NEXT WEEK: The other Beach Boys talk about their rocky success story and how their music has changed

MEDICINE MAN

LEAPING UP THE AMERICAN CHARTS!!!

SMASH! THE NEW SINGLE BY THE **BUCHANAN BROTHERS** POF 139

PAGE ONE RECORDS LIMITED
JAMES HOUSE, 71-75 NEW OXFORD STREET, LONDON W.C.1

DISC AND ECHO

Meditating with a Beach Boy – on the dodgems!

Beach Boys... Al Jardine, Bruce Johnston, Dennis Wilson, Carl Wilson, Mike Love.

MIKE LEDGERWOOD learns the mysteries

BEACH BOY Mike Love sat on a sofa, crossed his legs yoga-style, stared blankly out across Brighton seafront—and left us! His daily meditation had started.

Near him a weird woman with greying hair was rambling on about reincarnation, the mysteries of the occult and her belief that in another life I had been a great artist. On the sideboard stood pictures of the Maharishi Mahesh Yogi.

Earlier, in company with Bruce Johnston, we had watched Wimbledon tennis on the telly and been served with cream cakes and fresh fruit as afternoon tea by a trio of very attractive young ladies.

I was guest of the two Beach Boys at their transcendental meditation retreat in Sussex by the sea. "We love it here," confided Bruce. "It's so nice to get away from worries and things like that. We're even thinking of buying a hotel down here ourselves."

Bruce, wearing a pale blue boating cap and looking a little weary round the eyes, met me at the station. The sun was shining brightly and he announced that he'd been up since 9 am. A taxi took us to a tiny pub only a pebble's throw from the promenade and Bruce explained his personal belief in meditation.

"I'm not a great believer," he revealed. "I just find it relaxing. I don't try and spread-the-word either. I use meditation to dive inside myself and it helps me come to terms with life.

"Mike, though, is very serious. He does sometimes send it up himself—but that's only because I think he feels he shouldn't expect other people to understand everything he involves himself in."

Later we left to meet Mike at one of the two flats being used as meditation HQ. I was surprised not to find him attired in the now familiar white flowing robes. Instead, he wore a loose red jumper over brown suit trousers. The famous beard was bushy and his fair hair hung to his shoulders.

"Hi," he said. "Glad you could make it. Have a good journey down? Hang on a minute and we'll go and meet the others."

En route to the other flat, a few blocks away, we encountered Mike's younger brother, Steve, a sturdy fellow with fiery red hair and twinkling blue eyes, and his girlfriend.

Steve's been with the Beach Boys throughout their European tour. The trip was a gesture by Mike following his graduation success back home.

The other flat was cool and comfortable. From the verandah you could look out over the lawns to the choppy English Channel.

A friendly gentleman called Geoffrey, a sincere meditation man, organised tea for us which was served by three pretty pupils. Someone switched on the "box" and we all watched Wimbledon for a while.

"You don't have to meditate," explained Bruce. "Just relax and enjoy yourselves. That's what we're doing."

To illustrate his point the benign Bruce suggested a stroll along the seafront. "They've got some groovy dodgems down there," he indicated, with all the enthusiasm of a 10-year-old.

A few minutes later, just as the sun slipped behind a cloud and it began to spit with rain we arrived at the dodgems. "I hate the rain," revealed Bruce, screwing his face up. "I love Britain and everything about it—except the weather!"

Bruce must easily be the friendliest and most generous pop star I've met. He stops and talks to passers-by in the street, fusses over their pets and speaks to everyone as though he's known them all his life.

The dodgem cars were close to the seashore and a cruel wind swept over the shingle. Bruce pulled his hat on firmly and marched to a car. I secretly prayed that we wouldn't become human kebab while in the cars having read about the danger of water and electricity.

The next hour was utter madness. We must have raced round the track a million times in the rain. The cars skidded and shuddered, bumped and bashed their way along. We made the famous "Bullitt" chase seem like a funeral procession.

A small boy with National Health specs joined the fun and found it hard to believe that the dodgem he'd just rammed contained a Beach Boy. The loudspeaker blasted out, appropriately, "Do It Again." And we did!

Finally, after a plate of cockles from a stall, we returned to the sanity of the flat. Mike was busy doing a marathon 'phone interview and explaining for the umpteenth time that the Beach Boys were not really broke.

For the next 90 minutes I listened intrigued to Mike's views on meditation and his belief in the teaching of the Maharishi. His conversation with the woman who studied life-after-death was captivating. Talk revolved around the planets, about which Mike is currently composing a song, and about Piscean people and Aquarius Rising.

A lot of it, I must own up, left me cold. But after watching and listening I don't doubt Love's enthusiasm.

It was about this time that Mike left us to meditate. "You're welcome to join in," he invited. But, being cowards we opted for a drink round the corner and a game of table football in the amusement arcade.

Mainliners...

DENNIS WILSON (LEFT) AND JAMES TAYLOR...ACTING LEAVES A LOT TO BE DESIRED

Taylor, Wilson screen debuts

JAMES TAYLOR and Beach Boy Dennis Wilson have made their debut in one of those films that are "denied a general commercial showing" and so are getting an off-West End screening at The Screen On Islington Green in London, starting March 18. The film, Two Lane Blacktop, is one of the legion of "discovering America" films with James and Dennis as driver and mechanic of a souped-up 1955 Chevy. They make money to run the beast via drag races and challenges to car owners who think their cars can beat the rather beat-up-looking machine.

Both James Taylor and Dennis Wilson have great faces for films, but their acting leaves a lot to be desired. James has only one piece of dialogue that runs to more than "Fill 'er up" or "Rye in a glass of beer" and he blows that—it's just like a rehearsal for the scene. Dennis Wilson is a bit peppier as he leaps around with spanners and delivers his dialogue realistically.

Without actor Warren Oates playing a talkative, lonely romeo, who drives a 1970 Pontiac, the film would have been a total disaster. James Taylor has the voice and the face for films but not, I suspect, the desire. Dennis Wilson is another kettle of fish and he could be a Western hero any time he liked.

I liked the film—but don't know why. It's slow, sometimes puzzling, but it holds on to you and drags you across America. Its failure lies in its inability to get the emotions of the central characters over to you. The film also presented a delightful chick called Laurie Bird—who played a very strange part and seemed the cause of all the trouble.—GAVIN PETRIE

BEACH BOY DENNIS INJURY SHOCK

BEACH BOY drummer Dennis Wilson has lost the use of his right hand for at least three months, following a serious accident at his Los Angeles home last week.

Dennis was installing a pane of glass in a window frame when it splintered into large pieces, one of which fell directly into the palm of his hand. His wife Barbra said the glass immediately severed nerves in the hand. Wilson was rushed by ambulance to a nearby hospital, where a surgeon performed a delicate three-hour operation using a high-powered microscope to identify the torn nerves.

Medical specialists said the operation was successful but that 26-year-old Dennis would not regain full use of his hand for six months.

A Beach Boys spokesman told Disc that a proposed 10-day U.S. tour by the band would not be cancelled as a result of the accident—but Dennis was unlikely to make the trip. "If he does go, he'll likely sing but not play drums."

Part of the tour will include the taping of the Beach Boys first TV special in over two years.

Dennis is expected out of hospital next week—in time for interviews to tie in with the premiere of "Two Lane Blacktop," in which he co-stars with James Taylor. It is screened in New York on July 14. A British tour by the Beach Boys is now expected in November.

Gilt-edged Bruce is the Beach Boy who stayed a playboy

BRUCE JOHNSTON is the sort of pop star you can take anywhere. From the potted palm court of the plushest hotel, where ladies in long evening gowns tinkle away at the piano, to the real courts of royalty, where flunkies fawn at the feet of the nobility. In either, this bachelor Beach Boy, a playboy pop star still, is extraordinary at ease, exuding etiquette and cool courtesy at every move.

It was in the former environment that I found him last week, trying to escape the clutches of a middle-aged American millionairess, who claimed she'd known him for the past 10 years and could tell me anything I wanted to know.

Bruce smiled bravely and steered me to a corner table to partake in assorted sandwiches and Irish coffee in the company of his close friend and publicist Keith Altham.

Bruce Johnston will have been a Beach Boy for six years next April 9. And it's almost as if he was always with the group; although in fact he officially replaced big brother Brian Wilson. What satisfaction, I wondered, had the pop star status given him, apart from the obvious financial security?

"Mainly the opportunity to create and make music," he mused. "That's what I'm into now more than anything else. I'm no longer motivated by money; it's the artistic side of things which is grabbing my interest.

"I'm personally writing a lot now. I mean, I've always written songs—but they haven't meant much. Everything's better organised. I don't know whether the Beach Boys will record any of my material, but I do think I'm good enough to get them placed."

The group's current single, of course, the beautifully melodic "Tears In The Morning," is one of his songs; and he also sings lead for the first time. Sadly, too, it hasn't appeared to click with fans.

Bruce beamed. "I didn't decide it should be our single. To me it was just another piece of material. Actually, we believe it's a really good record—even if it doesn't work."

Nevertheless, the Beach Boys are determined to consolidate their success in Britain and Europe; to the point of actually settling here for around six months of each year.

"I like Britain the best of all of us," he confessed. "But it'll probably be me who stays behind in Los Angeles, and just joins the group for the tours.

"Mike and Al are talking about renting homes here, and I'm really jealous. But, you see, I'm the most mobile of the group, having no wife and family."

Bruce pricked up his ears suddenly, excused himself politely in mid-conversation, and strolled casually across to the lady pianist, softly picking out "Stranger In Paradise" amid the potted palms. He positioned himself at her side and carefully, with one hand, played "Autumn Leaves" at the same time, at the other end of the keyboard.

"I couldn't resist that!" he beamed broadly. Only the benign Bruce, with his cowboy shirt and clean-cut pop star appearance, could get away with that little episode. In fact, later, he took over the keyboard completely to play me another little piece. And nobody turned a hair!

Songwriting, it seems, is taking up much his time ("I'm finishing a song with Hoagy Carmichael when I get home," he explained. "He's dying to get back into the business; but I don't know if he knows what he's in for with the Beach Boys!"); yet he still finds time for the birds.

Why, I wondered, hadn't the suave Bruce succumbed to marital harmony. He's likely one of the most eligible—certainly the most likeable—bachelor pop stars.

"I think girls always look at your American Express card to see if it's green or gold," he grinned. "And they DARLING you accordingly. I'm being darling-ed pretty heavily at the moment!"

Apparently, American Express grade credit-card holders "Green" or "Gold" according to the size of the bank balance!

However, he admits that there was one special girlfriend, in New Zealand. And he's planning a surfing holiday over there when time permits. "New Zealand's an amazing country," he enthused. "I can really relax there."

But it's definitely Britain where Bruce plans to eventually expand his business interests. And aside from his songs, he also hopes to open a restaurant and jazz club.

"The Beach Boys' companies are finally very much together," he revealed. "Now it's simply up to all of us to make them work. We're even thinking of opening a London office of our record label.

"But at the moment," he concluded, "I just want to make music. Sit down in one place for a while and write songs. I think that's my biggest talent at the moment."

Word of warning

You'd think that after all these years together, a group like the Beach Boys would have overcome the desire to assert themselves individually on stage.

I watched last Friday's Finsbury Park Astoria show from the Wings and it was obvious throughout that Mike Love, Dennis Wilson and Bruce Johnston were competing against each other for the solo spotlight.

Love, of course is officially the Beach Boys' lead singer and makes a damn good job of it. But lately it's become blatantly obvious that Bruce and Dennis are struggling for personal stardom.

Dennis, for instance did solo numbers in the second show, yet appeared sadly devoid of either enthusiasm or presence out front. But he struggled defiantly through three songs when one would have been enough.

Later, seemingly not to be out done, bouncy Bruce interrupted the group during "Tears In The Morning" to take his solo entirely alone, except for his own piano accompaniment.

I must admit it went down a storm, and the song benefited from the simple piano-voice presentation.

But if you'd seen the expressions and heard the mutterings of the others of the group as they were ordered off it looked decidedly as though Bruce could find himself in the "doghouse."

Mike Ledgerwood

Beach Boy Dennis going solo?

DENNIS WILSON ... left the tour.

HAS Dennis Wilson left the Beach Boys? Do you expect me to have all the answers? I just supply the rumours. And this one has Dennis out of the group, supposedly planning to make albums of his own. It is fact that Dennis left the current Beach Boys tour in mid-November and returned to Los Angeles. Ever since Dennis hurt his hand the group has travelled with another drummer, Mike Kowalski, so Mike just took over all drumming for the remainder of the tour. No announcement has been made about Dennis's departure, whether it be temporary or permanent.

DISC AND ECHO

MURRY: BEACH BOYS DON'T HAVE ALL THE TALENT IN OUR FAMILY!

by Mike Ledgerwood

EVERY time Mrs Audree Wilson sees the Fred MacMurray TV show "My Three Sons" she thinks of her boys.

"One day I will write a book about them," she says. "It will make an interesting story."

In actual fact, her three sons, Brian, Carl and Dennis, have already made their mark—in the musical history books... as the world famous, highly-acclaimed Beach Boys.

A thing which makes Mr and Mrs Murry Wilson pop's proudest parents.

"It's all still so unreal," adds Audree. "I can't believe that people want to know all about my three sons. They're just normal people. Known always as clean-cut and nice."

Nursemaid

The couple were spending a few days in London at the end of a month-long European trip to promote "The Many Moods Of Murry Wilson," an album of music by the group's songwriting father.

I met them on the tenth floor of the luxurious Hilton Hotel. Mr Wilson is short, stockily-built, rather un-American looking. He smokes a pipe like his political namesake—and talks incessantly.

He admits to being "past 50" and has handled the Beach Boys' lives and career from their very first hit some six years ago.

"I'm manager, nursemaid, banker, business agent—as well as their father," he grins. "I was like a mother bear watching over her cubs at the start. But now they're grown up they virtually manage themselves. With just a little help from their dad!"

Murry Wilson was just an ordinary businessman in the days before his boys made it big. Usually behind in his HP payments, struggling to make ends meet, and with a family of four to support.

Today he's the figurehead of a multi-million dollar pop empire built from his sons' earnings through a group which has done for the States what the Beatles did for Britain.

"But the Beach Boys will never, ever, in the foreseeable future, be as big as the Beatles," he admits. "Even though this year alone they were the biggest money-earning group in the country. And they've been making records longer than the Beatles, too.

"When we started we were going to conquer the world, of course. I had no idea, personally, that the Beach Boys would be such a success story as recording artists.

"But Brian, my eldest son, sensed it. That boy has God-given talent. I hate the word GENIUS. I see it as extraordinary God-given talent.

"Of course, you can't compare him with Mozart or Schumann, though he is so close to having musical genius it is pitiful. Do you know, he can think in five and six-part harmony at one time?"

Beach Boys, apparently, have always been Beatles fans. Carl Wilson even sported a giant picture of the group on the wall of his room. They had all their records.

"The Beatles could never have such ardent fans. I used to call Carl a traitor," joked Murry.

"But when the Beatles happened my boys were quick to realise that here was the competition. Before then they were set to conquer the world! Soon they realised they had no chance."

Mr Wilson sees the release of his own album as something of a challenge to his singing sons—and to composer Brian, in particular.

"After 'Good Vibrations' Brian lost a lot of confidence. He didn't think he could ever write anything as good as that again. For eight months his songwriting was stagnant—until he completed 'Heroes And Villains'—which was really two songs strung together, anyway.

"With this LP I'm hoping to nudge my boys' competitive spirit. Show them that the Beach Boys don't have all the talent in the family.

"Brian may find new rejuvenation in his confidence as a result. They may all find new spirit to stay at the top."

Clean-cut

Added Mrs Wilson, a strikingly handsome woman: "My boys have always got along famously together.

"My advice to them was 'Earn money by doing an honest job. Don't let anybody down. And don't sing any dirty songs. Anything at all off-colour, lewd or connected with dope.

"As a result they've always had a reputation for being normal, nice and altogether a clean-cut group."

"I CALL THEM MY 'MONSTERS,'" LAUGHED MR WILSON. "BUT THEY'VE NEVER LET ME DOWN. HOW COULD I BE ANYTHING OTHER THAN PROUD OF THEM?"

Brian Wilson—the Beach Boy who, his father says, "is so close to having musical genius it is pitiful"—holding a picture of the other members of the group.

The Beach Boys! Since *Surfing U.S.A* they have had a string of hits and have become famous for the painstaking electronic ingenuity they give to their waxings, specially composed by their sixth, non-performing, member

ALL SET TO DETHRONE THE KINGS?

asks Graeme Andrews

THE Beach Boys, California's answer to the Beatles, are all set to dethrone John, Paul, George and Ringo in 1967. During the last twelve months the happy-go-lucky American quintet has built up a fantastic following for itself both at home, in Britain and the rest of the world.

A vital ingredient of the Beach Boys' appeal—as with the Beatles—is their attitude to, and way of, life, and not just the sound they make on their records.

The five come from the sunny west coast of America and rode to fame on the surfing craze with their record *Surfing U.S.A*. This blended the catchy tune of Chuck Berry's *Sweet Little Sixteen* with new lyrics which captured the fun of riding the breakers on a surf-board.

The brain behind this group who have gained fame by the electronic techniques on their records is the sixth Beach Boy, Brian Wilson. Brian no longer tours or performs with the other Beach Boys—instead he concentrates full time on composing and arranging their material and perfecting strange and intricate recording techniques.

Brian's decision last year to specialize on producing the Beach Boys' sound paid off handsomely. It resulted in the group's million-seller *Good Vibrations* which topped the British charts during the boys' sell-out tour of England. Brian thought up the basic idea of this record last April and worked on it for six months —using a special instrument called a therimin.

It took the five a lot of time and effort before they could perfect the sound that Brian wanted on the record. It took hours to record and the group made no less than 30 attempts at the song before Brian was satisfied. The end product was so unique that no other group has dared to attempt to record *Good Vibrations;* and even the Beach Boys themselves have difficulty recreating the sound of the record on stage!

This record clinched a wonderful year for the boys and ensured that their November visit was a roaring success. Everywhere they went the five—Dennis and Carl Wilson, Al Jardine, bearded, pipe-smoking Mike Love and Brian's replacement Bruce Johnston—received wild acclaim.

To coincide with the group's arrival the company issued an LP *The Best Of The Beach Boys* which included their smash hits *I Get Around, Barbara Ann, Sloop John B* and *God Only Knows,* plus popular tracks like *Surfin' Safari, Fun Fun Fun, All Summer Long* and *Help Me Rhonda*.

This is only the latest of the group's very popular string of long players, which include *Pet Sounds,* a superb album of songs all stamped with the Brian Wilson magic.

More recently the boys have been back in the studio recording their first LP for 1967 entitled simply *Smile,* and their follow-up single to *Good Vibrations* which has the intriguing title *Heroes And Villains*.

Their fans have high hopes that these discs will help the boys usurp the Beatles as the top pop group, for they have displaced the Liverpool lads in some popular polls already. And to try and entrench themselves at the top they are planning to come back to Britain for a much longer tour in May.

'Spirit Of America' — A Beach Boys Retrospective

Never have two monster groups been so united as the Beach Boys/Chicago tandem which is touring America like blood brothers.

by Michael Gross

Carl Wilson: In 1966, he was indicted for refusing induction into the U.S. Army. In 1969, he was cleared on the grounds that he was a Conscientious Objector.

Touring America is usually a matter of glorification. You go see one band, and maybe, if you're lucky, you get another thrown in. Sometimes on major tours there's a special guest. With luck that means Suzi Quatro with Alice Cooper. Without luck that means that some management firm or record company has forced promoters to take a second act in order to get the first—often at a distinct musical loss to the audience. But this summer's Beach Boys/Chicago tour is a different story. Two bands at peak popularity, both absolute sellout SRO headliners, are sharing bills across America as naturally as they put on their socks and tune their guitars in the morning. Everyone loves bands like the Beach Boys because, even in 1975, there's room for high spirits in the summertime. That's why albums of re-packaged hits like **Spirit Of America** (Capitol) and **Good Vibrations** (Reprise) do things like go gold a week after their release.

Good vibes and vigah: People were not too self-conscious about good vibes back in November, 1962, when a new group called the Beach Boys rose from the bleach blonde surfer dreamlands of Hawthorne, California, with a single called "Surfin' " and a debut album called **Surfin' Safari.** America had just lived through the Cuban Missile Crisis, and though the vibes were a bit threatened, America's spirit had emerged intact. The Beach Boys did nothing to disperse the clean-cut, 'go forth with vigah' determination of the Kennedy years. They sang all about matching sweaters and matching girls and toothy smiles and maybe, for fun, some riding of the waves or buzzing around in fast cars, like "409," immortalized for under two minutes on the flip side of the Boys' first single and now resurrected on **Spirit.**

Something about the Beach Boys' catchy melodies and uncomplicated world view caught the fancy of America that summer, and memory will tell you that, along with the Four Seasons, no one had more hit singles than the Beach Boys. Their albums began appearing fast and furious for almost two years, all with a similar motif of cars and girls and boards and good fun. **Surfin' USA** and **Shut Down** both appeared early in 1963. Classic singles poured from these albums, most of them on Capitol's last Beach Boys reissue, **Endless Summer.** Any image that caught that ideal—the good time—fit in well, and "Hawaii," from the band's fourth album, **Surfer Girl,** was typical of the band's idealization of any spot where the surf ran high and the girls would coyly flash their tan lines. "A Young Man Is Gone," "Spirit Of America" and "Custom Machine" all come from the fifth album, released less than a year after the first, **Little Deuce Coupe.** The Beach Boys, in the month before John Kennedy's assassination, were one of the most popular and prolific bands in America. Whether copping Chuck Berry riffs or creating their own, the Beach Boys, and most especially chief songwriter Brian Wilson, had caught a corner of carefree America, and framed it with a unique and totally joyous musical atmosphere.

Non-serious pop: That, of course, is all critical retrospect. No one took the Beach Boys very seriously as musicians back then. "This Car Of Mine" and a reworking of Frankie Lymons' "Why Do Fools Fall In Love" from **Shut Down Volume II** were not being held up for comparison with that era's serious pop music: jazz and folk. But then, neither were the songs of the Beatles, who'd burst into the American consciousness only a month before the release of that album.

The Beach Boys' offering, in the summer of '64, was **All Summer Long,** the classic album that gave the world "I Get Around," the song that knocked the British Invaders from the top of the pops and then played tag all through the summer, with the Four Seasons' "Rag Doll" for #1 spot on the hit parade. Buyers of the album were also being charged up for the summer party by "Little Honda," "Hushabye," "Drive-In," "Do You Remember" and "Don't Back Down"—all songs that, even in the early days of Dylan, SDS, Vietnam and Lyndon Johnson, seemed somehow closer to that traditional amorphous spirit of American good will and innocence that California represented and the rest of the world admired.

As 1964 wound to a close, two more Beach Boys LPs appeared. **Beach Boys Christmas Album** was standard Christmas carols, and **Beach Boys Concert,** which included "Graduation Day," represented the last period in the Beach Boys history when Brian Wilson played with them onstage.

Brian quits the stage: "Brian wanted to leave the group the first time in 1963," his brother Carl told Circus Magazine after the Texas concerts this spring. "He chose to leave that summer. Then there were some personnel changes." Brian's replacement, a neighborhood boy, played for awhile, but eventually quit to go to dental school. Brian rejoined in 1964. "Brian started working again, kind of enjoying it," Carl said. "But at the end of '64, in Houston, he packed

Dennis Wilson: It was Dennis, the family surfer, who first suggested that the band devote itself to music that celebrated California's #1 pastime.

it in. It was too upsetting for him. He couldn't handle it; being away from home, the sound level onstage was too loud for him, all that. Houston was the last time he played as a regular member. He was hearing a lot of things and it was frustrating for him not to be able to bring them into being. He still played on the albums. No one's ever come close to him in the studio. It's always been his music."

With Brian off the road and devoting himself 100% to composing, the Beach Boys' music took off for the stratosphere. "Dance, Dance, Dance," "Good To My Baby," "Please Let Me Wonder," "When I Grow Up," and a cover of Bobby Freeman's "Do You Wanna Dance" all appear on **Spirit,** but were originally in the hit-jammed **Beach Boys Today,** an album whose cover featured the band in lovely alpaca sweaters, the West Coast style of 1965. "Salt Lake City," from the next album, **Summer Days,** was a paean to the Utah city. "Tell Me Why" and "Barbara Ann" from **Beach Boys Party** represent the last offerings on **Spirit Of America** from this transitional phase of the band's career.

At first there had been the band with Brian. From 1964-5, the band kept playing, while Brian wrote, and though the songs were breaking out of the car/surf/girl/fun consistency of the Beach Boys' early work, their sound remained the same. "The Little Girl I Once Knew," a single released in October 1965, was typical of the period, displaying an advancing musical sophistication, but still undeniably in the mold.

Precious 'Pet': May, 1966 saw the release of **Pet Sounds,** an album that

Mike Love has said, "We're fundamentally a family unit. Brian was the overwhelming dominant creative force in the group just by virtue of his influence on his brothers, myself and his friends."

has now been released three separate times, only recently gaining the critical acclaim it deserves. Warner Brothers now owns the rights to this and all succeeding albums, but at the time, "Sloop John B," "God Only Knows," "Wouldn't It Be Nice" and "Caroline, No" all appeared on a Capitol label. Now, eight years later, they're reappearing on **Good Vibrations** this summer, thanks to the brothers at Warners. And the fact that ownership of material shifts as of **Pet Sounds** provides a convenient demarcation point between the old and new Beach Boys. Bye-bye cars and boards, hello heads and essences and music that was as thoughtful as it was beautiful. Brian Wilson began using orchestration and arrangement in a way previously unheard of in rock, paralleling, in a different dimension, the pioneering of The Beatles on **Rubber Soul**, released a few months earlier.

The story behind the shift in sound is a long one, told best by Paul Williams in his book, **Outlaw Blues**, where Brian's creative endeavors of the next year are fully explained. Suffice it to say that a masterpiece (co-produced by Van Dyke Parks) called **Smile** was due next, and it never appeared. Parks pulled out of the project and Brian, traumatized, shelved it where it stagnated. Instead, in the fall of 1967, **Smiley Smile** was released, and as far as public profile was concerned the Beach Boys went underground after the great rush of "Good Vibrations," that album's most popular track. The best example of what **Smile** might have been like was in a cut called "Heroes and Villains," now acclaimed as the strongest, and possibly grandest studio experiment Brian Wilson ever tried.

Wild Honey, released at the end of '67, was lost in the **Sgt. Pepper/Satanic Majesties Request** onslaught at the dawning of the Age of Aquarius, even though, as "Darling" shows, the Beach Boys had lost none of their punch. Only the title cut of **Friends**, "Do It Again" from **20/20**, and "Add Some Music To Your Day" from **Sunflower** (the only non-reissued Beach Boys middle period album) are represented on **Good Vibrations** to show what the Beach Boys did as the '60s turned to the '70s.

It was only with the release of **Surf's Up**, after the turn of the decade, that the Beach Boys regained the public eye. That album, again represented here by its title cut, also attracted new critical recognition: because of the LP's ties with the 1967 days through the title cut (it was originally recorded for **Smile**), critics and observers were forced to look back over the entire body of the Beach Boys' work. Luckily, that attention covered the commercial failure of **Carl and The Passions/So Tough**, and bridged the gap to the Beach Boys' last studio album, **Holland**, represented by the monumental "Sail On, Sailor." Excepting two more live albums, both considered failures by most critics, the Beach Boys oeuvre was complete. With the coming of the repackages, spearheaded by last year's **Endless Summer**, the Beach Boys' place as the quintessential American rock band was secured for all time.

Bouncing stages: "We weren't involved with **Endless Summer** at all," Carl explained, "but we do want the songs available for people. It makes you feel funny 'cause it's the third time it's been out. Then it goes to #1 and that's funky. I looked at the trade charts and thought 'My God!' It wasn't real to me. Al Coury at Capitol loves the group and he did it. We were pleased about it." So were audiences, who responded incredibly when the band re-tailored their stage set to make room for the suddenly-valid-again oldies they thought had been lost in the wash of history.

"The album was out," Carl explained, "and we like to ride the horse in the direction it's going so we changed the set. Sometimes, like at Madison Square Garden, it got scarey. The stage was bouncing. One of the light towers was shaking. But it's thrilling when people are getting off that bad. I don't want to sound corny, but we get off!"

There are still some questions, though, like the oft-asked one: is Brian Wilson crazy? Told of a conversation about Brian's state of mind, Carl was quick to reply. "My God, I can assure you Brian is not a vegetable. But that won't stop the rumors. I've heard outrageous stories about him, but he's far out. He does what he wants, when he wants."

These days he's often to be found in the studio, working with the rest of the band on a new album, their first studio set in three years, now due around November. "After we delivered the last Warners album," Carl said, "we just thought it didn't work for us anymore in the album grind, two albums a year. We decided to cruise and release an album when it gets released and it'll be an album we really like."

Then, asked about the feelings generated by this special tour, he went on earnestly. "The group feels honored that people are willing to let us participate in their lives. It may be difficult to relate to, but coming to play is very humbling. All that stuff about people being ego freaks is the biggest hype. Playing buzzes me out. It's so fascinating to make music, have the records come out, and then come out to play and discover they know about it. It's fascinating and it's wonderful."

The Chicago Connection

"Thanks to Jim, we've been working a little at Caribou and that's just a dream," Carl Wilson said happily. "Jim" is Jim Guercio, owner-operator of The Caribou Ranch, producer of Chicago, and long-time musician's musician. He's probably as much responsible for the Beach Boys' resurgence as the re-released albums.

"We wanted some assistance in the management/direction area about a year ago," Carl explained, "and when we were playing Denver one time, Jim invited us to the ranch. We got to talking while we were there. He's always been out front about liking our music, so we asked if it would be cool with Chicago for him to assist us. We needed conscious, responsible assistance.

"We got more acquainted and then he offered to play bass with us on the road which blew our minds. We got down to business and made an agreement for them to handle our comings and goings and that's how it started. Then several months ago, I think Jim brought up the idea of the two bands playing together."

Early this year, a logistical planning session was held in Hawaii, and the reality of a Beach Boys/Chicago tour began to take shape. Everyone who touched it was charmed and enthused by the idea and now, a few months later, it seems the feelings about it were right. Chicago, of course, is touring to support their most recent album, **Chicago VIII**, and the Beach Boys, one supposes, are touring because it's summer.

Onstage, at their tour-opening concerts in Texas, the Beach Boys began the set and were joined midway by Chicago. With the famous brass blasting away, Bobby Lamm sang "Surf's Up," Peter Cetera sang "Darlin'" and then Carl Wilson sang "God Only Knows." During Chicago's set, the Beach Boys joined in for "Old Days," "Wishin' You Were Here" and "Saturday In The Park." Then, as the finale, all seventeen musicians stood onstage and delighted the mellowed crowd with "Dialogue," "California Girls," "Harry Truman," "Fun, Fun, Fun," "Feeling Stronger" and, as the closer, "Jumping Jack Flash." By the end, the co-billing seemed entirely natural, as the audience realized that both Chicago and The Beach Boys were all-American bands. Regardless, wherever they go they draw the kind of crowds promoters love and give the kind of shows the audiences of America love. And that, as they say, is the big idea.

NEW TIMES 1976

Project DESKTOP: What is the Navy trying to hide?

New Times

APRIL 2, 1976   75 CENTS
THE FEATURE NEWS MAGAZINE

THE BEACH BOYS

Good Vibrations are back

NEW TIMES 1976

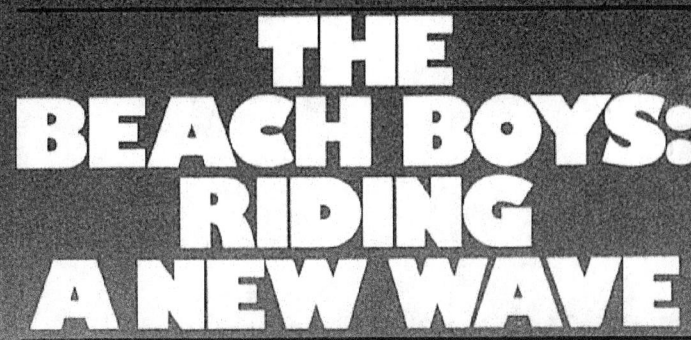

THE BEACH BOYS: RIDING A NEW WAVE

A whole new generation is turning out to hear replays of Sixties anthems. Says Mike Love, "We're inseparable from the white middle-class karma"

By Neal Gabler

On a small charter jet, Carl Wilson of the Beach Boys sits down next to me and hunches forward slightly to be heard over the thick hum of the engines. In the dim, yellowish plane light, he looks almost ethereal. "I've been thinking about the last time I went back to my old neighborhood in Hawthorne, California," he says softly. "I had this fantastic feeling. It seemed like such a big world when I was growing up. And now when I go back there it's just like... really small, you know. My car was too big to drive down the street. And then I saw a friend that I'd known since I was probably 9 or 10. He was still doing the same thing he was doing when I lived there. He was still in the garage working on a car. And it blew my mind. I felt—I was overwhelmed, like I was really going to have a very emotional experience, cry or whatever." He pauses to suck some coffee from a thin porcelain cup. "And when I was there I looked at our house, because he lived across the street. And I was looking over at it and I remembered the way it was when I grew up in it. And then after I moved away, my dad—you know we all had a lot of money and all that stuff—rebuilt it and it looked really different from all the other places. It had a lot of big tropical trees. It was really a mind-blower." He rolls his eyes away and tilts his head back again. "I think I just wanted to hang on to what was, and yet, by looking at it, I got to see the distance we've been since I was 12 or 13. Now we are flying on this crazy thing. I think it's incredible."

What is really incredible is not how far the Beach Boys have come, but how long they've managed to stay there. In the fragile ego-world of rock, where groups last as long as mayflies, the Beach Boys have remained intact for 15 years, practically an eon in their business.

Now, after nearly a decade of obscurity, the group has triumphed, beaten the cultural rap and become more popular than ever. "Good Vibrations"? Absolutely. Today, the Beach Boys represent the unchallenged kings of the 1970s rock 'n roll revival. Last July, during a smashing tour, the group set a record for the highest single-

NEW TIMES 1976

The way they were: the Beach Boys toward the end of their first peak in 1966. L. to R.: Mike Love, Brian Wilson and Carl Wilson. Bottom: Al Jardine and Dennis Wilson.

grossing concert ever. Three of their albums—full of early Sixties hits—made *Billboard*'s top 150 in 1975, and wherever the group plays, it is to sellout halls, at a $25,000 minimum. Twyla Tharp has written two ballets to their music, a concert with the Joffrey Ballet is being planned and Susan Ford has talked of inviting them to the White House. Investigators even found one of the Beach Boys' albums in Patty Hearst's otherwise explosive cache.

"Of course," smiles lead singer Mike Love. "She was a white kid growing up in America. If she didn't have the Beach Boys, then I'd have to say she was missing something."

Something a lot of people apparently want back again.

The main reason the Beach Boys have survived is that they are a family: the three Wilson brothers (Brian, who is 33, Dennis, who is 31, and Carl, who is 29); their cousin, Mike Love; and their high school chum, Alan Jardine. "I slept in the same room with Carl and Brian all my life," explains Dennis. "I've known Michael all my life. Alan all the way through school. We've done everything together. Shit, eat, fart, cry, laugh. Everything." Each member will tell you that there have been enormous tensions; it's not always smooth. "But even though they might do something outrageous,"

Neal Gabler is a graduate student in film at the University of Michigan. This is his first piece for a national magazine.

says Mike, "something that would break up another group, or cause a huge fight, the end result is that he's your cousin or your brother, and you've been through a lot of stuff together, and you love him."

Because they've been together so long, they have a history now, a cultural record. The Beach Boys are recounting that history while lazing in an exclusive Chicago hotel before a concert. The record begins, needless to say, back in California. Love grew up in Baldwin Hills. The Wilson brothers and Al Jardine grew up in suburban Hawthorne, just south of Los Angeles and a few miles from both Baldwin Hills and the beaches that rim the ocean. "We had a shitty childhood," Dennis Wilson says. "I mean my dad was a tyrant. He used to whale on us, physically beat the crap out of us. I don't know kids who got it like we did. His big number was, 'Don't ever lie. And if you lie, I'll beat the shit out of you. But if you go outside when it's raining, I'll beat the shit out of you!' So you go outside when it's raining and you lie to him and you get hit twice.

"I thought it was insane. But when we did anything with music, he'd just. . ." Dennis starts bawling like an ailing foghorn and rubbing his eyes."'. . .Gawwwd! It's beautiful.' Like a baby. And that was so real to see your father go through an experience, a change over your music. So we'd been singing since we were babies. We got off on the idea that three guys could sing harmony."

Wilson has long, wild hair parted down the middle and a full beard, and he looks like a radical from the mid-Sixties plopped down in the middle of splendor. Though he detests the label, he has gotten the reputation over the years as the wild Beach Boy, largely because Charles Manson lived with him for a short time before the Tate murders ("There's some things I don't talk about. It's kind of a shame. One day in a book maybe") and because he is the protagonist of the surfing legend. Back in 1961, as the story goes, Dennis came home from a hard day of surfing and asked brother Brian to write a song about it. "Surfin'" sprung full-blown from Brian's head. Their father, Murry Wilson, a businessman and frustrated musician, peddled the song at various record companies, until Candix bought it and dubbed the group the Beach Boys. "Surfin'" was a hit, Capitol Records signed and promoted the group and the rest is history—theirs and ours.

"Before the group, I was in the oil business for a while. Gas and oil, check the tires." In his room, as he talks, Mike Love stretches his long body over two chairs. His brother Stan was a professional basketball player in both the NBA and ABA, and the resemblance is obvious. At 34, he is the oldest Beach Boy, and his red hair is thinning, but he has a way of crinkling his face into a smile and gulping for laughter that makes him look 14, even with his red beard. "I was a sheet-metal apprentice at my father's factory too. I was married. I married a cheerleader when I was 20 and she was 18 and just out of high school. We 'had to get married.'" He traces quotation marks in the air and laughs. "Which is in the Great American Way. That's where we glean our experiences. So I had two jobs. And when we made this record and it became a hit, the decision had to be made to leave my father's firm. I can remember my dad saying, 'Well, what if this doesn't work out?' And I said, 'So if it doesn't I'll be back scraping shit off of metal.' I had no idea we'd be as successful as we are today for as long a time. But I thought it was worth taking off a year. So far it's been a pretty long year."

In fact, a year later the Beach Boys had turned out several hit records and had nearly every teen in America communing with California and hyperbolizing pond ripples into waves. "Surfing was the hottest craze since candy," says Dennis. "Everybody had something to do with being a surfer. I mean, you could not go anywhere without seeing woodies. I can remember as kids driving to the beach. We lived like five miles away, and there was a hill. There are always little hills before you get to the ocean. And I can see guys standing up on the back seat trying to be the first one to see the water. I mean our whole life was the ocean, and those things in our songs were real to us. What else did we have?"

Even for those of us who had never seen an ocean, the surf had profound and satisfying meanings. For any white kid growing up in Camelot, the Beach Boys seemed to condense the fantastic psychological space we called California, the comfy, expanding materialist ethos, and the sweet vibes of the high school subculture before it became a counterculture. When you listened to "Surfin' U.S.A." or "Surfer Girl" or "California Girls," you heard your own silly high school dreams perfectly articulated. When you listened to "In My Room" or "Be True to Your School" or "409," you heard your *experiences* being articulated. These were nothing less than folk songs for white, suburban, middle-class teens. That's because the Beach Boys were doing the same things we were doing and writing songs about them.

"On Saturday sometimes I'd sit on the curb with Louie Marrado and let farts and light 'em," Dennis recalls. "Skateboard all night. 'Let's go over to Margo's house and look in her window.' Play volleyball at the church. When we were driving—'Let's cruise A & W Root Beer.' At that turn in my life when I started getting a little bit of freedom out of the house, when I could stay out until midnight and sneak a beer—that's when the group happened. We went through all our teenage trials and tribulations on the road and in the music."

The result was a long string of hits and greater record sales than any other American group before or since. They were primitives, and their music was bathed in sentiment and sentimentality, but the sentimentality was credible because their fans had felt the same things and in the same ridiculously simple terms. That's why the Beach Boys could reify in their music a zillion wavering signals of American pop culture, while other, less naive, rock stars were out swiping T.S. Eliot's hubcaps. "When you're growing up, 17 or 18 years old, and you were going to the high school prom, and your dad gives you the keys to the car, gives you money to buy a corsage, gives you some more money to take the girl out after the date," says Mike Love, "how the fuck are you going to sit there and say on the other hand, 'OO-OOOOOOO-weeeeeeee! My baby's left me and what a drag,' and all that shit? Aspersions have been cast on our musical and lyrical integrity because we haven't been intellectual enough. Well, how the fuck are you going to get intellectual about a love for a little girl who spends all day on the beach? All you know is that you've got your teenage hard-on, the total hots, and so what's to intellectualize, I ask you."

The music itself was a combination of Chuck Berry and the HiLos, and the harmonies were so tangible you could almost bite them right out of the air. Carl says, "The lyrics for us were secondary. Because for us, it was the feeling we got, the experience we had of making the music. It was a very pure thing. And the lyrics were only a vehicle for our music."

While it lasted, the Beach Boys were the troubadours for a large segment of America. Then, around 1967, came the sudden fall, which didn't devastate them financially (they were set), but which wounded their pride. "There was a time," remembers Carl without a trace of bitterness, "when the Beach Boys were an uncool thing to be into." In some unregenerate precincts, they still are. Though most of these skeptics probably haven't heard any *new* Beach Boys music since 1966, nearly a decade, they seem to feel that they've grown up while the Beach Boys, like Peter Pan, never did.

"In 1965, when we did an album called *Summer Days, Summer Nights*, it started to bother us, doing this same stuff, because we thought we were trapped into having to sing about a certain thing," says Carl. He is soft and dreamy and a bit chunky. When he talks, he rolls his eyes lazily, and it is a little like watching a beatific gyroscope. "We'd been traveling around the world and having our experiences open up for us. So we were kind of humored at that time because people were saying, 'You guys are wearing striped shirts and white pants.' And we were going, 'Yeah, that's right. That ain't us, because the thing we were and are is the experience we create.' We were getting whomped on for wearing a particular kind of clothing, but we still experienced ourselves as valid musically."

Though a lot of teens might have denied it, the Beach Boys were maturing too. And they were concerned. They played benefits for the antiwar movement, and Carl fought through the courts for six years as a conscientious objector. Musically, the *Pet Sounds* album (1966), which includes "God Only Knows" and "Wouldn't It Be Nice," was pivotal. "A lot of people say *Sgt. Pepper* was the first concept album," says Carl, who acknowledges his respect for the Beatles. "But the truth is that *Pet Sounds* was really the first. It was thematic musically." On the album there was no mention of surf or

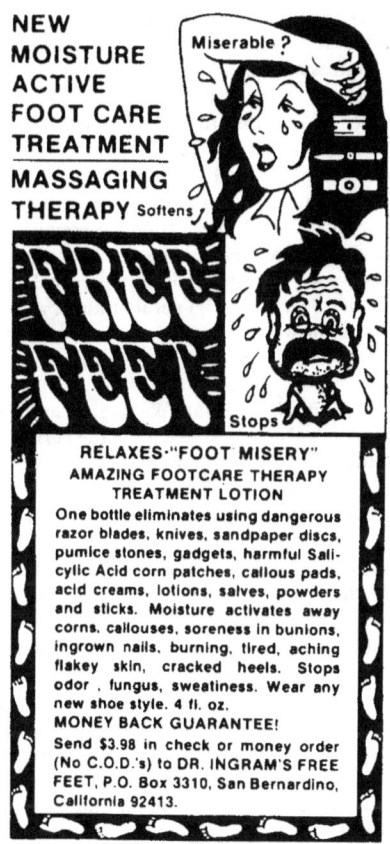

cars, only the post-adolescent pangs of someone (Brian Wilson) trying to come to terms with his life. The songs are mature and introspective, and the backups are so much more fully orchestrated than in the earlier albums that they are nearly symphonic. That album was followed by the classic single, "Good Vibrations," with its tempo changes, its cushion of sound, the eerie inclusion of music from a theremin and its simple mystic images. But the music wasn't political, it was personal, and the Beach Boys' general attitude, as Carl summarizes it, was that "politics is not necessarily the highest expression of life."

With the Vietnam War raging, and the seemingly sun-kissed days of the early Sixties gone, some people disagreed. Insofar as the counterculture revolted against both complacency and its own bourgeois roots, the Beach Boys were doubly cursed; they seemed complacent, and they were certifiably bourgeois. But the group blames Capitol Records for the slide, not the cultural change. "That's exactly why the decline was the decline," bristles Dennis. "Because of marketing. Because of packaging. We were so young when we signed a contract that Capitol could do virtually what they wanted to do with our records. Everyone has his own idea of how to sell a product: We'll put posters here. We'll call it the beach surfer buggy. We'll sell. . . . And pretty soon the public is beat to death with the surfing routine, the car routine, the blah blah blah routine. And they say, 'The fucking Beach Boys are just a plastic bunch of shit.' And then they grow up, right?

At the same time the aesthetic front of the counterculture was generating protest rock, it was also fissioning into blues, flower rock and drug rock. But, again, the Beach Boys were disregarded, aliens to the kids with whom they had grown up and for whom they had supplied dreams. "When we were getting to the end of our contract," Mike recalls, "Capitol wasn't promoting us because if they did, they would have had to spend enormous amounts of money to re-sign us. The San Francisco flower power people were saying peace and love, and we were geared right into that. But it never got transmitted across the media as well as the surfing and car stuff did."

Drug rock was a different story. "When drugs came in, we didn't want to commit to that," says Dennis. "I still smoke pot once in a while. Took acid a couple of times. Tried a little cocaine. Tried Quaaludes. I think I've done almost every drug except heroin. I've done opium. I've tried it all. But I don't deal with my problems with a drug. You notice all the groups that are really drug groups. Where are they?"

The group did keep experimenting with sounds, melding other components into its California idiom, but no one was listening because the Beach Boys seemed tacky and irrelevant. "I'm not saying we would have been universally revered," explains Mike. "But we would have been a lot better off had Capitol said, 'This is the Beach Boys' *new music*.' They didn't do it, so we were consequently known to just a very small core of intellectuals and music lovers who dug the Beach Boys from the level of art. There was no media hype going on for the Beach Boys, and there weren't top ten records going every day because Brian wasn't into that anymore. He went into producing albums, concepts."

For its concepts in new albums, the group built its own studio in Brian's living room, formed its own label in 1967, significantly called Brother Records, and kept on plugging. The results were artistic if not overwhelmingly com-

> "I was a sheet-metal apprentice at my father's factory," says Love. "I married a cheerleader. We had to get married—which is in the Great American Way. That's where we glean our experiences"

mercial. "Just after *Pet Sounds*," says Mike, "we did *Smiley Smile*, which was the antithesis of the superproduction race: the Stones did this, the Beatles did this, the Beach Boys did this. Brian went whooooo, 180 degrees, to real light stuff, and it was totally avant in that it was going in no direction that anybody else was going." In their most recent albums, particularly *Surf's Up* and *Holland* (made in Holland), the sound is denser, richer, a palimpsest of diaphanous layers of music. It fills the room like a vapor. The melodies are more ambitious, the musical routes more circuitous and the lyrics far more contemplative and imagistically more complex. There is no music quite like it.

"We went from a more direct look at the relative world of objects to a more introspective look at the self and then to a more universal awareness," says Mike. "The *Pet Sounds* album in 1966 began a more inner-directed approach to life and things. From there 'Good Vibrations' was a milestone, because we're directly dealing not with some outer phenomenon but with something coming from within, good vibrations. That's the direction we kept going."

The Beach Boys tried to refashion their public image to conform with their private one. They even joked about changing their name to Beach, short and pretentious. In 1971 and 1972, Jack Rieley, their manager at the time, worked to get them FM airplay and attract the college audience, and the group itself showcased its newer, more difficult material at concerts, reserving the oldies for the second half of the performance. "We wanted people to think we were good *now*," says Carl, "instead of looking at us as inferior to what we used to be. But the audience had different expectations."

I can vividly recall a concert in 1971 where the battle lines were pitched. The audience had come to camp it up and boogie in the aisles to "Surfin' U.S.A.," and from the first minutes it was like a showdown. The group's frustration was palpable. "We want to play something from our new album," Mike would announce, while the audience squirmed and snarled. "Play 'Rag Doll,' " someone yelled from the balcony, referring to the Four Seasons' falsetto hit. "Go soak yourself," Mike snapped, as the group slid into unfamiliar material. The tensions didn't subside until the Beach Boys came back ripping with the early hits. From its inauspicious beginnings, the concert ended with the entire auditorium on its feet (every concert does), but the whole experience left me with the distinct impression that the group would have rather been sunning itself back in California than having itself flagellated here in 1971's sinister version of 1961.

"The group had *treeeeemendous* pressure on it at that time," says Carl, trilling the word. "I'd been separated from my wife twice. Dennis had a couple of relationships falter. Michael had the same thing. And we had the problems with the record company, Capitol, rejecting us." At the same time, Carl was butting heads with his draft board, trying to get them to accept public service concerts as alternative service. After six years, he won his case. Then there was Dennis' involvement with Manson.

And finally there were Brian's continuing problems. Back when the Beach Boys were younger, Brian wrote all the music, arranged it, produced it and sang the lilting falsetto leads while Mike sang the deeper, rawer songs. He invented the rich harmonic idiom that had become the group's trademark, and at the unripe age of 20 he seemed to creatively command

"LEONARD COHEN, THE BEST OF."

A collection of some of the finest songs ever written:
Suzanne
Sisters of Mercy
So Long, Marianne
Bird on the Wire
Lady Midnight
The Partisan
Hey, That's No Way to Say Goodbye
Famous Blue Raincoat
Last Year's Man
Chelsea Hotel No. 2
Who by Fire
Take This Longing

By one of the finest writers who ever sang.
On Columbia Records and Tapes.

what this country needs is a good ten cent high.

The natural high of HIGH incense. Twenty aromatic incense sticks for just $2.00. Incense is the mood maker. Light a stick of HIGH and virtually feel your mood change as the delightful fragrance of Jasmine, Strawberry, African Violet or Black Raspberry fills the room, relaxing and refreshing your body and your head.

Order now and we'll send you a free special bonus—an unusually sensuous scent we're sure you'll enjoy.

Please allow 3 weeks for delivery.

YES, Send me _____ packages of HIGH incense in the scents checked below. I've enclosed my check for $2 per package. Please include my special free bonus scent.
☐ MUSK   ☐ COCONUT
☐ STRAWBERRY   ☐ JASMINE
☐ AFRICAN VIOLET   ☐ SANDALWOOD
☐ BLACK RASBERRY   ☐ VANILLA
☐ CHERRY   ☐ YELLOW ROSE
☐ ALL TEN SCENTS PLUS MY SPECIAL BONUS FOR ONLY $15

Name _____
Address _____
City _____ State _____ Zip _____

HIGH
P.O. BOX 368
Bellmore, New York 11710

---

an entire industry with the song structures he used, the bass lines he wrote, the arrangements he concocted and the independence he sought. But he was also shy to the point of being reclusive, insecure to the point of being neurotic, and that caused dissension and pain. Brian hasn't toured for a decade, preferring instead to concentrate on the music, and several breakdowns later he is no longer the "omnipresent, omnipotent dictator," in the respectful words of one Beach Boy. The rest of the group had to surface with their own musical expressions, and Brian became an elder statesman and collaborator, padding around his house like an exile, jamming occasionally with his friend Paul McCartney and constantly writing music, most of which he would never allow to be released. Brian is still a recluse; he doesn't travel, but the rest of the group have gradually come to terms with their problems.

TM was largely responsible. Carl shakes his head and grimaces without moving a facial muscle: "I've had the thought that had it not been for TM, I would have really had a hard time coping with all the pressures." The Beach Boys first met Maharishi Mahesh Yogi, the giggly main franchiser of transcendental meditation, in Paris at a worldwide TV hookup for UNICEF. It was 1967. Maharishi was sitting in the audience wrapped in his white robe watching Ravi Shankar rehearse. "I shook his hand and he goes—" Dennis makes a face like a Buddha. "And all of a sudden I felt this weirdness, this presence this guy had. Like out of left field. 'Live your life to the fullest.' First thing he ever said to me. So the next day I went over to his room, and he said, 'Tell me some words of your songs.' So we told him the lyrics to 'God Only Knows,' and he goes, 'That's the sun rising and the stars and the planets and it connects with. . . .'" Dennis scratches his beard wisely. "So I said, 'God this is great!' And he said, 'We'd like to initiate you into the program.' I said, 'What does that mean? How much?' And he said, 'We'll just do it to you tomorrow morning.' So I called Michael and all the guys in London. 'C'mon down here to Paris. We're all gonna meditate.' And then I got my mantra, and as Maharishi was giving them to us he says, 'What do you want?' I say, 'I want everything. Everything.' And he laughed and we meditated together. It was so wild."

Maharishi prophesied that if they continued to meditate, they would become the most influential group in the world. (He told the Beatles that if *they* continued to meditate, they would stay together.) The Beach Boys meditated hard. A few months after the Paris meeting, Mike Love took off for India to study with Maharishi, and both he and Al Jardine became teachers of TM. Then they planned a worldwide tour to introduce Maharishi to colleges and universities. But that was before TM became the chic way to raise consciousness, and few things *seemed* more incongruous (actually TM was a natural development from the early beach and fun philosophy, a spiritual counterpart) than our collective troubadour climbing out of a dune buggy to scale the Himalayas and meditate. The tour was booked into large halls, the small audiences were discourteous and the Beach Boys were forced to abort the project after two shows.

Only the last few TM-crazed years have vindicated them. In fact, one might even detect a cultural correlation between TM's popularity and that of the Beach Boys. Rick Nelson (not the singer) was West Coast coordinator for Students International Meditation Society when he met Mike Love and Al Jardine at a TM center in 1972. Mike invited him to dinner; he went to work as the group's sound man and was finally promoted to road manager. So for the last three years Nelson has seen every Beach Boys concert, which means he has seen the group over 250 times. "When I first started out with them, we were doing a lot of college gymnasiums, and since then we've started doing large, outdoor sellouts. No one can really say what's caused that, but my own personal theory is that the show is totally happy. I've never seen a down show. Night after night, it's up, up, up. The music is a positive, creative force (TM words). And people are ready for that these days. People need it or enjoy it or are looking for it."

At their recent concerts, the Beach Boys haven't played any new material (they have been working on an album for three years), but there is none of the old frustration that used to sour the shows. "I think we totally jumped out of the entrapment," says Carl. "I think it happened maybe a year or two ago when we stopped resisting our past and having people enjoy our older stuff." Mike Love concurs. "You never get tired of it. You see what those songs can do to an audience. It's fun and it's totally relevant. That's why we'll always have a public. There's no time limit now. We're like the Mills Brothers. A couple of them may die, they may change, but they've still got the sound." Dennis is even more sanguine. "I can tell you the day the Beach Boys will no longer exist." When? "Never. They'll be on stage in wheelchairs."

The way things are going for them,

The Beach Boys and supporting cast on tour last summer: The old hits are performed with new energy, and every night is up, up, up.

he may be right. There is a new generation of teens weaned on Nixon and glitter rock and without any positive, satisfying youth experience to cherish and stamp as their own. "I notice that our audience gets younger and younger," says Carl. "Four years ago we would play Carnegie Hall and schools, and we'd have a totally student audience. Last spring we played the Anaheim baseball park, and it blew Brian's mind to see 12-year-old people experiencing his music as new." For that

Maharishi Mahesh Yogi prophesied that if the Beach Boys meditated, they would become the most influential group in the world. He told the Beatles that if *they* continued to meditate, they would stay together

generation, the Beach Boys' music transports them back to the early Sixties, when people did go to the prom and scamper on the beach. It's manufactured nostalgia, by the audience rather than the Beach Boys—but it works and you can't knock it. The new Beach Boys fans may not be able to celebrate the good times and the good things they have; there's been too much innocence lost for that. But they can celebrate instead an attitude they don't have toward these things: they can romanticize the romanticization of things, and assuage their middle-class guilt at having too much. Through the Beach Boys they can plug in to the legendary innocence of the early Sixties. In a sense, then, the Beach Boys are doing in music what Gerald Ford was supposed to do in politics. They represent a kind of wholesome virtue, and they stand in roughly the same relationship to Alice Cooper or the Rolling Stones that Ford once stood to Nixon. "I just think there's a lot of agreement," explains Carl, "that we're one of the real things."

But Mike Love has his own theory, and it sets the Beach Boys in some final perspective. "They're all digging the Beach Boys," Love explains. "And there's only one reason for that. It's not because the music is abstract or intellectual or the blues or anything like that. It is because it has reencapsulated the same things that honestly and really identify with all kids growing up in a certain socioeconomic strata, and our experiences are indigenous to that." Love's long fingers flit through the air underscoring his point. "The Beach Boys are very much products of our society, and we're inseparable from the white, middle-class karma. And that's why I think a hundred years from now people will listen to the Beach Boys' music, and they won't be listening to a lot of other groups. They'll study it the same way they study classical music, Beethoven or someone like that. And 'Fun,Fun,Fun '—a guy will sit up there and show a hologram of somebody running through an A & W stand in a Thunderbird, or maybe *American Graffiti*. And he'll explain to them: 'This is what it was all like.'" ●

PERFORMANCES

Dennis the mystic covers his ears in distant reverie as the Beach Boys once again bring back echoes of old summer days and California nights.

Beach Boys
Anaheim Convention Center
Anaheim, Calif.

By GENE SCULATTI

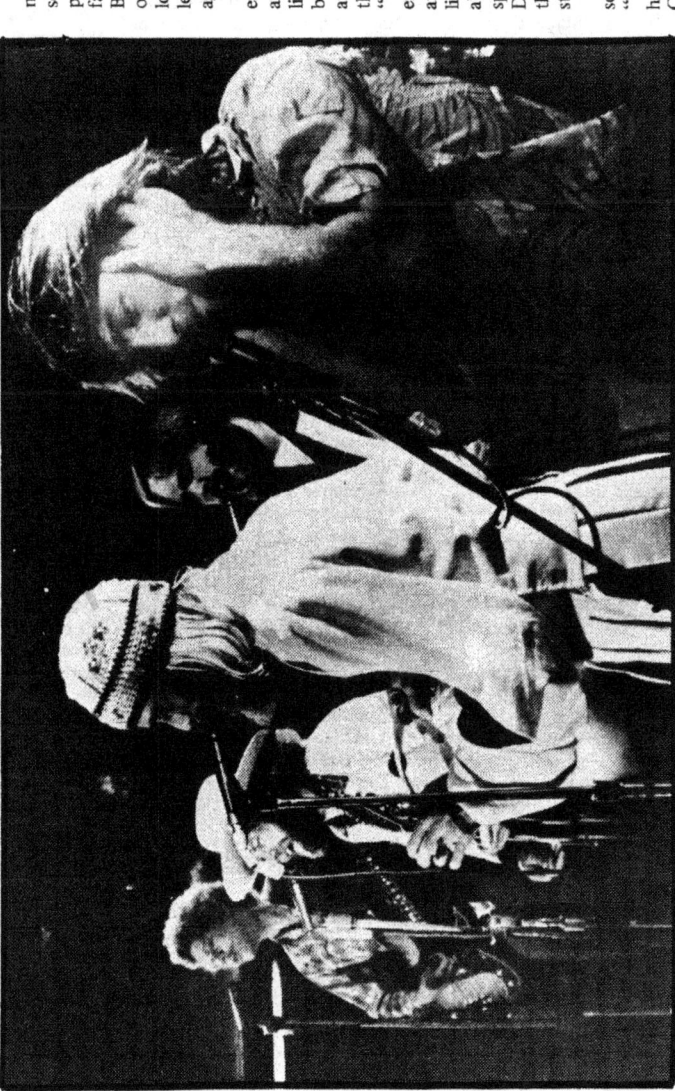

Where else could the Beach Boys preface a performance of "Surfer Girl" with, "on our way down here tonight, we passed within two blocks of where the girl who inspired this song used to live"? Elder brother Brian scribbled the selfsame sylph portrait one fine day in '63 on the way to his orthodontist's, somewhere down among the sweltering palms.

It's home territory. The Convention Center, that is, down Katella past the Westward Ho!, Rip Van Winkle, Ivanhoe, Candy Lane and Space Age motels, around the corner from the Matterhorn and the monorail.

Some spiritual home base, is what it is, 'cause there's no way these talented youngsters who call themselves the Beach Boys could get the kind of response in New York, Cleveland or anyplace else, that they draw right here.

Brian's homebound now and Al Jardine fills space on "Don't Worry Baby," and Carl warbles "Caroline No," but that doesn't change a thing to the home crowd. They've been cruising the parking lot since this afternoon, they're all casually dressed, primed for the event, and *they're all sixteen years old.*

They stir aloud during intermission. Lights dim and they scream in anticipation. The preparatory clap 'n' stomp starts, fades and restarts: "We want the Beach Boys! We want..." Intent on making one final adjustment, a lone equipment man enters stage left and the screams commence again.

Once onstage, their very presence inspires both rapt attention and pinch-me-is-it-real squeals; little Al, cherub Carl, foreign fireball Blondie, laid-back Mike Love and the rest, and always Dennis, the wandering focus for all that "mystique" talk. Toss-off references to "Brian", "Hawthorne" and "glad to be back" are greeted like gospel, repeated and verified, absorbed by an audience high on spirit and shiny from SoCal sun. Dennis points out his mother in the crowd and they give her a standing ovation.

Sure, there's a bond here. The songs, from Mike's arch nasalteen "Surfin' U.S.A." ("if ev'rybody had an O-shun...") to Blondie and Carl belting widetrack harmonies on a smooth "Sail On Sailor," get the kind of response that indicates they're accepted, acknowledged as some kind of South Bay birthright.

The dichotomy still exists; one clump of sophomores and juniors behind us shout themselves hoarse for "Oldies!", and two rows in front a blond chorus pleads for "Pisces Lady" ("Funky Pretty") and "Leaving This Town."

Four years ago, the group were reluctant to drag out the "Moldies", dressing them up as pitiable parodies. Now they can accomodate their entire career. And it's precisely the presence and persistence of their audience, growin' younger every day, that's accountable for the fact. *Greatest Hits, Pet Sounds, Wild Honey, Surf's Up, Holland* are served up as one sumptuous buffet and everyone partakes.

The audience sings along with every tune, drowning the group's clear-cut harmonies out completely by the end of "Fun Fun Fun" and the "Jumpin' Jack Flash" encore; all around the arena, from folding-chair floor to the high-up cheap seats, they're dancing in place, together, uninhibitedly goofing on this unique kind of California energy exchange right before their sunburnt orbs.

It's a bitch of a show. The hits and non-hits, all go down as smashes with this crowd. Mike brings the house down twice with the intimation of a "big party" to be thrown New Year's Eve in nearby Long Beach.

In Concert, the latest waxing, is damn good in *its* way too. You have to give it time, 'cause, unlike the kinetic explosion of the live show, its magic lies partially concealed. But it has special treats in abundance too; the strong new contender, "We Got Love," "Heroes And Villains" rendered with clarity, lyrics and melody breakdown notwithstanding, the buoyancy of "Wouldn't It Be Nice," "Marcella" as it never sounded on *So Tough*. It ain't the sweaty summerblast of their 1965 *Concert* (Cap. STAO 2198) and it might tame against the import *Live In London*, but it's representative of Beach Boys '73, and that's still one of the damn finest properties extant.

COLLEGE REPORTER CONCERT REVIEW

Concert Review
Beach Boys: A Triumphant Return
J. S. Douglas

The Beach Boys couldn't have begun last Saturday night's concert at Princeton University with a more symbolic song than "Good Vibrations" because those two words are the only two which begin to describe the atmosphere that prevailed in Dillon Gymnasium.

The standing ovation that greeted the appearance of the Boys on the stage was only the beginning as the entire evening was marked by thunderous applause from the 3,230 people that filled every available seat in the gym. The appearance of the Beach Boys did surprise some of those present; gone are the striped shirts, white coats and healthy, California-tanned shorthair look. In abundance are healthy beards, hair, leather and denim, and lots and lots of hats.

Unemotional piece of wood that I am, I cried when the Boys appeared on stage. It represented the triumph of the good, the hero-wins-in-the-end type of story to me, because I've been a Boys' fan for ten years; their appearance couldn't help but render a reaction of this kind when I remembered all the shit they've gone through in the years since 1968—the lawsuit when they broke with Capitol, the suppression of their albums by Capitol, etc. The nucleus of the group (Brian Wilson stopped performing in '66 to be replaced by Bruce Johnson who was replaced on the concert tour by Van Dyke Parks, and Dennis Wilson was out for this tour with a hand injury), was still the solid harmony of Al Jardine, Carl Wilson, and Mike Love; Mike and Al both sport beards and hats now to detract from the fact that the dome hair has gone to pasture.

Songs, News, Oldies

All these thoughts ran through my head in a couple of seconds. I sat down again after applauding and then wrote down the title of their next song, "Don't Go Near the Water" using the light from two flickering marijuana pipes directly behind me to illuminate my scratch pad.

The Beach Boys explained that they would entertain requests for

The Beach Boys explained that they would entertain requests for oldies during their second set after a short intermission, and then went right into "Wouldn't it be Nice" followed by "Student Demonstration Time". Their first set followed this trend, in that they would play one cut from their current album followed by an oldie, interspersed with news! Good news for us B.B. fans was that their lawsuit with Capitol was won by them, which means that their albums will again be available, and also that they'll be playing a three-night stand at Carnegie Hall in March. After ten songs, they left the stage to take a fifteen-minute intermission.

During the intermission everybody stretched but few left their seats to move around the gym; I was one of these as I approached the head of their student-run concert organization. He saw my note pad and pen and didn't seem at all surprised when I asked him how many people he could seat in the gym at one time. He replied that, due to a fire ordinance, they were limited to 3,200 people; however, to break even they had added 30 chairs for both performances.

I asked how they worked their concerts and he told me that they never booked warm-up groups, which saved them money, and also that they usually signed an agreement guaranteeing a group a certain amount.

Slow, Beautiful Ballads

The second set was different from the first in that the types of songs were grouped together. Instead of alternating with songs from their Surf's Up album with oldies, they performed mainly slow, beautiful ballads like "God Only Knows" and "Carol I Know". The band which was backing up the group didn't have a lot to do until the last few songs and the two encores which the audience demanded.

The actual Beach Boys consisted of Al Jardine, Mike Love, Carl Wilson, and Van Dyke Parks; they handled the main instruments—the Hammond B-3 organ, electric piano, standup organ, regular piano, lead and twelve-string guitar, and steel guitar—and were backed up by eight others, including two drumers, a bass player, two trumpets, trombone, saxophone, and another keyboard man. The sound was, as one girl around me screamed, "Better than their albums, even."

Show-wise, the Beach Boys were constantly entertaining with the verbal battle going on between Mike Love and the audience and between Mike Love and Al Jardine. The audience could discern a difference between the three in the way that they performed—Carl Wilson sang and played almost in a religious manner; Al Jardine joked around a little, but was mostly serious, even refusing a reefer from a girl in front of the stage; Mike Love, like his little four year old son who was constantly dancing around behind and beside the stage, was clowning and entertaining in vivid contrast to the other two.

Cheers and Applause Deafening

The entire two-hour concert was great, but the part that the audience enjoyed the most was the ending. The Beach Boys played "Better Watch Out What You Eat" from their new Surf's Up album, and then said good night. Everyone was on their feet by this time; the MC re-appeared on stage, said, "And once again, the Beach Boys," and they returned, did "California Girls," and retreated once more. The applause and cheers this time were almost deafening; people everywhere were laughing and clapping, screaming and crying; the MC surveyed the situation and repeated the magic words once more, and the Beach Boys were again back on the stage. Someone behind me said something to the effect that all this encore stuff was ridiculous, only to be mashed in the jaw with a pocketbook by a girl who told him, above the roar of the crowd: "Shut up—after three years of no recognition, they deserve this."

Crowd Went Bananas!

Any other exchanges between the masher and the mashed were lost as the entire crowd to a man went bananas; the Beach Boys played three of their best right in succession—"I Get Around," "Help Me Rhonda", and "Fun, Fun, Fun." People were throwing paper at one another, and jackets in the air, embracing one another, kissing, dancing, falling off chairs, but *everyone* was moving to the beat of the Beach Boys and singing along. As they finished, they again took up a recurring theme of the entire concert in that they asked everyone to please be sure to register and to vote.

As I left the gym, I stopped to wait for the rest of the entourage that had accompanied my date and myself to Princeton, and I watched the crowd file out. What I saw mirrored on their faces and in their excited words to one another was the same feeling that had come over me as the concert ended: the surf is indeed up for the Beach Boys; the Beach Boys are *back*, man, and they're back to stay for a long time.

ROCK MAGAZINE 1974

The Beach Boys
By Bill Reed

You couldn't count on fifty hands the number of times "genius" has been used in print in relation to Brian Wilson. Even Leonard Bernstein verified same in introducing number one Wilson son on one of his TV specials.

Accordingly, Brian has played the role, both publicly and privately (and consciously or unconsciously?) to the hilt. He is to rock as dramatist Alfred Jarry is to French arts and letters. Jarry's death-bed request for a toothpick (indeed his last pronouncement in this life) has met its outlandish match in Brian's "Fire Music" debacle. In what, in most respects, seems like a parody of mad genius, he destroyed all the tapes of a very expensive recording session of an extended piece entitled "Fire Music." Why? At the time of the session, a number of fires had unexplainedly flared up in L.A., and mere coincidence was not a suitable enough explanation for the composer. Consequently, he destroyed the tapes (burning them, of course), and "Fire Music" was lost to the ages.

There are a number of stories in circulation that go even farther in their depiction of Brian as Beethoven incarnate. Publicly, though, they're dismissed by his intimates as *just* "well, Brian's strange sense of humor."

Perhaps the "Seconds" episode is apocryphal, but it deserves another telling. In some of the middle period recordings, The Beach Boys showed the heavy influence of Phil Spector. Eventually, so it goes, Brian began to obsess on the possibility that Mr. Wall of Sound was out for revenge, angered by the fact that some of his highly original techniques had not only been copped but improved upon by Brian. This distraction absorbed his attention at a time when Spector was involved in a production deal with Paramount Pictures. That's the set-up.

Now picture Brian deciding to go to a movie, perhaps to get his mind off the Spector spectre. The film is, unfortunately for purposes of well-integrated Brian Wilson, the Paramount film "Seconds." Now, imagine Brian walking into the theater just as the screen is filled with a close-up of a character looking out and saying (in the context of the film) "Good afternoon, Mr. Wilson." The rumors vary as to the degree of Brian's upset, but significantly the whole affair was seen by our Brian as the upshot of a carefully timed, exquisitely wrought Goldfinger-like plot on Spector's part.

This was several years ago. Today Brian acknowledges the Spector-Ronettes

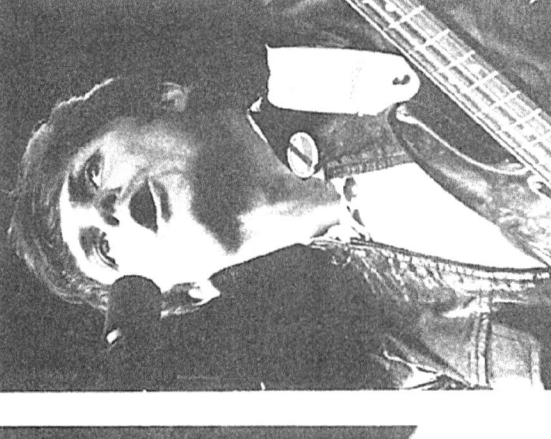

Photos: Emerson-Loew

Mike Love (above left) Carl Wilson (above right) Al Jardine (below left) Bruce Johnston (below right).

If only they'd called themselves the Band

"Be My Baby" as the *ne plus ultra* rock record. And coming out of virtual Garbo-like seclusion recently, he owned and operated a natural foods store in L.A., The Radiant Radish. His new toy amused him only a short while, for he soon gave up working in the store. But what a wonderful way to buy a Tiger's Milk Bar...from Brian Wilson.

And yet how could The Beach Boys possibly have known way back in balmier, pre-acid, surfin' days that their then-catchy name would ultimately be the cause of their undoing? If only they'd called themselves "The Band" back in '60.

With some of rock's most influential critics on their side, and after five years of movement away from their surfin' and striped-pants phase, Brian Wilson and company have yet to escape the stigma of their anachronistic agglomerate name.

Relatively few are aware that the group is still recording, and some of those who do know are laboring under the delusion that the group is still doing surf music.

So this greater participation by other members of the group hasn't been unsuspected. For years there were rumors of *bad* vibrations between members of the world's oldest living rock-and-roll ensemble, arising from the amount of control exercised by Brian. This may explain why the long-awaited *Smiley Smile* was so much less adventurous than had been expected. The legendary "Surf's Up" was gone from the record entirely, and "Heroes and Villians" was half its original length.

The new egalitarian tack accounts, in large part, for the group's overhaled sound. *Sunflower*, then, is "produced by The Beach Boys," not just by Brian Wilson. Even Carl Wilson is credited with co-authoring one of the titles.

Dennis Wilson is beginning to emerge as the second most well-defined entity of the group. If it has no other result, his highly publicized friendship with Charles Manson should affect the stubborn all-American image that has been anathema to the group in their attempts to gain a share of the attention they deserve. (Apocalyptic that the two swivet of creative frenzy.

"Good Vibrations," the group's number one single in 1966, marked the last time that The Beach Boys made much of an impression on the mass of record buyers. Since then their ability to capture the public's fancy has dwindled with mathematical regularity. Ironically, though, their only *really* interesting work has been produced during this period of waning popularity.

They've been very much boxed in. And, rather than fight fire with fire, they have refused to plunge indiscriminately into momentarily prevailing musical fashions. *Sunflower*, their very recent album, reveals only slight interest in what is being laid down outside rockdom. Several of the cuts fall outside even the broadest definition of "rock."

Paul Williams remarked on this quality in the group's music when he wrote of their 1967 album, *Wild Honey*. Williams then read this seemingly regressive tendency as a way of countering the post-*Pepper* hysteria evidenced by a lot of the music being performed and recorded during that acid summer. "Dylan," he wrote, "told them what to do, he's leading the way again with *John Wesley Harding*. He's told everyone to go back to simplicity and forget wild production albums and just put it where it's at. And then all of a sudden I realized Brian had been there first with *Wild Honey*." Williams came to appreciate the album, but only after he'd listened to it for a quite lengthy period. I had a very similar reaction to that same album. At the time I too was puzzled by the simple compositions and the sparse construction of most of *Wild Honey*. With its Webcor-in-the-garage sound and one-take texture there was nothing initially for me to latch on to. Even some very good groups were coming out with some very bad Sgt. Pepper imitations—over-extended compositions based on dubious "concept" themes.

In the midst of all this, there was Brian, just screaming rock blues past the top of his range, backed by the funkiest bass lines this side of "Louie, Louie." Nothing on *Wild Honey* lasted longer than two minutes and forty seconds.

Next they presented us with *Friends*, as difficult to approach as the pre-*Honey Smiley Smile* album, but curiously even simpler compositionally than *Wild Honey*.

Each successive album has been not only as good as the last, but has also presented us with a radical departure from the one before. Perhaps only The Beatles have mastered the art of musical surprise quite as well. Unlike The Beatles, though, each new Beach Boys release meets with increasing public indifference. This blessed flux in their music is one other reason for the "Boys" shifting popularity. For one group that occupied such a fixed place in the public's mind, this constant change in musical approach proved just too confusing.

All of this is compounded by The Beach Boys' deportment during live appearances. A Fillmore East concert of a year and a half ago was a near disaster. They came onstage decked out in matching ice cream-colored suits. And since, generally, Fillmore habitues like their groups gungey, raw and *au courant*, the Good Humor hallucination on the stage couldn't help but bring out the sadistic side of the audience. By the end of their set, the aging "Beach Boys" were like panicky circus ponies. Granted, they got it on approximately during the last number. But the previous fifty minutes of self-deprecation had taken its toll. Too much goosing and horsing around betrayed the fact that they really were ashamed of being simply The Beach Boys.

At the time, and for several years prior to this, Brian hadn't been performing with the group in public. Instead, he opted to seclude himself in Belair, California, and act as producer and arranger-writer for the group.

Until very recently, then, the group has traveled without its nucleus. This lack of focus has obviously contributed to the overall shabbiness of a typical "live" Beach Boys show. It's not, as has been suggested, that they're "incapable of sounding good live," but rather like the "old" Byrds, they just don't know how to approach the problem of performing outside studio walls.

Until the release of *20/20*, each Beach Boys album was of a whole cloth. *Pet Sounds* betrayed the heavy influence that Phil Spector had on the group. And also (gasp) a touch of Martin Denny. *Smiley Smile* had Van Dyke Parks and, presumably, LSD as collaborators. *Friends* bore the imprint of the group's controversial association with The Maha(ha)rishi. And til *20/20* all of the albums were almost exclusively the end result of Brian Wilson research. But the latter album and the recent *Sunflower*, even more so, are indicative of a much more democratic apportioning of responsibilities. Apparently Brian is no longer the sole instigator of the group's musical direction. *Pet Sounds* reportedly had Brian playing almost all of the instruments, composing all the material, and mixing the album in a months' long

figures mentioned most frequently in connection with Manson are (1) a member of The Beach Boys, and (2) Terry Melcher, son of the high priestess of the American cult of prolonged virginity, Doris Day.)

Sunflower amassed a set of almost unqualified raves, and generally Dennis' name is mentioned in reviews with almost as much frequency as Brian's.

During the last three or four lackluster years, these grand purveyors of post-scarcity, California, sun-baked hedonism have been helped, in large part, to get by because of a little help from their musical friends. Such strange bedfellows as James Morrison and Paul McCartney have repeatedly praised the excellence of the group's efforts. And, too, rock journalists and a small but staunch group of loyals have lent support. Because of this they've been able to maintain a sort of celebrity during the year and a half of musical silence brought about by the legal encumbrances of Capitol Records. Their recent contract with Reprise gives them the creative autonomy that was sought, but never achieved, during their eight year relationship with Capitol.

Incidentally, the disparity between the generally highly favorable reviews for *Sunflower* and the skimpy amount of airplay that the work has received on the hipper New York FM outlets goes a long way in reinforcing the contention of those who insist that rock journalism doesn't really have that suffocating control over the mind of the rock fan that it's often been accused of having. I log a lot of hours during the week listening to "underground" radio, and yet I've only heard one track from *Sunflower* played on the air during first month of

continued on page 31

But astonishingly, they've come through it and now are indicating, to what will be hopefully an ever-widening audience, just how "seriously" they should be taken. Their integrity and the certainty of their musical vision are in no way better underlined than by Brian's decision to tour with the group again.

Their performance at the October 3rd Big Sur Folk Festival marked their belated initiation into the ways of the music festival. Their success at Big Sur could come as a real surprise only to those unfamiliar with *Wild Honey*, the one album that really shows they're capable of something other than the brilliant recording-studio surgery typical of most of their other albums. And only *Wild Honey* displayed well the extent to which each member of The Beach Boys deserves being considered a first-class musician.

Those attending had a chance to experience this first-hand when The Beach Boys played at Big Sur. Perhaps the best indication, though, that The Beach Boys are out front and have a clearly-marked path staked-out for themselves is the simple one of Brian's submission to the tradition of interview, a tradition he has conspicuously ignored for quite a few years.

It was just three days after the group's performance at Big Sur that an extremely open Brian Wilson spoke with me on what is one of my favorite subjects, The Beach Boys. Also participating in the conversation were Beach Boy Carl Wilson and publicity aide Jack Riley. The interview was conducted via a long-distance phone call, (the brevity of many of Brian's remarks arises from the fact that he was having a hard time finding an extension in his home that worked properly. Carl came through loud and clear; it's obvious that he enjoys acting as a spokesman for the group. He appears to be very dedicated to The Beach Boys, and his enthusiasm for all facets of the group's activities is close to peak. Amazing, considering the ten-year association with one group.)

How was the response at Big Sur?

Carl: It went fine. I only wish we'd had a little more time. There were a lot of

things straight.

Carl: Well I've always been amused by it. I know what you're talking about, though; and I suppose we all feel a little bit differently about it. Like at Big Sur after the show you'd see one person turn to another and say, "Did you dig it?" And the other person would say, "Well, I don't know? Did you dig it?"

A little paranoid about comitting themselves.

Carl: Yeah.

How do you get together now on producing an album?

Carl: Well, *Sunflower*, I'd say, is the truest group effort we've ever had. Each of us was deeply involved in the creation of almost all the cuts. Say, someone would come to the studio early and put down a basic track, and then someone else would arrive and think of a good line to overdub....

So it really is accurate to say "produced by The Beach Boys." (At this point Brian interjects a question that still has me a little baffled. Who in his right mind wouldn't want to do the following?)

Brian: Bill?

Yes, Brian?

Brian: Have you ever talked to Mick Jagger?

No, I never have. Why?

Brian: Are you going to?

I'd like to, sure. But I don't foresee it in the near future. Why?

Brian: I think you should.

What do you mean?

Brian: I think he would be a really interesting rap. He's in this movie "Performance" where he's dressed like a girl, and I just think he'd make a good rap.

Okay. Are you tired of being asked about "Surf's Up"?

NO

Do you think it might make it onto a future album?

Brian: No.

Why?

Brian: We lost it.

No dubs or anything?

Brian: Nope, its gone.

Carl: I think we still have an eight track on it.

Brian: I don't think so.

And one of things noted was that you were going to do a soundtrack for an Andy Warhol movie about a spade gay surfer.

Brian: A what?

A spade gay surfer.

Brian: SPADE GAY SURFER?

Uh-huh.

Brian: That's what I thought you said. Nope. Never even met Andy Warhol.

What individual projects are you guys involved with, right now?

Brian: Dennis is doing a film, acting. Carl is producing an album for a South African group, The Flame. And I'm working on an album with a country singer.

Who's that?

Brian: (Faintly, because of bad connection) Fred Veil.

I can barely hear you. Fred V A L E? Like Jerry Vale?

Brian: Jerry Vale? No, V E I L. We've just finished the instrumental tracks but still haven't had a chance to get down the vocals.

What sort of a singer is he?

Brian: He sounds sort. of like Johnny Cash.

Carl: (laughing) A very far-out Johnny Cash.

Brian: (also laughing) Uh-Huh, a veryfar-out Johnny Cash.

What kind of group is The Flame, Carl?

Carl: We were in London finishing up a tour when we heard them.

Are they black?

Carl: Well no, I don't think so. They're Malaysians who grew up in South Africa.

What kind of music?

Carl: (laughing) Rock!

Following the tradition of The Beach Boys, how will the next album differ markedly from Sunflower?

Brian: We actually went out and bought a Moog synthesizer. All of the albums from now on will have more Moog. We used it on "Cool Water" on *Sunflower*. We're also working with quadraphonic sound. "Cool Water" is recorded quadraphonically.

Carl: The industry is trying to hype the public into believing that you have to buy a lot of new equipment to get

ROCK MAGAZINE 1974

the album's release.

Apparently The Beach Boys will continue to prevail though. Several incidents indicate that the group is moving into a phase of their career that will prove more exciting and productive than anything that has occurred up to this point.

A recent tour of Britain met with at least half as much raw excitement and press coverage as would have been accorded to The Beatles if they were back on the touring circuit again. The trip coincided with the unexpected success of a single of "Cottonfields" that Capitol culled from 20/20. The Beach Boys topping the charts in several European countries had the makings of an exciting comeback story. By the time the British music press finished with them, The Beach Boys found themselves emanating a sort of charismatic urgency that had been missing from the British music scene for quite some time.

By the standards of the music world, The Beach Boys have been through some "perilous" territory these last few years.

acts so even with two sets we didn't get a chance to play as much as we'd have liked to. I liked playing there, though.

Has your approach to live performing changed much? Are you still concerned with trying to duplicate the recorded sound in "live" performances?

Carl: We're not so much trying to re-do the records now, although we still travel with that big sound system. We're loosening up in our interpretations. It seems like a much more realistic thing to be doing.

What material are you using in public performances now?

Carl: Well, "Darlin'," "Aren't You Glad," "Vegetables." Like that.

Newer material, too?

Carl: Some stuff from *Sunflower*.

Brian, did you perform with the group at Big Sur, or during the recent English tour?

Brian: No, but I'm going along for the European tour in mid-November.

Was the group surprised with success of "Cottonfields" in England?

Carl: Well, its really Al's record. We weren't surprised because Capitol told us they were going to promote it in England, but not in the States. Since we've split with them, they're not expecting to make a lot of bread off 'the Beach Boys in this country. But because of the steam the group has built up in other countries, everyone was pretty sure it would be big in Europe.

With the people I talk to, I find a lot of ignorance about what the group is doing these days. When someone asks me my favorite group and I say "The Beach Boys," most often I get those hipper-than-thou raised eyebrows. Of course, it's easy to remedy the situation, all I have to do is put on "How She Boogalooed It" from Wild Honey to set

Brian, do you ever listen to any classical music?

Brian: A little Beethoven, but that's about all.

What happened with Capitol that made the group split after such a long time?

Carl: They were against *Pet Sounds* and all the albums that came after. They wanted us to stick with surfin' and hot rod records, you know. But we said, Well you know, we don't want to do that. We're doing other music now. But they really weren't going for it. And so they had all these hundreds of people in their organization pushing another thing. People were bound to get the wrong impression about the group.

So the public was stuck with the ideas of The Beach Boys, circa '63.

Carl: Exactly.

Wasn't there also some dissension in the group about just how progressive your music should be.

Carl and Brian: No!

Brian: And I don't think The Beach Boys have ever really been that far out.

Come on, now. Smiley Smile?

Carl: Well, maybe that one.

Brian: There's a drug abuse clinic somewhere in Texas that uses *Smiley Smile* to help people out of their bad trips.

(*Thinking that perhaps my leg is being pulled, long distance) Come on!*

Jack: This drug abuse clinic, when someone on a really bad acid trip comes in, helps them calm down and gets them back into a good head by playing *Smiley Smile*. They don't tell them what they're going to hear, but they play *Smiley Smile* on headphones. And in almost every case the people suddenly start smiling.

Brian, Rolling Stone ran a short piece about the group a couple of months ago.

four-channel sound. But a system developed by a company in Philadelphia, Dynaco, has devised a recording process where all you have to do is have two extra speakers and a little bit of lamp cord.

And with "Cool Water" played with the system, you can actually get four distinct channels of sound?

Carl: Yes. It was on the front page of *Billboard* a few weeks ago. And you can hear "Cool Water" quadraphonically by wiring up the speakers according to a very simple circuit.

When does the European tour begin?

Carl: On November 18th. And we've got a couple of gigs before then. The Whisky a GO GO.

I guess you'll be pretty busy till then, so I'll let you get along. Just one more thing Brian, have you ever considered producing an album for the Chordettes?

Brian: (pause) "Sh-Boom", right?

Nope, *"Lollipop"*.

Brian: You mean(proceeds with a few bars of same.) Yeah, I love that record.

The Chordettes, huh?

Perhaps I planted a seed. The Chordettes Sing the Brian Wilson Songbook?

Chatting with The Beach Boys, even on the telephone, is a semi-celestial experience. Like rapping with angels. Deleted from the above transcript of our conversation is a period of about five minutes of blithering encomium from my end of the wire. About how their music helped me through the "blecch-est" periods of my life, etc. My "pleth" of praise seemed to be accepted as sincere, though; it really sounded as if they were as excited talking with me as I was with them.

Still, it's a shame they didn't call themselves The Band.

CARL & PASSIONS PROMO LP FACT SHEET

Artist

The Beach Boys

2MS 2083
L5 2083
L8 2083

Album Title

Pet Sounds/Carl and the Passions - So Tough

Side 1	PET SOUNDS	
Title	Composer	Time
1. WOULDN'T IT BE NICE	Wilson/Asher	Not Available
2. YOU STILL BELIEVE IN ME	Wilson/Asher	Not Available
3. THAT'S NOT ME	Wilson/Asher	Not Available
4. DON'T TALK	Wilson/Asher	Not Available
5. I'M WAITING FOR THE DAY	Wilson/Love	Not Available
6. LET'S GO AWAY FOR A WHILE	Wilson	Not Available
7. SLOOP JOHN B.	Arranged by Wilson	Not Available
Side 2		
1. GOD ONLY KNOWS	Wilson/Asher	Not Available
2. I KNOW THERE'S AN ANSWER	Wilson-Sachen	Not Available
3. HERE TODAY	Wilson/Asher	Not Available
4. I JUST WASN'T MADE FOR THESE TIMES	Wilson/Asher	Not Available
5. PET SOUNDS	Wilson	Not Available
6. CAROLINE, NO	Wilson/Asher	Not Available

PET SOUNDS produced by Brian Wilson. Recorded at Western, Colombia and Gold Star Studios, Los Angeles, 1966. This recording is monophonic sound, the way Brian cut it.

Side 1	CARL AND THE PASSIONS — SO TOUGH	
1. YOU NEED A MESS OF HELP TO STAND ALONE	Brian Wilson/Jack Reiley	3:26
2. HERE SHE COMES	Ricky Fataar/Blondie Chaplin	5:08
3. HE COME DOWN	Alan Jardine/Brian Wilson/Mike Love	4:40
4. MARCELLA	Brian Wilson/Jack Reiley	3:52
Side 2		
1. HOLD ON DEAR BROTHER	Ricky Fataar/Blondie Chaplin	4:42
2. MAKE IT GOOD	Dennis Wilson-Darryl Dragon	2:34
3. ALL THIS IS THAT	Alan Jardine/Carl Wilson/Mike Love	3:57
4. CUDDLE UP	Dennis Wilson/Darryl Dragon	5:42

CARL AND THE PASSIONS—SO TOUGH produced by the Beach Boys

It's been ten years since the Beach Boys first changed the course of rock music. Now, a specially-priced two-record set, PET SOUNDS/CARL AND THE PASSIONS — SO TOUGH marks the beginning of a new era for one of California's (and Hawthorne's) most important exports.

FLYING TIME
Time sure flies when you're having a good time. It hardly seems possible that the Beach Boys have been around as long as they have, but it's true. And they've gone through more changes than can comfortably be discussed at one sitting. Yet the Wilsons and friends continue to amaze everyone but the most diehard skeptics by always coming up with creatively loveable music.

Last year's *Surf's Up* was lauded by practically everyone for its ingenious harmonies, that seem to lie only within the capacities of the Beach Boys. The songs were kind of "laid back," having taken a 180 degree turn from the uptempo numbers for which the boys are best known. It was the album that many knew the Beach Boys were capable of — an LP that must truly rank among the best of the year.

SPECIAL PACKAGE
Here it is 1972, and the Beach Boys are honoring us with this very special package. *Pet Sounds* was released previously, as every record fan should know, and it is being included in this package because it went largely unheard in 1966. Too bad, because it is one of the Beach Boys greatest musical creations, containing "Sloop John B," "Wouldn't It Be Nice?," "God Only Knows" and some numbers that were probably ahead of their time. They should be appreciated now, at a time when the old "surfboard image" is at long last disappearing.

The all-new, recently recorded half is called *Carl and the Passions — So Tough*, which at once compliments and contrasts *Pet Sounds*, depending on which cut you're listening to. It's yet another direction for the inimitable 7 man group consisting of Brian, Dennis and Carl Wilson, Mike Love, Alan Jardine, Ricky Fataar and Blondie Chaplin.

Even before its release *Pet Sounds/Carl and the Passions — So Tough* has created a great deal of interest among the record devouring public. Maybe it took ten years for everyone to realize that the Beach Boys are not just Hawthorne heavyweights, but a group of immense musical and cultural significance.

PET SOUNDS/CARL AND THE PASSIONS — SO TOUGH is scheduled for release in May. 2MS 2083 is list priced at $7.98; L5 and L8 are list priced at $7.97.

Other albums: RS, M5, M8 6382 SUNFLOWER; RS, M5, M8 6453 SURF'S UP.

PROMOTIONAL PHOTO

IN CONCERT PROMO POSTCARD

ADS

Two Big Albums • Packaged Together • By The
BEACH BOYS

First, Their All New, 1972 Event: SO TOUGH. Plus, the Re-issue of Their Legendary PET SOUNDS ("Sloop John B.," "Wouldn't It Be Nice," & Co.)

Two Full Albums at a Special $7.98 List Price. On Brother Reprise.

2MS 2083 / Also available on tapes.

Artist	Song	Cat. No.
HURRICANE SMITH	My Mother Was Her Name	DB 8943
MARY HOPKIN	Mary Had A Baby	RZ 3070
CILLA BLACK	You You You	R 5972
MICHAEL JACKSON	Ben	TMG 834
FOUR TOPS	Keeper Of The Castle	PRO 575
BEACH BOYS	Barbara Ann	CMS 2
BLUE MINK	Stay With Me	RZ 3064
KEN DODD	Just Out Of Reach	DB 8947
BENNY HILL	Fad Eyed Fal	DB 8940
JONI MITCHELL	You Turn Me On, I'm A Radio	AYM 511
ARTHUR LOWE	My Little Girl, My Little Boy	DB 8956
VINCE HILL	And I Love You So	DB 8939

20 of your Favorite Hits by
THE BEACH BOYS
ENDLESS SUMMER

Surfin' Safari * Surfer Girl * Catch A Wave * The Warmth Of The Sun
Surfin' U.S.A. * Be True To Your School * Little Deuce Coupe * In My Room
Shut Down * Fun, Fun, Fun, * I Get Around * The Girls On The Beach
Wendy * Let Him Run Wild * Don't Worry Baby * California Girls
Girl Don't Tell Me * Help Me, Rhonda * You're So Good To Me * All Summer Long

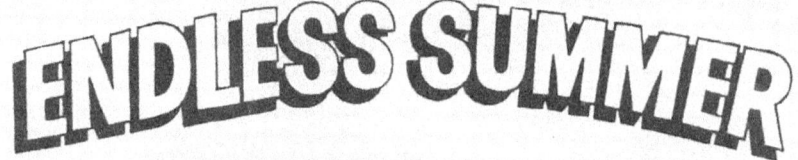

TWO-RECORD SET INCLUDES FREE! ENDLESS SUMMER POSTER!

Capitol®

2-LPs $5.88
SVBB 11307

8-TRACK $6.88
8XWW 11307

 ALL RECORD STORES IN THE DELAWARE VALLEY ARE WELL STOCKED WITH THIS ALBUM OF GOLDEN HITS

THE ROCK MARKETPLACE

on **THE BEACH BOYS**
and hear them sing their New Single
"I CAN HEAR MUSIC" (2432)
from the
20/20 ALBUM (SKAO 133)
KRAFT MUSIC HALL
9:00 P.M.
(E.S.T.)
WEDNESDAY, FEB. 19

John Smith Productions Presents
CRYSTAL PALACE BOWL
garden party III
sat June 3

BEACH BOYS
JOE COCKER
& the 12 piece Chris Stainton all stars
RICHIE HAVENS
MELANIE
SHA NA NA

groups in alphabetic order

TICKETS £1.75 in advance
£2.00 on the day if available

AGENCIES — harlequin record shops 01-636-1348

FREE CAR PARKS
GATES OPEN AT 12 NOON
Good Food at proper prices

TICKETS AVAILABLE BY MAIL

Mailing Address
GARDEN PARTY
42 KING'S COLLEGE COURT
PRIMROSE HILL ROAD
LONDON N.W.3

DOWARD PROMOTIONS PRESENTS

THE BEACH BOYS IN CONCERT

Tuesday, May 16th Two Perfs. 6.30 p.m., 9.00 p.m.
CITY HALL, NEWCASTLE

Monday, May 22nd Two Perfs. 7.30 p.m., 10.00 p.m.
TOP RANK SUITE, READING

Wednesday, May 24th, Two Perfs. 6.30 p.m., 9.00 p.m.
BRIGHTON DOME

Tickets from usual agents or separate venues
Enquiries: **Doward Promotions.** Tel: Shoreham (07917) 62600

PETER MARTIN PRESENTS

THE
BEACH BOYS

for the first time in their own complete show.
MAYFAIR, BIRMINGHAM
Next to New Street Station
Thursday, May 18th at 8.30 p.m.

Advance £1.10 from Mayfair or usual local agents or by post from C.T.E. 60 Stratford Road, Birmingham 11. Tel.: 021-772 4731.

CONCERT ADS

HOLLAND AD

Operation

CARL WILSON: Los Angeles spread out behind him.

THE MORNING AFTER the Beach Boys hauled themselves back into Los Angeles after their self-imposed six months exile in Holland, Carl Wilson awoke in what he told me was "a state of shock".

The delicate process of attempting to re-adjust his chromosomes to the paranoia of L.A. after what Wilson terms "the civilised tranquility" of the Netherlands was just too acute for his nervous system to assimilate in one day.

High above garish Sunset Strip — 11 floors to be precise — but not high enough to eradicate the incessant noise of the nose-to-tail traffic — Wilson details some of the traumatic circumstances that led up to the mammoth Beach Boys airlift last June . . .

A meticulously-planned exodus which, at a cost in excess of half-a-million dollars, was to take the Beach Boys lock, stock and 16-track recording studio out of the Hollywood Hills and set them down amid the picturesque windmills and canals of Baambrugge, just a 20-minute fast limo ride from the centre of Amsterdam.

Such an ambitious operation, it should straight away be pointed out, wasn't the result of a mere flight of fancy. It was borne out of the eroding effect that living in L.A. was having upon the Beach Boys' creative resources — with the end product, namely the "Holland" album, more than justifying the means.

Together with their 70's masterwork "Surf's Up", "Holland" represents the renaissance of a band — now in its 11th year — which, at its previous creative peak ('66/68), was neglected in its mothercountry or dismissed by ill-informed trendsetters as little more than America's definitive Golden Oldie party band.

"Things had reached a point where we just had to move out of L.A. and find a fresh environment," Carl Wilson explains.

"We all feel that it's getting to be very un-natural in this town, with just about everything changing too fast for comfort. You've seen it yourself . . . a lot of people are freaking out".

A statement of fact underlined that particular week by a spate of senseless thrill-slayings, a minor earth tremor and the thickening of the yellow smog cloud that invariably blots out the sun and threatens one day to completely asphyxiate the city.

Looking out across the impressive view from his balcony, Wilson continues, "People are a part of nature and, when their environment suddenly becomes un-natural, something drastic is bound to happen.

"Smog", he utters the most obscene of Californian four-letter words, "like the kind you get here in L.A., is nerve gas. And as such, it has a most alarming effect upon people.

"They get edgy, nervous and sometimes very violent . . . you can feel the tension. You can't blame anyone for wanting to escape."

Though they weren't aware of it at the time, the first hint of the Beach Boys malfunctioning

OPERATION AIRLIFT

Airlift

ROY CARR REPORTS FROM LOS ANGELES ON THE 'HOLLAND' EXPEDITION

How seven Beach Boys, wives, children, in-laws, pets and maids — plus engineers and custom-built studio — escaped the smog of L.A. and found true happiness in Holland

DEVISED BY the Beach Boys themselves, execution of "Operation Holland" was put in the hands of Hollywood PR-man Bill de Simone.

Having to contend with Holland's acute housing shortage, de Simone's first and perhaps most arduous assignment was to secure suitable accommodation for: Brian Wilson, his wife, two children, sister-in-law and housekeeper; Dennis Wilson, his wife and child; Carl Wilson, wife, two children, mother, brother-in-law, housekeeper and two dogs; Mike Love, a wife, two kids and a maid; Al Jardine with the same contingent as Love; Ricky Fataar, wife plus in-laws, and Blondie Chaplin with a female companion.

De Simone also had to find shelter for chief engineer Steve Moffitt with secretary and son; additional engineers Gordon Rudd (plus wife), Jon Parker (plus lady) and Thom Gellert (plus admirers); Russ Mackie (the band's travelling attaché); and Jack Reiley (Brother Records main man) with his secretary Carole Hayes (plus Mr. Hayes) and Rieley's dog.

By way of an encore, de Simone also commandeered 14 automobiles along with stereo sets and pianos for each household.

As it turned out, Dutch recording facilities weren't conducive to Beach Boys requirements either, nor was sufficient studio time available.

So it was agreed that a sophisticated studio would be designed from scratch and constructed in California, then broken down and airlifted to Holland and re-assembled in a converted farm building.

And all this to be completed in 90 days.

This unenviable task befell Steve Moffit who, assisted by physics whiz-kid Gordon Rudd, started work on a 24-hour shift basis. With a 30-input console with 20-channel monitor system, 30-quad pans, 30-stereo pans plus a 1,000-hole patch bay, there was no slacking.

There are four daily flights out of L.A. to Amsterdam and, for nearly five weeks, the components for this custom-built studio occupied each and every outwardbound flight, while additional electronics came from London. Crates alone totalled 5,000 dollars for the 7,300 pounds of technological deadweight.

Even the Beach Boys can't estimate the overall cost of the operation but, chances are, the sales alone from "Holland" won't recoup the outlay.

"THERE'S A FOG upon L.A.," George Harrison once sang, but when Carl Wilson, Russ Mackie and I drove to the top of the immortalised Blue Jay Way, it was one of those precious clear days when you imagine you can almost see forever.

As we gaze at the city sprawled some hundreds of feet below us, I ask Carl Wilson if "Holland" could have materialised so effectively "down there".

"It probably wouldn't have had the same direction," he replies, "and therefore could have easily turned out like 'So Tough', which I consider to be a very strange album.

"Music comes out anywhere, but the environment will definitely have a different effect on your moods, and there's a definite mood to be found in Holland.

"After a couple of false starts, even Brian was persuaded to move both his house and family. In fact, just recently Brian was talking about going back."

Various aspects of the "Holland" album came up for discussion as Carl turns his attention from the scenic view. "We've always been extremely meticulous when recording, but, on all the 'Holland' sessions, things came together very easily and also very naturally. This album has a much better blending than ever before, with both Blondie and Ricky now an intricate part of the Beach Boys as a unit.

"Fundamentally, we did the basic tracks and then maybe added an extra vocal bit or effect on top, but nothing more adventurous than that.

"Of all the cuts, 'Only With You' was the easiest to complete. We did the entire song in approximately 2 hours."

Referring to what the Beach Boys affectionately call "Brian Wilson's gift" — the "Mount Vernon and Fairway" bonus 7-inch mini-album presented with "Holland" — younger brother Carl declares: "That was a lotta fun to do, and something completely different than anything we've ever done before."

In fact, after periods of spasmodic activity, Brian Wilson is gradually emerging from his life as a recluse, and managing to contend better with the unfortunate "20th Century Genius" tag that got hung around his neck.

"Reality is reality", says Carl Wilson, "and it sometimes frightens people. And because Brian was a little too sensitive, he wasn't prepared to cope with it so . . ." He stops mid-sentence, leaving you to draw your own conclusion.

"When Brian feels like working, he's ferocious . . . it's a joy to watch. He's got some great music people haven't heard yet, but give him time."

OF THE LEGEND that the Beach Boys are musical perfectionists, Wilson has this to say: "Look, everyone who goes into a recording studio wants their music to sound as perfect as they can get it. However, if we have two takes of one song and we have to choose between the one that's technically accurate and the one with the best feel, it would undoubtedly be the one with the best feel.

"At a session, we always let nature take its course and, as far as this band is concerned, it seems to be the right approach. The great thing about this band is that we really do enjoy playing, touring and recording together."

Wilson puts the Beach Boys 1973 in their correct perspective when he concludes. "Today, people are getting into the sounds coming out of the speakers and not getting hung up on our striped shirts."

came with the release last year of "So Tough" — Carl & The Passions".

It's an album which, as an entity, Carl doesn't particular care for. "I can only enjoy listening to the songs separately" he offers as that collection's only redeeming quality.

1973

The Perfect Wave
BEACH BOYS LOOKIN' BACK

"I love to make records that my friends like to hear."
—BRIAN WILSON

THERE'S A ROCK N' ROLL myth that says groups are discovered harmonising on street corners, or on tiny regional labels, and are instantly catapulted to fame.

There's another that says rock n' roll stars enjoy only a brief stay in the limelight before sliding back to that street corner or car wash. (The exceptions, of course, offer the rule's conclusive proof).

Another says that instead of giving philosophical or emotional interpretations/insights of the world around him, which is the artist's role in society, the rock musician will regurgitate the lifestyle of his peers — in essence, reinforce the rightness of a teener's way of living in the face of Establishment opposition.

To anyone who implicitly bases his involvement with rock on these myths which surround and support it. The Beach Boys must loom large within his lexicon.

For The Beach Boys were born and nurtured in the heart of these myths, and are now one of the major forces destroying and altering those very same myths, not to mention all our assumptions on which they were based.

The Beach Boys hail from Hawthorne, California, part of the Los Angeles sprawl, but to the south, near the endless miles of beach and surf.

Teenage life invariably consisted of being blond, going to pep rallies and drive-ins, cruising, and most of all, surfing.

The three Wilsons, Brian, Carl and Dennis, with cousin Al Jardine and friend Mike Love, moved through this Shangri La in a number of teen

Apart from "Do You Wanna Dance", "*The Beach Boys Today*" maintains itself on a very restrained level. Everything swirls in a refined Spector symphony of sound, telling melancholy tales of love.

The only response is to cuddle your girl a little tighter and sigh at appropriate moments.

"When I Grow Up" features a different mix to the single and "Help Me, Rhonda", is entirely different from the 45.

Just in case you think the Boys are getting serious, the album ends with "Bull Session with the 'Big Daddy'", in which Marilyn brings the group hamburgers and Earl Leaf interviews them about Europe. Dick Clark's liner notes add appropriate icing.

THERE WERE four perfect summer albums in the 60s, and The Beach Boys claim two. "*Summer Days (And Summer Nights!)*" was the ultimate '65 teenage dream.

California equalled summer, and Brian was extending the border to the Atlantic coast (and by implication, the world), spreading clues through "Amusement Parks USA", with ...... from "Palisades Park" ...... "Little Egypt", "Salt Lake City", and "The Girl from New York City", which is an incredible rocker made transcendent through honking sax and wailing falsettos.

The entire gamut of summer life was chronicled, even to "imprisonment" in the hilarious "I'm Bugged At My Old Dad" (he doesn't even know Where It's At), which is a new twist on Brian's stalk tracks.

In contrast to "*Today*", the tone is ebullient, with a sparse, rocking sound for the most part.

combos, most notably as Carl and the Passions, playing for their friends at the usual sock hops and parties.

Finally, Brian decided to exercise his claim to fame, lifted some Chuck Berry riffs, and wrote "Surfin'," which extolled the virtues of "the latest craze to invade the sun drenched Pacific coast of Southern California" (to quote some early liner notes), even though Dennis was the only one who surfed.

Released on Candix and its subsidiary X label, with "Luau" on the flip side (which never appears again, though somebody mentions it on "Beach Boys Party"), it was an immediate local hit, causing Capitol Records to sign them to a long term contract.

The next song was "Surfin' Safari," and world wide fame was theirs. Al Jardine had left for dentist school, and neighbour David Marks replaced him; father Murry Wilson managed them. The albums followed soon after.

THE BEACH Boys have released 24 albums, and to this day all are eminently listenable. Even "Surfin' Safari," recorded over ten years ago, shows their infatuation with technology, both from a production standpoint and lyrically, as "409" readily attests.

There are interesting allusions to older vocal styles, especially "Surfin'," as well as homages to their gods in a highschoolish "Summertime Blues," and "Cuckoo Clock," which sounds remarkably like "Palisades Park," as well as "Moon Dawg," which was a contemporary to the likes of The Surfaris and Ramrods and others jumping on the surf wag on.

Most important is the evocation of the California myth, to which The Beach Boys are irrevocably linked.

Because of them, The Promised Land now means a land where the carefree girls are the most beautiful anywhere, where cars are not mere transportation but a kinetic art form, opening to the teenage driver a world of cruising, drive-ins (both food and film), hearing "our song" on the radio, and most important, access to the sea, where the bummers of the world could be banished in the search of the perfect wave.

Technology was the machine of loving grace that gave us Utopia, and the reality of cost never entered.

Capitol, having found a major source of income, started to really churn the records out. "Surfin' USA" soon followed, the title song again being rewritten C. Berry, and then "Surfer Girl" (file under Surfing Music). Ballads were beginning to make inroads, and even strings appear.

By now Brian was producing, adding subtle touches like the two seconds of harp in "In My Room." Philles records were making a large impression on him and he was hot on the trail to Spector City.

Cars were also gaining more prominence, and the next album, "Little Deuce Coupe" (file under Hot Rod Music), was entirely devoted to those chrome and candied dream machines so ardently epitomised on the cover.

Along with the title song were three others making their second appearance — Capitol was really out for bread. By now the quarter mile was replacing the perfect wave in rock consciousness, and the surf sound (twangy guitar, pulsing organ) that characteris'd previous Beach Boy albums had disappeared.

Influences were shown in "Car Crazy Cutie," a lift from "Young Man Is Gone" ("This daring young star died while in his car . . . He died without a cause"), sung acapella.

Also of note are "Spirit of America," an ode to Craig Breedlove and his "jet without wings," and "Be True To Your School," which is minus the cheerleading effects of Marilyn Wilson and Diane Rovell (otherwise known as American Spring) which made the single such an anthem.

WITH THE untamed thunder of tuned exhausts reverberating through Hollywood, "Shut Down Vol. II" was only a short matter of time. Among the Stingrays and Bonnevilles the title cover is Al Jardine, who had decided stardom was more favourable than dentistry, and David Marks vanished with the woodies and surfboards.

The classic of this album is "Fun, Fun, Fun," possibly the most accurately titled song of 1964. Its wit and preciseness of lyric shows a new level in Brian's songwriting, and it also reaches new levels of California myth, though now it is a conscious striving.

The Wilson pursuit on Spector reaches new heights in "Don't Worry Baby" and "Why Do Fools Fall In Love," both of which sound remarkably close to Dave Edmunds' recent sounds.

More homages appear with "Louie Louie" and "Denny's Drums," which is similar to Sandy Nelson's "Drum Beat Pt. 2." Also there is "Cassius Love vs. 'Sonny' Wilson," the first on a series of talk tracks which show Brian's own particular sense of humour.

"All Summer Long" is the first of what have become classic Beach Boys albums. For a start it contains "I Get Around," easily the best song of their early period, and arguably one of the best songs they've written.

The California myth is finally no longer implied but detailed: "We always take my car because it's never been beat/ And we never miss once with the girls we meet/None of the guys go steady 'cos it wouldn't be right/To leave the best girls home on a Saturday night".

"All Summer Long," which follows, continues the gay, carefree life: miniature golf, Hondas, occasionally hearing "our song."

The production is much more complex than before, and the sound fuller. The talk sections continue with "Our Favourite Recording Sessions," and the nostalgia continues through "Don't Back Down," the first surf song since "Surfer Girl," and "Do You Remember" (all the guys who gave us rock and roll), possibly the first rock nostalgia/revival song (this is '64 after all).

California myth continues with "Drive In" ("if you say you watched the picture you know you're a liar"), merging with the humour strain in "Carl's Big Chance," which uses the rhythm of "Long Tall Texan," over which Carl picks some gritty surf guitar.

BRIAN WILSON'S infatuation with Spector caused him to record "The Beach Boys Christmas Album", the second rarest BB album to find. Side one is B. Wilson originals and Side two Xmas standards, with the former winning by a mile. "Little Saint Nick", one of the best Xmas rock standards, was released as a single with an acapella "Lord's Prayer" on the flip, showing up nowhere else.

The other highlights of the album are "Santas Beard", which tells of little brother being reassured he is seeing the real Santa, and then him pulling out the pillow and eating the beard — but all is well, because "he's just helping Santa". "We Three Kings of Orient Are", which at four minutes stands as the longest Beach Boys song until 1971, and "Christmas Day", which exhibits some fine Berryish guitar.

"Beach Boys Concert" also stands as a classic ("file under Teen Best Sellers"). Recorded at Sacramento, California's capital city, the liner notes tell us that instead of beefing up the audience reaction on the record, as is commonly the case, Capitol's recording engineers had to use all their know-how to subdue audience sounds so The Beach Boys could be heard!

Through the pandemonium, the Boys sing a selection of their hits, as well as "Monster Mash", "Johnny B. Goode", "The Wanderer", marking Dennis Wilson's vocal solo debut, and "Graduation Wey", an acapella ode to The Four Freshmen. Brian's major vocal influence.

They rip out some fine surf sounds on "Lets Go Tripping" and even do "The Little Old Lady From Pasadena", which Brian wrote for Jan and Dean. (It should also be noted that on "Jan and Dean's Greatest Hits Volume Two", "Deadman's Curve" is sung by Brian. It's actually the demo he gave the duo).

Overall, it's a fun album, and at the time of its release was a party favourite.

"Beach Boys' Party" concludes the first BB era. Brian had stopped touring shortly before to concentrate on writing and recording (he had written the better part of twelve albums in three years), and Glen Campbell, then a top L.A. session man (he played on most of Spector's later recordings, and worked in duo with Len Russell), joined for a short while, succeeded by Bruce Johnston, a fixture of the L.A. music scene who had recorded with Terry Melcher (friend of the Byrds and producer of The Byrds) and as a solo.

The idea for the album was that they would hold a party in the studio and record it. The atmosphere is loose and relaxed, filled with chatter.

The music is acoustic, with lots of falling about as they meander through standards like "Hully Gully", "Alley Oop", a selection from the Lennon/ McCartney songbook, a touch of Spector, one or two B. Wilson compositions, and even "The Times They Are A Changing".

Like "Concert", it was a party favourite, and the Beach Boys position in the stars seemed more assured than ever. Little did Brian know how prophetic this choice of Dylan was.

NEXT WEEK: "Pet Sounds" to "Holland".

JOHN INGHAM

Lyrics "I Get Around" reproduced kind permission Burlington Music Ltd.

A Surf Patriarchs Credo:

Helping People Find That Perfect Wave

by Michael Gross

Whatever happened to the endless summer, watching the surfers on Wide World of Sports, sipping iced tea and listening to "Surfin' USA" on a Japanese transistor radio that would cough itself to death in September? Whatever happened to the Beach Boys and rooting for "I Get Around" to move from number two to number one — and put the Four Seasons and that sappy song "Rag Doll" out to pasture? Anyone who passed through New York in those golden days of summers past might wonder, too, whatever happened to the Good Guys who gave the world the stupid yellow smile on Good Guy sweatshirts, not knowing it would soon be the symbol of the endless summer, for another summer. But the Beach Boys are the subject at hand... those wonderful lads who used to look like frat brothers, ride around in woodys, croonin' 'bout cruisin' the burger stands of southern formicalia. But they transcended that to an extent and were able to make their dark-haired, untanned brothers and sisters from Omaha to Detroit to Central Park dance, dance, dance, right along, and no one even cared if Daddy took the T-bird away. Whatever happened to the endless summer? It's a question that comes to plague you when you come to see the Beach Boys today, without Brian, with long hair and beards and white wicker furniture onstage and Gerry Ford nominating Hot Rocky as VP that very week. I know some people who think this may be the endless summer. The unpardoned, the Ron Zieglers, for whom August will ring, over and over. How's that California Water, there, Ronnie-boy? Can't be as hot as the D.C. swamp, now can it? Hey, and if it gets too bad there Ronnie-boy, you can always take some lessons in TM, from a Beach Boy, and try to find the endless summer. TM — that's transcendental meditation for the unenlightened amongst ye. Remember that? The Maharishi and the Beatles and Ravi Shankar and the Beach Boys and bad jokes about Indians? Hold hands and we can all bliss out together and it'll be... well... it'll be an... endless summer with psychic waves breaking through your mind, each one of them perfect. Mike Love, a Beach Boy, has kept the faith where others have fallen. Lennon went to Yoko, Paul went to Nashville, Harrison bets on a dark horse, but Mike Love and Al Jardine teach TM — helping people find the perfect wave. A wave that carries the carved physique of Ultimate Surfer, and on his back, you guessed it, Surfer Girl, and all the time that he's shooting the curl and hanging ten (didn't you love it when people talked like that?), he's blissing out on the ultimate good vibes of the whole thing. No big bad wave is gonna come and splinter Ultimate Surfer's board, or turn the curved, blonde, string-bikinied bod of little surfer girl into a mourned, seaborn relic. Those high cheekbones and white white teeth will live on, for Ultimate Surfer and for all of us because it's the endless summer. Don't worry baby, the heroes are on our side, the villains only come out at night, and Ultimate Surfer is at the peak of the curl.

☆ ☆ ☆

Mike Love, a Beach Boy, sits under a tent backstage at Roosevelt Stadium in New Jersey. The tent breeds flies like Northern Jersey breeds bad odors, but no flies go near Mike Love. He wears a straw panama hat. His beard is carefully trimmed. The fact that the girl at his side is not blonde scratches the veneer of perfect unity but does not make it crumble. Love spoons vegetable salad out of an avocado. Love is dressed in white. He seems not to sweat, though the air breathes water and the lights beneath the tent are harsh. He sips spring water from a beer cup. His feet are encased in white sweat sox and sandals. The sandals have no heels. Love stands at ground level. The girls shakes her head and a scarf peaks out from behind her neck. It says Dior. Love smiles at her. She smiles back and drifts away. He bows his slightly balding blonde head towards the table and spoons another bit of veg-delight into his mouth.

He is asked about the re-release of a new/old Beach Boys album on Capitol Records, *Endless Summer*. "I gave them the idea for the title," he says softly. "It has to do with a perennial uplifting, outdoor vibes, summer tours. It's a lasting title, a lasting, timeless image. It implies forever."

A girl approaches the table shyly. She smiles and Love smiles back. She speaks softly for a few moments. Love answers when appropriate, acts nonchalant and positively charming. As she turns to go, the girl looks back, one last time, at a symbol of the endless summer. "Debby meditates too," she says, blushes, turns, and disappears. Love smiles, spoons, chews and turns.

"Our music," he says slowly, emphasizing each syllable, "has, more than ever," he pauses a micro-second, "borne the test of time."

In the past few weeks the backstage scene at Roosevelt had been slightly frantic. People wandered, disappeared, came back smiling, screamed about why they *had* to be onstage or in the trailer or in the port-a-san, and somehow made everything seem brittle, easy to shatter. At Emerson, Lake and Palmer's appearance, the harshness had been most apparent. The road crew then were all on edge, and the sudden appearance of T-shirts, proclaiming, "No Head, No Backstage Pass" only brought out slight smiles.

Agents congregated backstage at Roosevelt, with beautiful women on their arms, seeming in ceaseless motion. Only the limousine drivers and the few fans who finagle their way to the inner sanctum seemed content to just sit on the grass and act like the Woodstock Generation. Before most of the shows ended, the backstage area would be close to empty, as getting out of Roosevelt is hard, and leaving early, sacrificing the encore, meant getting back to the City and Max's, The 82 or JP's without getting mired in Jersey traffic, being forced to listen over and over to eight-track Bachman-Turner tapes, pouring out of VW's and Gremlins. These people didn't need to be reminded that "Taking Care Of Business" was this endless summer's summer song.

The Beach Boys/Eagles show was different though. Backstage was cool, mellow. Just fill in the mid-sixties adjective of your choice. That's what it was. Organic, even. Blonde hair, tanned faces and bellies and loosely tied clothing flowed all around the backstage area. People smiled, some meditated. Roosevelt's security heavies didn't even put up the restraining ropes that keep the backstagers from the stars until moments before the Beach Boys took the stage.

Road manager, Rick Nelson, a small, harried, but pleasant man explained that the road crew liked a clean stage, and, in fact, the stage was filled with clean, respectful people. The intense crowds that surrounded ELP were nowhere to be seen. Only one person was forcibly removed from the stage, and that was when he sat on one of the wicker couches the band used as stage props.

"What the hell is he doin' there??" one roadie yelled.

"I'll ask him," another screamed back. The boy was escorted from the stage, smiling. The roadies doing the escorting were smiling. When he was gone, they shook their heads in bemused confusion. Had it been another band, that boy might have suffered multiple fractures from a bumpy flight down the stage stairs.

☆ ☆ ☆

"TM has expanded my ability to create," Love had said, a few minutes before disappearing to meditate, moments before the show was set to start. "We've all been writing." And if one wondered about lost Beach Boy, Brian Wilson, there was a pleasant answer. "Brian's mostly a cousin. He's a unique individual. Very reclusive. He was there when we recorded *Holland*. His presence is always there. It's implied."

Onstage, the boys are (may it be said?), kicking out the jams. Within three numbers they put their recent live album to shame. A white carpet covers the stage. Love sings, barefoot. Wicker furniture and palm trees accentuate the positive. "California Water" is followed by "Do It Again." Mike dances, smiles at the loving, but frantic crowd. It's hot and sweaty down there in the human sea, pushing against the fences and each other, but no one minds as Ultimate Surfer flies across Northern Jersey.

Love introduces "I Can Hear Music" by saying it's been released as a single. "It's in your hands from here, folks," he explains. Carl sings it, sweetly. "This is a socially significant song. This is one of the things that makes the world go 'round," Mike quips, as the band launches into "Little Deuce Coupe." They play everything you want to hear.

"Sail On Sailor" inspires a Texas-bred roadie. He slips a joint out of his cigarrette pack, lights it, draws deeply and exhales, nodding at Jim Guercio, the newest Beach Boy (Caribou-bred), whose bass playing, learned at the feet of Jan and Dean, has combined with two drummers to drive the band with inspired force. Guercio is the one who doesn't fit. His hair is short, glasses old-fashioned. He is wearing chinos and a button-down shirt.

"He's like mah old frat brothas at SAE," the roadie stage-whispers. "But boy, that mutha can play *some* bass. Shiiit."

Love sits in a wicker throne. He commands, and receives, quiet. He introduces a TM-inspired song, "All This Is That." "It's an indication of a nice feeling," he muses, shuts his eyes, leans back, and croons. Three keyboards work at once, creating a tapestry of sound, and Love's calm combines with it, and the vibes...the vibes, to make a home for Ultimate Surfer, before we take a trip to endless summers past. "Surfer Girl," "Heroes and Villains," "Help Me Rhonda," "I Get Around" and "Good Vibrations" flow one after another. One muses on the Beach Boys and comes up with words like "anachronism."

One wishes it were all somehow simpler. They look different, but they sound the same. Close your eyes and it's '62, or '64 or even '67, when even TM could be called a "trip." Open your eyes and notice how little equipment the Beach Boys need to get it over. The crowd doesn't care. They're frantic and happy. Ultimate Surfer sits on a cloud and smiles down. He kisses Surfer Girl with closed lips, then squeezes her hand.

Love leaves the stage, slips into a long black car, that glides quietly back to New York City. He thinks, perhaps, about the studio Lp the Beach Boys will work on in September and October. He considers his upcoming trip to Hawaii to polish the songs the Boys will record. He is, more than anything else, serene.

"We try to make touring purposely enjoyable," he muses. "We're going to do a world tour for the World Wildlife Fund sometime soon. The reason is that the Beach Boys have always tried for a positive, harmonious, loving approach. We say to ourselves, 'Let's do something positive.'"

Roosevelt Stadium empties slowly. Traffic is at a standstill. In Hamburger Heavens all across Northern Jersey, the kids swig Coke and munch on ratburgers. They listen to BTO and get a little misty when the radio crackles, the DJ cries "OLDIE" and "Surfer Girl" wafts through the airwaves. In endless summer heaven, Ultimate Surfer sips a glass of pure, sweet spring water. He smiles at Surfer Girl and softly caresses her straight, sun-bleached hair. He looks down and spies a long black car gliding out of a tunnel into the jungle of the city. He hoists his lady onto his shoulders, mounts his board, looks to the horizon for the next of the endless series of perfect waves. The frothing water appears like clockwork, and the bronzed golden couple rides off to the sunset. He doesn't look down. He knows, that soon enough, another endless summer will come along. As he reaches the peak of the curl, he begins to sing, softly, a smile crossing his face. Surfer Girl looks down, smiles with him, and hums a sweet harmony.

"Good, good, good...good vibrations..."

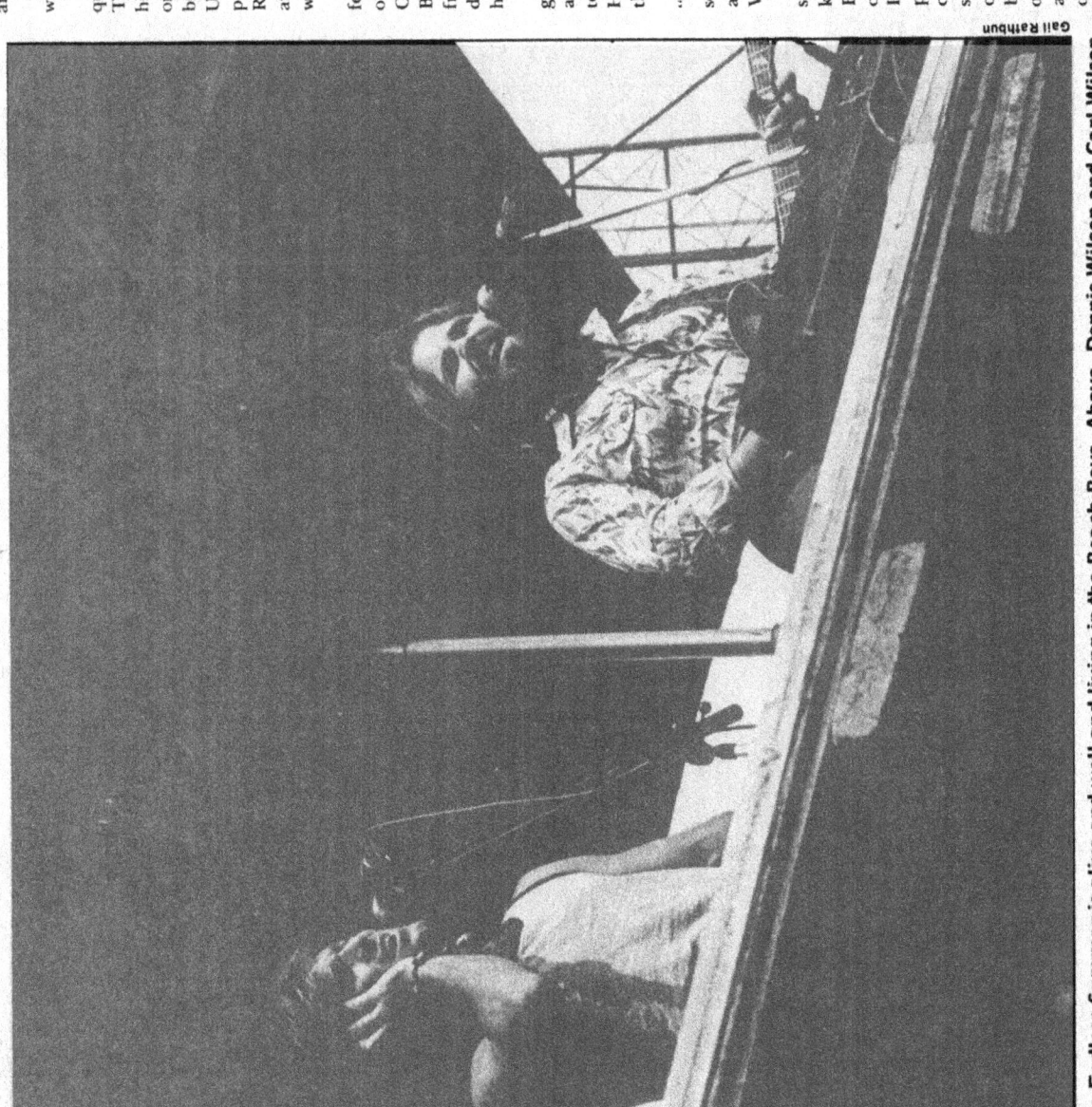

Gail Rathbun

The Endless Summer is alive and well and living in the Beach Boys. Above, Dennis Wilson and Carl Wilson kick out the jams. Mike Love, opposite, presides barefoot from a wicker throne

DENNIS WILSON: "I LIVE WITH 17 GIRLS"

SAID Dennis Wilson, a bemused frown on his face: "I don't know why I'm telling you all this..."

Well, whatever Dennis's reasons (if any), the fact that he spoke so openly and for so long does imply an element of trust. May be he said things he'd rather not see printed. Maybe he was so willing to tell the truth, the whole truth, about himself and The Beach Boys that he didn't mind seeing it all laid out before the lucky readers of the RM. Anyway, I've had to exercise some sort of judgement so here folllows a compromise — PART of what Dennis said over food and drinks at the Hilton a few days ago:

LAST TOUR?

"This could be our last tour. See, when you go on tour you could be recording. I guess we've done more touring than just about any other group in the world. Now we're thinking of doing maybe ten days a year and, for the rest of the time, getting right down to it in the studio.

"The public is evolving too. A couple of years ago we got very paranoid about the possibility of losing our public. We were getting loaded, taking acid, and we made a whole album which we scrapped.

"Instead, we went to Hawaii, rested up, and then came out with the 'Smiley Smiles' album, all new material. Drugs played a great role in our evolution but as a result we were frightened that people would no longer understand us, musically.

DENNIS WILSON — Explains it all to RM's Griffiths

"We no longer feel that way. I know I am now more in tune with my mind, I feel easier and more confident of myself and I am completely involved in communication with others. That's all there is, it's the most fascinating thing..." Noticing how civil he was to the (mostly) girls who came up asking him to sign photographs, I asked Dennis if he ever becomes short-tempered about these trivial demands on his time. "Not at all — talking to people who are interested in The Beach Boys gives me a very warm feeling."

And what Beach Boys recording does he regard as most worthy of our attention? "No doubt about it—'Good Vibrations'. Perhaps in two or three years time it will be played again and re-evalued as being ahead of its time."

Perhaps so, Dennis, but aren't such recordings difficult to reproduce in concerts because of the electronic treatment that goes into their sound? "Yes, but we can reproduce most anything onstage these days. We're travelling with 30 musicians."

Expensive, isn't it? "Yes, but we've reached the stage where we can afford what we want. I'm not saying we could book a full Philharmonic but if I really lock into some idea about musical backing I can, within reason, afford to hire the required musicians."

CRUDE SAX?

Which brought me to the most disappointing Beach Boys track of the year — "Transcendental Meditation" on the "Friends" album. What was the idea behind that amazingly crude bit of saxophone playing? "Well, we wanted to get away from anything that sounded too pompous, too religious. It would have been easy to do something very peaceful, very Eastern, but we were trying to reach listeners on all levels. The guy who played that sax didn't blow my mind but he had a certain quality of 'come on, let's try transcendental meditation...' And listen to the chord structure, it says a lot.

"I still believe in meditation and I'm not experimenting with tribal living. I live in the woods in California, near Death Valley, with 17 girls. They're space ladies. And they'd make a great group, I'm thinking of launching them as the Family Gems."

How did you come to meet up with no less than 17 girls? "It happened strangely. I went up into the mountains with my houseboy to take an LSD trip. We met two girls hitch-hiking. One of them was pregnant. We gave them a lift, and a purse was left in the car. About a month later, near Malibu, I saw the pregnant girl again, only this time she'd had her baby. I was overjoyed for her and it

BEACH BOY DENNIS WILSON — Death Valley pad

was through her that I met all the other girls. I told them about our involvement with the Maharishi and they told me they too had a guru, a guy named Charlie who'd recently come out of jail after 12 years. His mother was a hooker, his father was a gangster, he'd drifted into crime but when I met him I found he had great musical ideas. We're writing together now. He's dumb, in some ways, but I accept his approach and have learnt from him. He taught me a dance, The Inhibition. You have to imagine you're a frozen man and the ice is thawing out. Start with your fingertips, then all the rest of you, then you extend it to a feeling that the whole universe is thawing out..."

Are you supporting all these people? "No, if anything, they're supporting me. I had all the rich status symbols—Rolls Royce, Ferrari, home after home. Then I woke up, gave away 50 to 60 per cent of my money. Now I live in one small room, with one candle, and I'm happy, finding myself."

DAVID GRIFFITHS

1975 TOUR BOOK

1975 TOUR BOOK

© 1975 American Productions

For additional copies of this book,
send $2.50 per copy (postage and handling included)
to The Beach Boys, 8600 Melrose Avenue, Los Angeles, California 90069.

Designed by Gary Nichamin/Boom! Graphics; Photographs by John Rose, Gary Nichamin, Mike Phillips, Tim Sylvia/Coastway Photography, and Stu Fine.

1975 TOUR BOOK

1975 TOUR BOOK

1975 TOUR BOOK

Alan

1975 TOUR BOOK

1975 TOUR BOOK

Brian

1975 TOUR BOOK

1975 TOUR BOOK

1975 TOUR BOOK

1975 TOUR BOOK

1975 TOUR BOOK

1975 TOUR BOOK

1975 TOUR BOOK

1975 TOUR BOOK

1975 TOUR BOOK

Mike

1975 TOUR BOOK

1975 TOUR BOOK

AN AMERICAN BAND

Because of their success, on many levels, throughout the previous fourteen years, it may now be possible to speak of the Beach Boys in perspective—in terms of popular music in general, and in terms of their own growth.

Their success lies *not* in the fact that they have sold more records than any other American group; it is that their music has had inestimable influence on the very nature of the medium. No dinosaur, no "living legend"—the Beach Boys *remain* a vital force in the arena.

Beginning with the earliest efforts that were certainly responsible for the worldwide surfing phenomenon—they at one time made the Fender Telecaster a household word and everygroup necessity—"Carl and the Passions" from Hawthorne, California have been true innovators. Their influence in promulgating the "California Style" is obvious; their recording of "concept" albums set a precedent that has affected *every* album recorded since by anyone.

(The Beach Boys were, in fact, the first successful contemporary "concept" group—a "surf band"—which evolved *naturally* inland to *The Beach Boys,* neither boys nor of the beach.)

Through all of this, the primary motivation for the group has been the music itself. Brian Wilson, Dennis Wilson, Carl Wilson, Alan Jardine and Michael Love—the "original" Beach Boys, and the nucleus around which The Beach Boys are structured today—are utilizing their energies to grow as musicians. As a musical endeavor, they are still evolving, changing, growing. These changes are noticeable in their onstage demeanor, their willingness to experiment with form and content and their expansion of the traveling band format. Their show now includes such things as tympani, electronic instruments and whatever else is needed to present their music *totally*, not a slim copy or packaged self-parody. With each member proficient on many instruments, they have avoided the pitfalls of tedium and sameness that affects many otherwise-talented groups. And, as always, what The Beach Boys derive in the studio, The Beach Boys play onstage—all over the world.

As individuals, The Beach Boys have pursued their separate interests ranging from a dedication to the principles of Transcendental Meditation, to acting, to sports, to the operation of a health foods store. And typically, the energies invested in such endeavors as these are of the same intensity with which The Beach Boys approach their music.

As in any evolving creative effort, there have been changes; and the personnel is an example. But it is important that The Beach Boys of today are the same Beach Boys that changed the sound and shape of American music. Brian Wilson now concentrates his energy in the recording studio and on his writing, while Carl, Dennis, Alan and Michael, along with other carefully-selected musicians, devote a large part of their time to playing music on the road.

They have brought politics and philosophy to concerts, and vice-versa. They have had lasting effects on culture and songform. The success of The Beach Boys—spanning much more than a decade—is full of special events and memories; but the success of The Beach Boys is today. Everybody *has* an ocean, and The Beach Boys are music from America.

1975 TOUR BOOK

1975 TOUR BOOK

1975 TOUR BOOK

The Beach Boys are: Dennis Wilson, Michael Love, Carl Wilson, Alan Jardine and Brian Wilson.

1975 TOUR BOOK

Tuning in to those Good Vibrations

AFTER being idolised and trailed through every city in America Paul Revere and the Raiders, currently on tour with the Beach Boys, find it strange to walk almost unhindered through the streets.

I spoke to lead singer Mark Lindsay in his plush hotel room before the opening of the Birmingham concert.

"It's very strange to be able to walk down the street and do some shopping. This visit is a great chance to relax," 26-year-old Mark told me. "The pressure comes when we get out on stage though. You can sense people wondering what it's about. If something goes wrong it creates a lasting bad impression. It's the same as if, say, the Chromium Zip were playing with the Raiders in the States!"

The Raiders have had a consistent stream of hits in America, which have enabled them each to own several cars, including a Buick, Pontiac, Volkswagen, Phantom V Rolls-Royce and a Ferrari. Lead guitarist Freddy Wheller in fact owns five cars. "He needs five because he lives on a corner," Paul Revere explained, "Then he has a car pointing in each direction!"

Paul and the Raiders, Keith Allison—bass guitar, Freddy Wheller, Mississippi Joe Junior—drums, and Paul himself on organ, have been hosting a highly successful U.S. TV series for two years. The show is a fast moving pop spectacular, including comedy sketches. "I usually get the pies thrown in my face," Paul lamented.

During our conversation Birmingham resident Carl Wayne visited the group's room. Then after typically English tea and biscuits publicist Valerie Bond, Mark and I set off for the Odeon After collecting several bottles of wine and trying to reach the stage door via the one way system—each time in vain—we decided to leave Mark to walk to the theatre.

The concert was opened by a massive negro singer, Joe Hicks, who 'socked it to 'em' in true soul style and provided a lively opening set.

The Raiders were fronted by Mark Lindsay, who worked hard, leaping about with his long hair flowing down his back

The group opened with a beaty number "Him or Me", which typified their hard rock style. In contrast Freddy Wheller stepped to the fore to sing his own gentle country version of "Games People Play", which at the time of writing is number two in the U.S. country and western charts. Freddy, incidentally, has also released a solo album in the States

Another Raider who has 'branched out' to an extent is Keith Allison, who went to college with Monkee Mike Nesmith, and has since composed tunes with him, and played on the Monkees "Birds Bees and Monkees" album, and on "Stepping Stone". Joe Junior has interests in the jazz field, which are highly disapproved of by the rest of the Raiders, and he has also worked on records for Tommy Boyce and Bobby Hart, and Ike and Tina Turner. The Raiders themselves have an album, currently on U.S. release, due for release here shortly.

During their act the group featured a

THE BEACH BOYS seen backstage on their current tour (RM pic.) and inset, MARK LINDSAY of Paul Revere and the Raiders, who talks to RM's own Val Mabbs.

beautiful Jim Webb composition "Hymn From Grand Terrace" and their latest release "Let Me" which was greeted by screams.

Paul Revere and the Raiders were well received by the audience although they were unhappy about the sound mixing involved with the Beach Boys' equipment.

"Although the equipment is tremendous, and suitable for the Beach Boys," Mark explained, "we find when we move from the mikes to balance our sound the Beach Boys' engineer increases the power and brings the sound up again!"

During the second half the Beach Boys took to the stage, with Mike Love dressed in a flowing white monk's style robe, and Carl Wilson and Al Jardine also wearing white, in contrast to the bright red satin shirt sported by Dennis Wilson.

The boys opened their set with "In My Room" and after making light-hearted quips about their financial status they continued with "Get Around", "Sloop John B", and "Do It Again", which displayed incredibly well balanced and perfectly reproduced harmonies.

One of the highlights of the group's act was their current release "Break Away", which must renew every fan's faith in the Beach Boys' musical talent.

On their return from the Continent the Beach Boys and the Raiders were delayed at customs for several hours while every vitamin pill was carefully analysed, and the group gleefully related tales of this from the stage.

Al Jardine was highlighted during the act with "Cotton Fields" from the "20/20" album, and Carl Wilson excelled with "God Only Knows".

The Beach Boys closed an enjoyable and memorable show with "Good Vibrations" and left the capacity audience well satisfied.

Whether the group always have the time to actually sing on their records or not, they proved that they are definitely capable of reproducing live the sounds for which they are so famous.

VALERIE MABBS

RAVE INTERVIEW 1969

The Rave

DENNIS WILSON is the walking contradiction in the Beach Boys, who provides the motor for the group with his powerhouse percussion and unlimited energy. Dennis Wilson is the gentle-savage, the intellectual primitive, full of wilful pride and enforced humility.

He lives his life at breakneck speed with scarcely a backward glance behind him, but tempers his own velocity with daily meditation which stops him burning up in the atmosphere as he defies the laws of gravity.

Here is a man who cares for no one and everyone with the greater part of his devotion directed towards his music. He cares almost fanatically about his work and the group's performance. When the backing musicians failed to measure up to standard in Berlin, it was Dennis who steamed off stage after the show and tore into the musicians' room to deliver a scorching sermon on professionalism and sack everyone in sight. Fifteen minutes later he had cooled down and reinstated them, but the warning was enough to ensure the group one hundred per cent effort from the men on the next show!

Here, then, are a few impressions of the Beach Boys' guided missile. You may read between the lines or over the lines or under the lines or through the lines but be careful not to tread on the lines because there is a train coming. Which you might be excused from thinking has nothing to do with Dennis Wilson unless you realise he is the train!

What other work are you doing independent of the Beach Boys?

"I am recording a friend of mine—'Medulla'—who is a singer-guitarist who played a long time ago on one of our tours as a backing musician. He writes all his own songs. I have completed an album with him and when Brother Records are launched this year I hope to have him on our label."

What would you say for you was the happiest time you spent with the Beach Boys?

"Right now, because of the mere fact that I'm alive *now*. I live now—I can look back at the past and dig it, but there is more you can do about enjoying life now."

You live your life in an apparently fearless manner, but is there anything that frightens you?

"Fear is nothing but awareness. I was only frightened as a child because I did not understand fear—the dark, being lost, what was under the bed! It came from within.

"Sometimes the Wizard frightens me—Charlie Manson who is another friend of mine who says he is God and the devil! He sings, plays and writes poetry and may be another artist for Brother Records."

Do you think your marriage broke up because you were a Beach Boy—because you have to spend so much time working away from home?

"Maybe—but that was just a small part of it. It was just a question of growing apart, changing taste, direction—growing out of a shoe. The fact that you are a part of a successful group means you can do a lot of things you could not do before for your family, so it balances out."

Is this story true that you are living in a cellar in California at present?

"Yep—it's a little room about half the size of this hotel room. I look at it as my mind. There's a piano in there and a bed and that's all I need. People fill their lives and their rooms with so much stuff that they don't need—watches, furniture, cars—and they pour their life into keeping and acquiring these things. They spend all their time working to pay for that car, which they keep in a parking lot all day long.

"I could live anywhere I want. I've tried living in luxury, living in the mountains, living with my family and my favourite place is that little room!"

 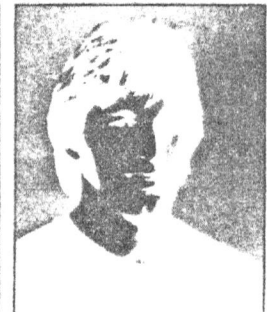

Subject
Dennis Wilson

Interviewer
Keith Altham

Situation
Beach Boys
Hotel

 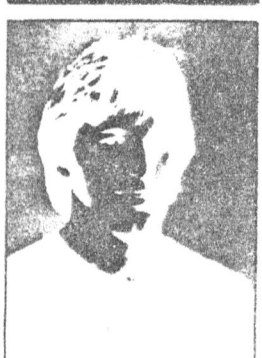

RAVE INTERVIEW 1969

Interview

How important is a hit single to you?

"Oh it's a lot of fun—it's all just for fun. It's good for your self-esteem. It's like bumping into a friend and saying 'Here's where I'm at'—I love it."

Why did you become involved in transcendental meditation?

"It's a very personal, fulfilling thing. It stimulates the mind and body and gives you a greater appreciation of life. It puts you in communication with something infinitely greater and more important than self."

Which people have most musical influence over you?

"I like parts of things—that is I can appreciate a piece of one thing or another for its chord structure, or its melody, or its lyric, but it's silly to nominate a whole thing which you probably only   in part. I very much admire Phil Spector, but I wouldn't say I loved everything he does.

"One of the most impressive groups to emerge from America in recent months is CTA—their whole structure is fantastic. They do everything tastefully, and progressively—boom! Mark my words!"

Why is it that the Beach Boys have never related to films?

"I don't think the Beach Boys are a visual thing in that way like the Beatles were. I can dig it for myself. The fun part of it—the glamour and the people. I'd love to play something like the Hunchback of Notre Dame or a Shakespearian role. I loved that Evelyn Waugh film, 'The Loved Ones'.

"Someone has just got to do a version of that book, 'Stranger In A Strange Land' and I think I know someone who has the rights to it anyway—he wanted Paul McCartney to play the role of the Martian. That is a fantastic book. I've only ever read three books, 'Black Beauty', 'The Prophet' and 'Stranger In A Strange Land'.

"I dislike censorship in films —art should be an entirely unrestricted medium in which the artist imposes his own limitations. There should be no boundaries."

What do you think has kept the Beach Boys together?

"A great love for each other and respect. The fact that we grew up together."

Are those stories true about you giving your money away?

"Sure—I give everything I have away. What I am wearing and what's in that suitcase is it. I don't even have a car. I have a 1934 Dodge pick-up truck which someone gave me.

"I could have anything I want. I just have to go out and get it. If it's worth having, it's worth giving. The smile you send out will return to you!"

Are you conscious of having moved away from the slightly philosophical content of albums like *Smiley Smiley* with your recent recordings?

(In mocking tones) "Philosophical—dat's heavy, man dat's really heavy, dat's de heaviest ting I ever hoid damn! Some people say we are tools and some people say we must polish the tool and others say we must use the tool. Who knows? It's all down to you."

How long can the Beach Boys go on being the Beach Boys?

"We can go on for ever—until we're eighty-three! Maybe when my son gets a little older—when he gets to eleven. . . ."

Would you like your son to be in a beat group?

"He can do anything he wants to do. He likes to play the piano and he likes to sing but he would rather wrestle or go swimming and fishing, hiking, get dirty or watch me race a motor cycle . . . who knows?"

Did you ever want to do anything else other than be a drummer?

"I wanted to join the forestry commission—have my own trees to look after, the peace of a piece of land. I wanted to be a gardener and skipper of a boat.

Who are the people who have had most influence over your life?

"Christ, Maharishi, Buddha, my Father, Brian and me."

   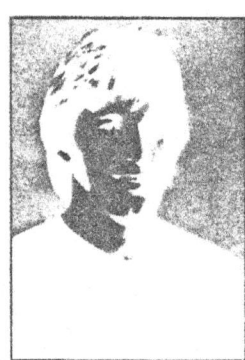 

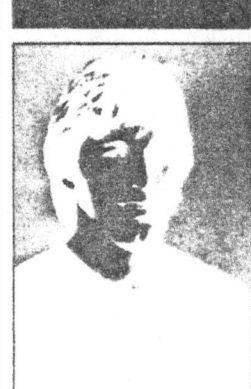   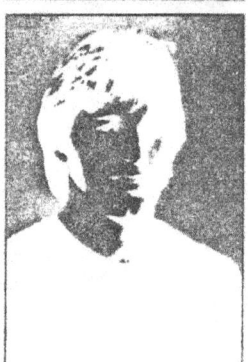

The Beach Boys: It's a Family Affair

By Dennis Metrano and Jim Miller

Jack Rieley is officially the manager of the Beach Boys, although he assumes numerous other responsibilities, from travelling secretary to publicity director. His lyrics appeared at several points on Surf's Up, with music by Carl and Brian Wilson; he also sang the lead on "A Day In the Life of a Tree," and often performs back-up vocals with the group on record.

Rieley, 29, has been in large measure responsible for the renewed popularity of the Beach Boys. Moreover, as several members of the group pointed out, Jack is as much a close friend as he is the band's manager. He was nominated for a Pulitzer Prize at the age of 21 for exposing the Ku Klux Klan in print, helped run the West Coast's first "underground" radio station, was NBC's Latin American correspondent, and has suffered at least one heart attack. His promotional and organizational skills, as well as his obvious sensitivity to and love for the Beach Boys' music make him an ideal spokesman for the group.

Real Paper: Will the complete *Smile* ever appear?

Jack Rieley: Yes, in late 1973, in stereo.

RP: What songs will be on it?

JR: The original uncut version of "Heroes and Villains"; "Wind Chimes"; "Wonderful"; "Surf's Up," possibly with an extended "The Child is the Father to the Man"... "The Old Master Painter" that's very important... And of course the elements suite: "Vegetables"; the legendary song about fire, "Mrs. O'Leary's Cow"; "I Love to Say DaDa" (part of which has appeared on *Sunflower* as "Cool Cool Water"); and "Good Vibra-

drive over he kept asking me about these stories he'd heard. By the time we pulled into Brian's driveway, I had convinced him that although Brian had done all those weird things, that was in the past and Brian was a very normal, regular guy now. Getting out of the car I heard a voice say, "Hi, Jack." I looked over and there was Brian, half his face painted red, half green and wearing only a black cape. So much for normalcy.

RP: To perform?

(Rieley shrugs and smiles.)

RP: There are several members of the Beach Boys who receive little attention...

JR: Yes. The Arp player is Daryll Dragon, son of Carmen Dragon, who is the conductor of the Hollywood Bowl Orchestra. Toni Shearer, who does lots of keyboard and percussion work, has a musical opention.

RP: What is your personal reaction to being considered part of a living musical legend, the Beach Boys?

CW: I've never considered it. I don't relate to that.

RP: What was it like when you were fifteen and "Surfin'" happened?

CW: Well, we were all pretty naive. We were just a group that made a record that happened to hit. That's all.

RP: Yes, but you followed it up very quickly.

CW: Hmmm. It was a while before we started to get into it.

RP: Well, what was it: six months between "Surfin'" and "Surfin' Safari"? And then it was "Ten Little Indians," if I remember, which was a bomb. And then it was about nine, ten months at the most until "Surfin' U.S.A."

CW: Right. The first records we made were recorded very simply. Just used a one track machine. Brian played drums on a can with pencils. Alan played stand up bass. We usually got it all down the first time. Very funky.

RP: How come there's no falsetto on your first album? It seems like a strange omission, since falsetto practically became the Beach Boys' trademark for a time.

CW: Well, we recorded that at Capitol records, and a lot of things didn't work out. It took us time to get into the recording process and learn.

RP: How did Brian end up producing his own records at that early date? Wasn't it unprecedented for a rock group to go into a major label and, having made only two or three albums, to start producing

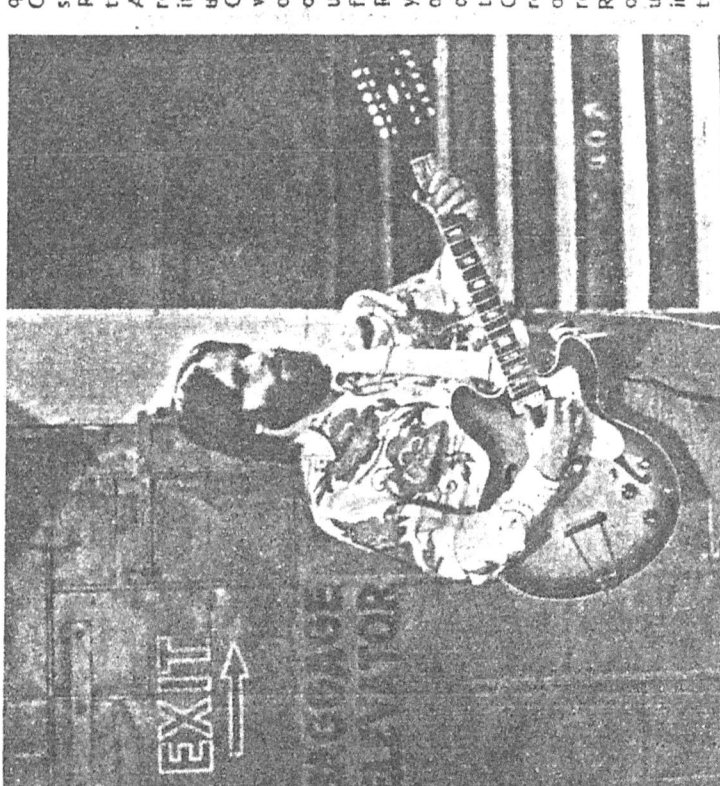

PHOTO — JEFF ALBERTSON

REAL PAPER EARBOOK DECEMBER 1972

tions," which is the section on air.

RP: Will you use the already existing versions for some of these songs?

JR: No, probably not. Brian still has the original instrumental tracks for most of them, but we'll probably re-record all the songs.

RP: Will *Smile* be issued with the original graphics and booklet?

JR: Believe it or not, Capitol records claims it has lost the original album cover! Ben Edmonds of Creem magazine has a slick of the cover, and perhaps we'll use that. I doubt if we'll keep the original photos, since everyone has gone through so many changes since then — Carl looks like a child in them. The booklet is pretty outdated.

RP: Was there ever a Beach Boy/Who album planned?

JR: Keith Moon mentioned doing a joint album, but it never really advanced beyond the talking stages.

RP: It has been rumored that the Beach Boys' money has been invested in oil wells, real estate, etcetera. Is this so?

JR: No. The Beach Boys have their own corporation. American Productions, that handles their finances. We are currently involved in suing their former business management, who had them invest in several hundred "prime" acres of land called Simi (pronounced, incredibly enough, "seamy") Valley. It turned out to be worth considerably less than the price they paid for it. The Beach Boys ended up losing over a million dollars on that deal.

RP: How has the tour been received so far?

JR: We toured the South for the first time in several years, and were amazed to find how much the South is into the Beach Boys, not only the surfing and hot rod Beach Boys, but what we are doing today. Also, it is interesting that a year ago we played to considerably less than a full house in Boston, and tonight we've sold out two shows. We are planning to record live at Carnegie Hall and the Capitol Theater in New Jersey for a live album. Brian will be at the Carnegie

Carl Wilson

ing on Broadway called "Mother Earth," Ed Carter, on bass and guitar, would have taken Brian's place instead of Bruce Johnston if Ed hadn't decided to go back to college.

RP: How's Brian?

JR: Brian is very excited about the new album, *Holland*, which should be out in January. He is also writing a lot of new songs. There will be a seven inch disc included with *Holland* of a fairy tale Brian has written, a lot of which sounds autobiographical, to me. Brian does the Pied Piper and I narrate the rest. It contains fragments of five new songs that may eventually appear in full form. Brian very much wants this released as a 45 and we're having a hard time explaining to him that it just won't get top 40 and juke box play. An interesting footnote is that Brian wrote the fairy tale letter by letter with those little stick-on letters you find in dime stores; it took him months!

RP: Ah, yes, Jack. The stories about Brian's idiosyncrasies . . . .

JR: They're all true. He *did* put a sandbox in his living room so that he could play the piano with his feet in the sand; he *did* have a tent erected in his kitchen. But my favorite Brian story is when a friend of mine who is a musician, and has always dug Brian's music, came to town and asked to meet Brian. On the

RP: So what is Brian *really* like? How does he spend his days?

JR: Brian is an extremely shy person, and very sensitive; he'll get upset by apparently harmless remarks. He's also very conscious about his weight. He keeps irregular hours. He'll be up for three days, and then sleep for the next three days. He spends a lot of time listening to old R&B from the Fifties. And of course he composes new music, plays the piano; he's writing now like he's never written before.

Carl Wilson rarely speaks for mass consumption. A reserved, soft-spoken person, he seems extremely fatigued from playing a string of one-nighters. By contrast, brother Dennis is buoyant and tends to enliven things with his sense of humor.

RP: Do you still have to do C.O. work? [After spending several years in the courts, Carl won the privilege of fulfilling his conscientious objector requirements by working with music for social improvement.]

Carl Wilson: Yes. Recently I've been doing mainly voter registration. The Beach Boys registered over 300,000 new voters this last year. I usually put more than 40 hours a week in. I've done some prison and hospital things, but the last six months it's been mostly voter registra-

CW: I don't think so; everyone started doing it at that time. I remember that the Four Seasons did their own producing.

RP: I thought Bob Crewe produced them.

CW: He did, but the real influence was Bob Gaudio.

RP: Was there any sense of competition between you and the Four Seasons in the early days? That was rather hyped up, especially on the East Coast, as a battle between the two big American bands.

CW: It may have caused us to set a standard for each other. It was something to reach for — to match each other's standards. It was really pretty innocent; it was just a very simple thing.

RP: How do you react to the criticism that with *Pet Sounds* the Beach Boys' recordings became too artsy?

CW: I'm not aware of that criticism, but I'm not worried about it. We are just making the music that we make.

RP: What effect has the fact that Brian is considered a reclusive and eccentric genius had upon you?

CW: It hasn't had any, because we've always had the same relationship, and it's very different from the hype and rumors about Brian. Those stories haven't affected our relationship.

RP: Has the responsibility of being the de facto leader of the group after Brian stopped performing been a burden?

CW: Well, it's really just a matter of helping organize the music.

RP: How calculated were the lyrics on the early records? Dennis was the only surfer, so in a sense they weren't true. Did you think in terms of "this is what our audience wants to hear"? Did you take the lyrics seriously?

CW: I think we related in terms of the audience in those days. But primarily we just tried to make the best sound we could. We were into the sound, the vibrations, more than the lyrics.

RP: What's your favorite Beach Boys' song?

CW: It's hard to say. For a time it was "Wouldn't It Be Nice," and then it was

[Continued on page 22]

Beach Boys

[Continued from page 20]

"Caroline No," and then "Surf's Up."

RP: You said your early stuff was very simply done. By the time you got to "Wouldn't It Be Nice" and Pet Sounds, how were the records being made? How many over-dubs? Were you using session musicians? How long would it take to do a track like that?

CW: "Wouldn't It Be Nice" sort of sticks out in my memory. We did ten sessions on the vocals alone just trying to get the sound right. No session men.

CS: There's probably four tracks of vocals, two for the lead and two for the background. You see, then we weren't really into recording. I'm really into recording now. I enjoy recording all the time.

RP: About three months after "Wouldn't It Be Nice" was released, I saw you in Chicago. Mike Love came out on stage and said some very sarcastic things about that song and "God Only Knows," something to the effect that Brian was writing songs that you couldn't sing in person anymore. I sensed a distance then between the performing unit and Brian. At the time there were rumors about a possible Beach Boys break-up. Was there any kind of strain between you, the band, who were performing the songs, and Brian, who was composing them?

CW: I think that was a consideration at the time, but we chose to make better records. It's true that the concerts were very different than the records. After Pet Sounds the concerts of course were different from the records. You can't make the same sound.

RP: What direction do you want to take as an individual writer? You've written two outstanding songs, "Long Promised Road" and "Feel Flows," and I understand you've done two more songs on Holland. You've blossomed on your own as a writer.

CW: I just got inspired and started writing...

words relating to sound rather than relating literally.

RP: What has meditation done for you?

CW: It's helped a lot. I couldn't do this road thing without it.

RP: How often do you meditate?

CW: Everyday, thirty to forty-five minutes. It's a scientific yet natural thing.

RP: Do you think it's made you more creative?

CW: Definitely. It affects you subtly; you

humorous and lengthy story about brotherly rivalry involving Carl and Dennis pulling each other's ears when Dennis was five and Carl was three. Carl responds as if he is unsure whether the story is true or not.)

RP: How much has being a family helped the Beach Boys to survive? After all, eleven years is a remarkably long time for a band to stay together.

DW: Oh yeah, we're in love.

PHOTO — JEFF ALBERTSON

don't suddenly create songs because of it. If it were to change someone's nature, it would be over a long period of time.

RP: You, Billy Hinsche, Alan and Mike recorded a song, "T.M.," at Inter-Media Sounds in Boston with Charles Lloyd the last time you were here.

CW: Yes. It's a simple tune: "T.M., T.M., in the AM, in the PM"....

RP: What do you think is the most under-recognized Beach Boys album; there was a time when not many Beach Boys albums were being sold in this country.

CW: Smiley Smile or maybe Friends. (Dennis comes out of the bathroom and sits on the floor.)

RP: How do you and Dennis get along? (Dennis immediately plunges into a

CW: It's as if you put a group of friends together, that you've known all your life. You don't get so upset at their idiosyncrasies as you might with someone you've just met.

DW: Or you can look at the group itself. In the beginning Alan didn't know if he wanted to be a Beach Boy or not. David Marks and the rest of us never really got along; there was a lot of trouble. So Alan, who had gone to dentistry school, and who was like a brother, came back into the group. And with Bruce, it was constant bickering between Bruce and myself.

RP: Bruce Johnston was in the group for a pretty long time for something that ultimately didn't work out.

CW: He really likes to write and perform music at the piano. He really wants to be a soloist. He should be doing a solo piano act, and I'm sure he will.

RP: I think he's remarkably talented.

DW: He's a giant! He's an exceptional writer as a soloist. He's a romanticist. It's just the bag he's in. He'd sit with my mom at the piano. He likes to get very emotional.

RP: How much did Paul McCartney do on "Vegetables"?

CW: He attended the session, but he really didn't do that much.

DW: It blew our minds. I couldn't believe he was there.

RP: Other than Brian, who are your favorite musicians?

DW: My all-time favorite would be Wagner, especially the prelude to Tristan and Isolde.

RP: Ever consider doing a rock opera?

CW: Yes, a long time ago.

DW: Brian had been listening to Wagner and considered it.

RP: Dennis, you have two songs on Holland that you don't sing. Why?

DW: It's just that Carl can do them better.

RP: Carl, weren't you disappointed when Dennis pulled two songs from Surf's Up?

CW: I wanted very much for them to go on. Dennis wasn't satisfied, so they didn't go on.

RP: Dennis, why weren't you satisfied?

DW: I can't explain it. When you write a song, you should feel done with it. Those didn't feel done.

CW: The whole thing with Dennis is if it sounds right we'll go with it, if not, we'll wait.

The show that followed was a professional presentation of the Beach Boys' music, including three songs from their upcoming Holland LP. The band betrayed some signs of weariness, but by midway through the second half of the concert, the audience's evident enthusiasm had transferred itself to the stage. The group did "God Only Knows" beautifully, and Blondie Chaplain ripped through a positively searing "Wild Honey." The Beach Boys remain one of America's greatest rock 'n' roll bands.

■

RP: I was excited when I saw *So Tough* by "Carl and the Passions," and yet there was really no Carl, no new songs by you on the album.

CW: Well, that's true. A lot of people didn't understand that. The name was just a put-on that Brian did a long time ago. It was just a rock 'n' roll name. Just a joke.

RP: Are you pleased with your songs?

CW: (laughs) Sometimes. I liked the bridge on "Long Promised Road," especially where the Moog is turned up high.

RP: What do you think of Brian's fairy tale?

CW: Well, it's really different. I don't know how many people are going to appreciate it. It's not like a normal record. It's a story, a narration with sound effects.

RP: Have ever thought about sitting down and putting together an obvious top 40 single again?

CW: No. I don't like that idea at all. Certain people, like Warner Brothers, say to us, "Why don't you guys make a single record?" I'd rather make albums.

RP: I thought "Long Promised Road" should have been a top 40 hit.

CW: I think possibly it demanded too much attention.

RP: Is Van Dyke Parks going to do any of the sessions on *Smile*?

CW: He could. He and Brian have been hanging out together a lot lately. (Dennis Wilson enters the room to go to the bathroom.)

Dennis Wilson: I'm going to have to slam this door to shut it. Sorry, Carl. SLAM! (Carl grimaces and smiles at the same time.)

RP: Van Dyke Parks writes very obscure lyrics.

CW: I just really like his poetry. It's really far-out. He loves sound. He chooses

Overlooked Treasures: Greg Shaw

TEENAGE HEAD by Flamin' Groovies (Kama Sutra). This may have been 1970's best album by an American rock group. Like the Stones might sound like as a young group today; like more groups oughta sound. Currently in England, the Groovies may yet find the recognition they deserve.

BAD RICE by Ron Nagle (Warner Bros.). Now this could've been a big album, if Warners hadn't been pushing a hundred other releases that month. Nagle came from a legendary San Francisco group called the Mystery Trend, and with the aid of Ry Cooder, Jack Nitzsche, and the West Virginia Creeper, he produced a real gem of an album in the Van Dyke Parks/Randy Newman vein. The songs are about people with names like Uncle Frank and Chuckie's mom, told in inventively bizarre lyrics.

RISE by Louie & the Lovers (Epic). Remember this group of teenage Chicanos, produced by Sir Doug Sahm a couple of years ago? Their album was an unmitigated delight, bringing to mind shades of Moby Grape, the Byrds, Kaleidoscope, and Creedence, yet maintaining a distinctive personality of its own. This is one even I had forgotten until today, but the songs spring into my mind when I read the titles and I can't wait to hear it again.

REFUGEE by The Savage Rose (RCA). Any of their three albums would have done as well, but this is the most recent and it almost produced a hit single with "Revival Day." Wish it had, then I wouldn't have to try and describe the ineffably strange and attractive voice of vocalist Anisette. The group consists of several rich art school kids from Denmark, and their music simply must be heard. It's not pretentious art-rock by any means; it contains influences from R&B, rock and classical, and sounds like nothing else in this world.

ROCKPILE by Dave Edmunds (MAM). This guy is England's premier rocker, his work with Love Sculpture deserves to be on this list too. He produced for Shakin' Stevens the only rock revival album worth a shit, he's currently producing the Flamin' Groovies, and this album is one of the amazingly few that no one I know has grown tired of. Songs from Chuck Berry, Fats Domino, Neil Young, Dylan and others take on new vitality in his hands. If you like Gary Glitter, here's where it all came from.

WALK AWAY RENEE by Left Banke (Smash). Here's an oldie that's been passed by while the likes of Count Five were being enshrined in history. Only the first group to effectively synthesize rock and classical/chamber music, they had two fair-sized hits and one great album. You won't believe how "Lazy Day" rocks, and most of the other songs are in a class with their hits. Leader Mike Brown is now in Stories, another fine group with a new single that sounds like Slade. Speaking of whom, their PLAY IT LOUD album on Cotillion has certainly been overlooked.

HIGH TIME by the MC5 (Atlantic). I could as well list Back in the U.S.A., for after the political naiveté of their first album nobody seemed to notice the subsequent efforts of what turned out to be one of our best domestic rock 'n' roll bands. Check out "Teenage Lust," "Shakin' Street" and "The Human Being Lawnmower," and on HIGH TIME just try and tell me every single song isn't a killer. If they ever get back from England we'll find out again what high energy's all about, meanwhile these albums are easy to find for under 50 cents each.

LOOKIN' THRU YOU by The Herd (Fontana). An import. This group, led by Peter Frampton and Andy Bown, was among the forerunners of England's late-Sixties lightweight pop movement, and produced some of its best music. "From the Underworld" was a large hit over there but they didn't catch on here. Bown went on to Judas Jump and Frampton to Humble Pie, leaving behind this tasty biscuit.

WHERE WERE YOU WHEN I NEEDED YOU by the Grass Roots (Dunhill). Probably the ultimate folk-rock album, eclipsing all the works of P.F. Sloan, Barry McGuire, the Turtles, and even the Byrds in my opinion. Aside from Dylan's "Ballad of a Thin Man," a "Tell Me" that puts the Stones to shame, "I Am a Rock" and "Ain't That Lovin' You Baby," all songs are Sloan/Barri originals from a time when that team was at its peak.

REDWING (Fantasy). Here's a group that should've really gone somewhere. For a first album theirs was one of 1971's most refreshing, with a youthful vigor and a sense of rock 'n' roll basics that delighted the critics but seemed to go unnoticed by the record-buying masses. Their second album was more of the same, and that's what it received too. Pick up both of them and ask yourself why. And if you figure it out, let me know.

MEDIA INFORMATION

BEACH BOYS

A newspaper reporter was interviewing Carl Wilson on The Beach Boys' fifteenth anniversary, asking him what the significance of the group was, what it all meant. Carl told him that The Beach Boys didn't <u>mean</u> anything, that their music was an <u>experience</u>. Then the reporter asked him what the new album was going to sound like. Carl shook his head. He was 15 years old when the group had its first hit. He's now 30. "It'll sound like us," he said quietly, "It'll sound like The Beach Boys."

Almost everybody knows what The Beach Boys sound like: that high, tight wall of harmony, counterpoint and background, with rich vocals and orchestration leaning in and out of rising balanced music with a shape and energy of its own, clear and powerful. Music you can ride; music that could have only come out of the beach and sunshine culture of Southern California in the 50's and 60's.

Brian Wilson went to Hawthorne High School. It was a California school that had more lawn than asphalt and where the kids were taught to play fair in teams. Brian played baseball and football. His cousin Mike Love went to Dorsey High and ran on the track and cross country teams. Both of them loved music and on the way home from youth night at the Angeles Mesa Presbyterian Church, they'd harmonize on Everly Brothers songs. Brian loved the Four Freshmen too, and spent hours at the piano picking out parts to songs like "Polka Dots and Moonbeams." When he got it he'd give Mike the bass line, then he'd give brothers Dennis and Carl the baritone and tenor: he'd take one of the high parts and give the other to whomever was around and sometimes that meant his mother Audree. Then Al Jardine, a football teammate, recovered one of Brian's fumbled pitch-outs and got his leg broken doing it. The two became friends and Al, who had a strong lead voice, played stand-up bass and loved folk music, started singing with them. Carl was the only truly accomplished musician when they started, and he played lead guitar. They put some drums into it, and for a while Mike Love even played the saxophone. They called themselves "The Pendltones," and although it was all very new to them, they began thinking that maybe they had a band.

All of them loved rock and roll, Chuck Berry especially, and that's the kind of music they began working on. For a while they put their words to other people's music. Then they started to write songs of their own. They played some parties and a couple of shows and then Al found somebody who wanted to record them. In fact, the man thought Al was bringing him a folk group that was going to do a Kingston Trio kind of act; folk was still king around then and Al let him think what he wanted. But Dennis had just begun to surf and he talked a lot about it. One day, on the way home from the beach off the Redondo Pier, he and Mike first talked about maybe writing a surf song. Mike was ready to do the words if he could just get Brian interested enough to do the music. He did: that first record, for a label called Candix, was titled "Surfin'," and when it was released in the winter of 1961 it went to number ten on the Los Angeles charts. Carl was a sophomore at Hawthorne High then, Dennis was 17, Al and Brian were 19, and Mike was just 20. It was a time when a lot of groups came and went in four weeks, but The Beach Boys, as they started calling themselves, all played and sang well. And Brian seemed to have extraordinary talent.

Candix folded almost immediately but under the aggressive management of Murry Wilson (Brian, Dennis and Carl's dad) the group signed a contract with Capitol Records. By the time they'd done their first two albums they were wildly popular and had already begun to chart their course as a premier California band. They were writing many of their own songs by now, rock and roll songs about miles of beach, where the sun shone almost all the time, and where the simple promise was fun. The lyrics were full of lines like, "She's the head cheerleader, she dates the quarterback" and "Be true to your school, just like you would to your girl or guy." When Mike Love said not long ago that The Beach Boys were inseparable from middle-class karma, he was right. The music and the lyrics from the period are such a funky, honest collection of California moments and fascinations and moods that it all came together and burst into myth, one of America's best myth's so far: Endless Summer, the eternal surfer, the perfect wave.

In 1963 they made their third album, Surfer Girl, and Brian took over all production chores, artistic control such as had never happened in rock and roll before. Brian's arrangements put his own clear falsetto together with Mike's boyish voice on leads; the backgrounds grew richer; the musical patterns more complicated; and for the first time Brian's melancholy began to show through, on a powerful ballad called "In My Room," a hymn to solitude.

Another album, Little Deuce Coupe, followed the same year. It was a collection of car songs and on it Brian took another step toward the sound he'd been chasing on the other albums. On the next one, Shut Down, Vol. II, he got it: a sound that owed bits and pieces to people like Chuck Berry, Phil Spector and The Four Freshmen; but which emerged as original and surprising, far beyond what any other rock and roll group had tried in terms of musical sophistication and production. "Fun Fun Fun" was the album's rouser, a car song still, but with a hint in it that it was time to move on. And the album had two quiet triumphs on it: "The Warmth of the Sun" and "Don't Worry Baby."

In 1965 The Beach Boys recorded two songs that are still among their most popular: "Help Me Rhonda," a rocker about the end of one romance and the beginning of another, and "California Girls," which may be the quintessential Beach Boys song from the early years. It's an up little fantasy, full of rising chords, and it still brings people to their feet wherever it's played.

Early in 1965 Brian stopped touring with the group. He never had a skin thick enough for that part of the work and the longer he did it the worse it got. Shy, eccentric, creative in ways that won't take a lot of interviewing, uncomfortable in a room with even one stranger, he finally told the rest of the group that although he wanted to go on composing and producing for them he couldn't perform anymore. It was a great loss and very traumatic for the group. Carl, although the youngest, inherited leadership of the band on the road because of his steady temper and accomplished musicianship.

Around this time Bruce Johnston, a talented L.A. musician, joined the group to sing Brian's parts on tour and he was just one of many good people who drifted in and out of the group over those years. Daryl Dragon, son of composer Carmen Dragon, played keyboards with the band for about 6 years. Then he met Toni Tennille, (the only girl who ever toured with The Beach Boys), and the two of them ran off and became The Captain and Tennille. Glen Campbell played one tour with the group, and there were others. But it wasn't the same without Brian, but The Beach Boys, five years after they began, were still one of the most successful rock and roll bands in the world: every single they'd released to this time had reached the top 30 on the national charts.

In 1966, under Brian's direction, the group recorded its most ambitious album. <u>Pet Sounds</u> contained some of their best work ever and to this day remains some of the most interesting musical architecture in all of rock and roll. Songs like "God Only Knows" and "I'm Waiting for the Day" showed the group at its most romantic. The music and arrangements soared and although the single "Wouldn't It Be Nice" broke into the top ten, the album itself sold poorly and presaged a time of declining fortunes and commercial trouble for the group, that was broken only by "Good Vibrations," a single in 1966. That song took six months to produce and many critics think it to be the group's strongest single piece. It came out of the confusion of those years, out of the psychedelic revolution that finally overran everything. It was different in its way from anything else that they had done but it was still unmistakably The Beach Boys: a simple positive feeling wrapped in music that ran a mood range from galloping highs to moody lows. Because of its elements and construction, critics began to speculate that if Brian had lived in another century he might well have been picking out parts to Beethoven sonatas on his piano after school, and then trying to out-do their beauty with his own music. "Good Vibrations" is still the largest selling hit The Beach Boys have ever had.

Over the last part of the 60s there were more albums, (by now, for Warner/Reprise instead of Capitol) and there were more personnel changes. Van Dyke Parks collaborated with Brian as lyricist on Sunflower and Surf's Up. Blondie Chaplin took Bruce Johnston's place and Rickey Fataar took over drums from Dennis, who had cut his hand badly.

At the age of ten the group continued to make music. They had always spent a lot of time touring and though they were drawing well, it wasn't possible to match the heat and speed of those early years. Those were hard times for the group, professionally and personally, but they were moving through them. They began meditating and Mike and Al went to Spain to become teachers of TM. Later, Carl and Dennis took est (Erhard Seminars Training) and both say it was an incredible experience and has added a great deal to their lives. And always, through everything, they were a family: five guys, all different from each other, all intense and dedicated in their lives and work.

In 1973 they made the Holland album. It was recorded over six months in that gentle country and it signaled a new movement for the group. It was an ambitious and sustained album, their first in a while and it took the California theme way beyond cars and surfing with songs like "The Trader," "Sail On Sailor" and the three-part "California Saga" the album's strongest piece musically and lyrically: Mike Love and Alan and Lynda Jardine teaming up with poet Robinson Jeffers to pay tribute to Big Sur. They wrote and arranged it themselves. It was a clear sign that The Beach Boys, 13 years after they became a group, had places to go, things to do.

Still, if you ask Carl what it all means--"For a few minutes while they're listening to a Beach Boys song maybe people like being alive a little bit more," he says. "That's the experience and it's up."

A Beach Boys concert is the best place to feel just how up the experience can be. There's really nothing like it and they take the audience through all that music, from way back then to now, through all those moods and themes; "I Can Hear Music," "Catch A Wave," "Heroes and Villians," "Surfin' USA," "Fun, Fun, Fun." Somehow they take that technically-demanding music onto the stage with energy and precision and by the time they do their encore the thirty-year olds in the audience are in a memory frenzy and the younger kids are just as crazy over something that's new to them. "It's the positivity of our music--a natural expression of our way of life that makes The Beach Boys music come alive," says Mike.

Last year, when America turned 200, The Beach Boys turned 15. Their birthday present to themselves and to us was an album recorded at Brother Studios called Fifteen Big Ones. The first side included original compositions (written by Brian and Mike), and the second side favored classic rock and roll songs arranged for this album by Brian. It was the first time the group had been in the studio together for 3 years and they worked on the album five days a week for two months. When Rolling Stone did a feature on the session they called it, "The Beach Boys: Big Brother is Back," because Brian got involved on the album in a way that he hadn't for a long time. It excited the group to have his full energy back, along with his humor, his voice and all his other fierce and sweet musical powers.

Most of the new songs were Brian's: "Back Home," "That Same Song," (both with Brian singing the lead), "Had to Phone Ya," and "It's OK." Mike Love wrote "Everyone's in Love With You," and almost everyone's on that track; The Captain and Tennille did the background vocals, Charles Lloyd played the flute and Mike's sister Maureen Love played the harp.

The oldies on the album were all done by other groups originally but given The Beach Boys sound. Mike sang lead on "Rock and Roll Music," Mike and Al had the lead for "A Casual Look," Brian on "Chapel of Love," Carl, on "Palisades Park," and Dennis sang "In the Still of the Night."

When they finished, Mike Love talked about the album this way: "It's a great new moment in the history of The Beach Boys. That's what's neat about the group; you have a history to look at. You can appreciate the group in its different periods, its moods and its changes. You can begin to appreciate The Beach Boys more like you would the work of an artist; and therefore, appreciate the whole of its life's work and not judge it by whether it has reached number one on the record charts."

The next year saw Brian in one of the most productive periods of his life. To many observers the sight of the Beach Boys' Big Brother determinedly holed up in the studio day after day recalled the commitment of the Pet Sounds era. And the music on his latest work The Beach Boys Love You, didn't dispute the comparison, especially the series of touching ballads headed up by "I'll Bet He's Nice" on Side Two.

Brian had written over two dozen tunes for the album and 14 sparklers made it onto the final mix. Each song was a concise, unabashed celebration of the classic pop form. The atmospheric quality of the music was heightened by discarding the natural bass for the bottom of the mini-Moog, creating highly ambient textures a perfect match for all those BB harmonies.

Many of the numbers brimmed over with youthful enthusiasm. The boy-girl songwriting mode was back in the hands of the master. The upbeat "Roller Skating Child" checked out courtship at the skating rink, and, if the recent Southern California seaside skating boom keeps exploding "Roller Skating Child" could put the Boys on top of another outdoor craze a la skateboarding and surfing. "Honkin' Down the Highway" and Brian's homage to Phil Spector, "Mona," were two more future car radio standards.

The Beach Boys Love You capped off a year of varied Beach Boys activities for Brian including concert appearances, a television special for NBC and presentations on the Grammy and Rock Concert shows. He has no intention of slowing down the pace. "I do feel more like a member of the group again," he has said. "It's a little easier to cope now. I played about 35 shows last year, and it was a little scary to be out there, but it was a thrill for me to be part of the Beach Boys thing. I'll be out there again."

BIOGRAPHY: ALAN JARDINE

Al is an easy-going thoughtful man, and you can see it in his face: bright eyes above a comfortable smile and a country beard. He loves animals and the land; and could talk all day about the whales that migrate up and down the California coast, or how to build an ecologically healthy bass pond.

Alan played football with Brian Wilson at Hawthorne High and was an original member of the group although he took a year off to finish his pre-dental studies in 1962. He has always contributed to The Beach Boys' musical soup: Alan brought a knowledge of folk music to the group when they first started and it led to Brian's arrangements of "Cottonfields," which was a big hit in England and Europe, and "Sloop John B." Al also knows and collects classic rhythm and blues records, and he had a hand in choosing the old rock and roll standards that went into Fifteen Big Ones. His fascination with the Robinson Jeffers/John Steinbeck country around the central California coast led him to create (with Mike Love) "The California Saga Trilogy," one of the group's most ambitious and beautiful pieces. Alan is The Beach Boys' on-stage rhythm guitarist, harmony and occasional lead vocalist. Although he has always participated in the creation of Beach Boys' music, the Friends album was a major step in his career; it contained five songs written or co-written by him.

Alan lives with his wife Lynda near Monterey where they raise Arabian horses in a canyon ranch. The horses have to share their barn: most of it has been done over into a complete recording studio that is a funky combination of modern technology and rustic woodwork done by local craftsmen. Alan's main interest at home besides restoring his beautiful historic ranch is a working dedication for the preservation of California's beautiful coastline.

BIOGRAPHY: MIKE LOVE

Mike Love is first cousin to the Wilson brothers and the four of them grew up in nearby neighborhoods. When they made their first record Brian wrote the music and Mike wrote the words, combination has made many of The Beach Boys biggest hits over the years. Mike likes to write spontaneously and thinks he's done some of his best work that way; he says that he wrote the lyrics to "Good Vibrations" in ten minutes driving down the Hollywood freeway on the way to the recording session. He and Brian wrote "Fun, Fun, Fun" in the back of a taxi between a Holiday Inn and an airport in Salt Lake City.

Mike has always been articulate and energetic, and those qualities helped launch the group in 1961. In the beginning he involved himself with the group's business matters, but now his brother Steve handles financial affairs. Mike teaches Transcendental Meditation, and has practiced it for eight years. "We met the Maharishi Mahesh Yogi in December, 1967, when we did a United Nations show in Paris. The whole group now meditates; Al and I are teachers. Any group is only as strong as its members. I don't think I'd be in the group if it wasn't for meditation.

"It raises your tolerance to tension and stress. It helps against the fatiguing effects of physical and mental activity."

To spread the word about the benefits of TM, Mike spends much time lecturing to groups across the country. Today, he is one of TM's most visible and most eloquent spokesmen.

Mike continues to write music and lyrics and when he is not living the fast life on the road he lives very quietly in Santa Barbara on a bluff overlooking a surfing spot; there he spends most of his time in a one room cliff house with stained glass windows.

BIOGRAPHY: BRIAN WILSON

> "Brian Wilson is The Beach Boys. He is the band. We're his messengers. He is all of it. He's everything."
> —Dennis Wilson, quoted in
> Crawdaddy, June, 1976

It would be difficult to overstate Brian Wilson's influence on The Beach Boys" sound. From the beginning, he was the band's leader, bassist, chief songwriter and producer. Often, he was lead vocalist as well; and it was Brian who was responsible for the wide-open harmony vocal arrangements that became an early Beach Boys trademark. Even during his protracted absence from The Beach Boys' live performances and recording sessions, Brian was the undisputed spiritual leader of the band; the felt-if-never-seen presence that served to cohere the group's sound and image. The term "genius" has been applied to Brian more than once.

Though the Wilson brothers' father Murry was a part-time composer, Brian's first taste of formal musical training came while he attended Hawthorne High. "Unfortunately," he recalls, "I allowed my position on the varsity baseball team and my involvement in a rock group called the Pendletones to distract from my music lessons...I stopped doing my assignments, and ended up with a 'C' in the course."

The Pendletones changed their name to The Beach Boys in time to record a Brian Wilson composition entitled "Surfin'," originally released on the local Candix label. Even that first Beach Boys record showed evidence of what was to come: a combination of Four Freshmen harmonies and Chuck Berry beat that was as effective as it was eclectic.

Weary of constant touring, Brian retired from that aspect of The Beach Boys' life in 1965 to concentrate on songwriting and recording studio work.

As The Beach Boys' sound refined itself, producer Phil Spector and his distinctive "wall of sound" instrumental and vocal arrangements became absorbed into Brian's consciousness, blending with earlier influences and with his own very personal perceptions and culminating in the 1966 album, Pet Sounds. Ahead of its time in many respects (as a cohesive "concept" album, it predated Sgt. Pepper by 18 months), the album is more highly regarded today than it was at the time, when sales were disappointing despite enthusiastic critical reaction and the inclusion of three hit singles: "Wouldn't It Be Nice?" "Sloop John B.," and "Caroline, No"--the first and third being Brian Wilson compositions.

Though Brian Wilson compositions have appeared on virtually every Beach Boys album since the very beginning, his involvement with the band decreased steadily from 1967 (he was replaced as vocalist in 1969 by Grammy award winner Bruce Johnston, who remained with The Beach Boys for two years) until 1976. Until then, Brian's most recent full production had been an album by his wife, Marilyn, and her sister Diane Rovell who recorded under the name Spring. It was released in 1972. This year, he has become again fully involved in writing, producing, and singing with The Beach Boys.

In addition to his musical pursuits, Brian is a student of Transcendental Meditation and has recently embarked upon a concentrated physical fitness program (briefly, some years ago, Brian owned and operated a health food store called the Radiant Radish in West Hollywood). He, Marilyn, and daughters Carnie and Wendy, live in the Los Angeles suburb of Bel-Air.

BIOGRAPHY: CARL WILSON

Like older brothers Dennis and Brian, Carl Wilson was born in Hawthorne, a Los Angeles suburb five miles from the Pacific Ocean.

"My family had a lot to do with my early musical life," he says. "During Christmas, we would usually gather around the piano and sing carols. My mother Audree is a good piano player and my father Murry had already written quite a few songs. They were definitely a big influence on my music!"

Carl was one of the first members of the group to play a musical instrument, inspired by a family friend who played guitar. Carl's first formal lessons were held in the back room of an accordian studio. Depressed by the formality of the situation ("I just wanted to rock!"), Carl dropped out. John Maus--who later went to England as one of the hitmaking Walker Brothers--helped Carl develop his technique as a rock and roll guitarist.

The most obvious of Carl's early influences was Chuck Berry, though he credits such rockers as Little Richard and Fats Domino for their inspiration as well.

In addition to playing the guitar, Carl often sings lead, frequently plays keyboard instruments, and has produced some of The Beach Boys' records.

Carl produced the albums Surf's Up, In Concert and Holland. His contributions as songwriter include "Long Promised Road," "Feel Flows," and "The Trader."

Carl was initiated into TM by Maharishi Mahesh Yogi in December of 1967, and has called it "a real blessing." Carl is also a graduate of est stating, "It has added a lot to my life for which I am really grateful to Werner Erhard. I love him. I would like to review the training again."

Carl, wife Annie, and their two sons Jonah and Justyn, live on the beach near Los Angeles.

Among his goals for the future, Carl says that he'd like to take some formal training in orchestration. All of which is part of Carl's continuing desire to expand his tastes and abilities as a musician; an already-wide range that's more than a little responsible for the all-inclusive Beach Boys sound.

BIOGRAPHY: DENNIS WILSON

Dennis, the middle of the Wilson brothers, is the only member of The Beach Boys to qualify as a genuine surfer. It was his interest in the sport that started the band's climb to success in the early Sixties.

"We'd been writing some of our own songs, about girlfriends and the usual kind of things, and playing a lot of current hits and rock oldies," he recalls. "But one day in 1961, I came back from a hard day of surfing and asked Brian to write a song about it." Brian obligingly composed "Surfin'," which the band promptly recorded. To tie in with the tune title, someone at the record company decided that the band should call themselves The Beach Boys.

From the beginning until 1971, Dennis was the band's drummer ("Denny's Drums" is an instrumental solo on an early album). A hand injury in that year forced him to switch to less-taxing keyboard instruments. Since then his hand has healed 100% and this year he's in full swing as The Beach Boys' drummer.

In the recording studio, Dennis likes to take an active hand in the group's sound, occassionally to the point of producing songs that he has written. "Brian is really the leader, but we all like to get involved in what we put down. It helps us, and makes for a better sound on record."

Much of the music that Dennis composes has a classical feel, which he credits to his early musical background. He has written numerous tunes for the group, including "Steamboat," "Only With You," and "Got to Know the Woman." "I usually write from experience," he says. "I find that when you're more honest, the songs turn out better."

Dennis not long ago began studying acting and co-starred with James Taylor in the acclaimed film Two Lane Blacktop. "There's a parallel between what we do as musicians and acting," explains Dennis. "What we're there to do in both cases is entertain the audience. And that's what we do best."

0377

BEACH BOYS

Ken Barnes examines the sudden Beach Boys bonanza.

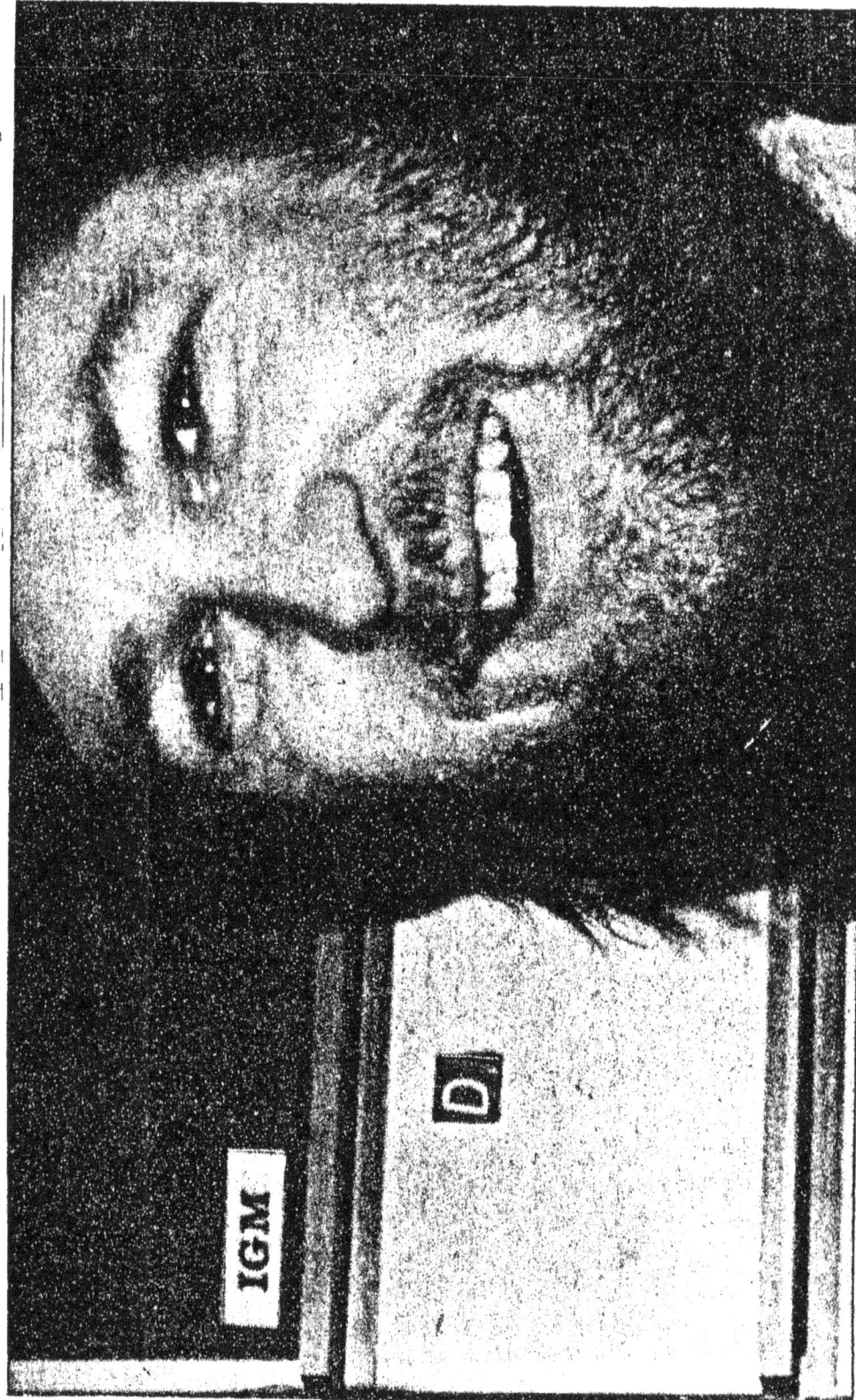

A rare shot of Brian Wilson, taken during an even rarer radio interview, August 1974. When asked about "Surfin' U.S.A." being on the charts again, he said, "I saw it, but I didn't believe it". When asked about touring again with the Beach Boys, Brian replied, "I'd like to. If I could just lose some weight........"

PHONOGRAPH 1974

It's Surf Revival '74 time, and there are signs indicating it may actually happen this time. If it doesn't, of course, next year PRM will present Surf Revival '75 and will continue to ram the concept down the public's throat until it all comes back.

Seriously, though, First Class's emergence and the profusion of summer-themed song titles on their own point to a new wave rising. But the highest tidings of the '74 surf scene are the facts and figures pertaining to the true oceanic patriarchs, the Beach Boys. They're more popular than ever, with a whole new audience flocking to their concerts; and this summer, success has come so fast for them it appears as if it were overnight.

It's nothing of the sort, of course; the Beach Boys' resurgence is more along the lines of a gradual groundswell. When they resumed active touring in 1970, their reception was ecstatic, and ever since they've been on the road almost constantly. And anyone who's been to their concerts has noted the odd audience mixture of aging Surf nostalgists and teenagers who were in the kindergarten corps when the first surf boom hit. Whether they come for the mystique or the music, they've helped to boost the Beach Boys into the top echelon of in-person attractions.

Record-wise, however, it was much tougher sledding (to mix seasonal metaphors rather carelessly). 1973's *Holland* and *In Concert* finally attained respectable sales levels, but still didn't approach the magnitude of the live Beach Boys phenomenon. And singles dropped like flies—since their last reasonably big hit in 1970, "Add Some Music to Your Day," they've had nine resoundingly unsuccessful releases, with highest chart penetration in the eighties.

Then early this summer Capitol Records, carefully noting the success of nostalgic TV record packages (and no doubt lavishing special attention the exploits of *High Water*, a two-record Pick-ick budget compilation of Beach Boys tracks that received a big TV campaign and has topped the nation's budget charts for months on end), dredged deep into their still-extensive Beach Boys catalog (apparently extending from "Surfin'," to the *Party* album of late '65, with Warners owning the rest), and emerged with *Endless Summer*. Though this two-record set was rather hastily assembled, contains dubious choices and in no way could be termed definitive, it includes the bulk of the surf-era classics, with an attractive, high-powered TV assault to go with it.

And it took off like Craig Breedlove's *Spirit of America*—as of August 24, it was No. 15 in *Billboard*'s LP charts, higher than any Beach Boys album in years and still climbing. It's ahead of Marvin Gaye's live LP, the Souther-Hillman-Furay Band and Sly, and is aspiring to join the ranks of such certified superstars as Quincy Jones, Robin Trower, Rick Wakeman and Loggins & Messina.

Warners, who'd re-released *Pet Sounds* for the third time last spring to moderate success, responded with a reissue of the out-of-print *Wild Honey* and *20/20* albums. This package, with no surf totems anywhere to be found, is billeted and bulleted at No. 82. In October, *Friends* and *Smiley Smile* are scheduled to receive the same treatment, and perhaps they may go so far as to compile an album including the brilliant non-LP single "Celebrate the News," and its equally stellar flip, *Smile*-era tracks and other oddities still languish in neglected cans.

Recently L.A.'s top-rated station KHJ ran an all-time Top 500 contest, which was won by a huge margin by none other than "Surfin' USA." Capitol promptly reissued it as a single, and it's on the charts with a bullet, receiving new-record airplay on some stations and increased oldie rotation on many others. It might even make it.....

As for the whys of it all, I'd prefer to avoid delving into some esoteric theoretical discussion about how hearing the Beach Boys makes the years drift away and your hair feels like it's been bleached blond. Again, it seems like the reasonably natural result of a gradual build-up—dramatically increased in-concert popularity, the new power of TV advertising, the timely emphasis on the group placed by the *American Graffiti* soundtrack, the never-slackening onrush of nostalgia, etc.

Also, acts like 10cc, First Class, Roy Wood, Flash Cadillac, and Abba either show strong Beach Boys influences or have directly paid tribute to the group recently. Elton John and Chicago have employed Beach Boys back-up vocal stylings this year (not forgetting B.J. Thomas' pseudo-surf backings on "Rock & Roll Lullaby 2½ years back, a real pioneer). But I'd say TV power combined with growing recognition of the strength of Beach Boys music are the big reasons for their new ascendancy.

The big problem is what to do next. It's been 20 months since the last Beach Boys studio album, and no signs of a new one beyond rumors of recording at Guercio's Caribou caravansery. The group may feel boxed in, as if they can't sell records without reverting to a style they feel they've outgrown. Perhaps not necessarily so, however—"California Saga," a fairly obvious attempt in that direction, didn't sell all that well, and in concert the young partisans are just as receptive to the new material as the goldens—cries of "Funky Pretty!" fight it out with the "Little Deuce Coupe" calls.

Still, seeing decade-old material power-shift up the charts where contemporary efforts stalled can't help but have some constricting effect. There are no easy solutions to this dilemma. The Beach Boys are back on top again thanks to the brilliant specters of their past, but the next move is up to them. One can remain hopeful that the Beach Boys will reap their just rewards, win through to a new revival on their own terms, and in general do it again.

Two of the classic early Beach Boys album covers. The guys in the woody can't believe it takes all five of them to carry one surfboard, little knowing it was their first time on a beach!

PHONOGRAPH 1974

PERFORMANCES

Are they really just blond-haired Children of the Damned, shoved onstage and totally devoid of any other power other than to do musical tricks in perfect harmony?

The Beach Boys
The Eagles
Roosevelt Stadium, New Jersey

By LANCE LOUD

The Beach Boys ARE American Pop. They have managed to come up with a bit of heritage somewhere in all that surf, sand and burger stand. They have the fantastic knack of seducing passing fancy to stay a while. The Beach Boys have as many emotions as you could fit on a telephone dial, maybe a little fewer than that, because that is an important part to their winning sweepstake ticket to Heritage.

Their obviousness is their mystery; they have no secrets, but like surfing Greta Garbo's, they have always remained semi-detached from the rock world at large. They just tour and record and break up and reform and make quiet little decisions and go back on them, always making other arrangements, cutting off a few friends, finding new places to rent houses, never really coming out and explaining the thing that to me, they seem to taunt the answer for, the Secret of California.

It DOES get boring, chatting up, or putting down, the West Coast. The Beach Boys take all that Golden Goodness, that Wishy Washy perfection (capitalization is essential here to make these things sound like Birds Eye frozen vegetables you would get at any supermarket) and turn it into Quick Tan Pleasure.

They have nothing to offer but their sunwashed selves but they offer it up beautifully. The divine mystery boy Brian Wilson is so pragmatic that I would shy away from even attempting to scratch his surface but in their records they will remain beached sleeping beauties, allowing us, through the miracle of widescreen Vinyl, to view bits of their dreams.

In concert. How would you, Beach Boy fans, LIKE to see them in concert? Do you think that they try and arrange performances the way they would like best to be viewed? Or do they just drag themselves around, being shoved onstage like those little blonde haired, gold eyed Children of the Damned from the horror film of the same name but in this case, totally devoid of any other power other than to do musical tricks in perfect harmony?

The Eagles were tuning-up when we arrived, either that or they were jamming. Actually they were better than I had thought they would be, I was prepared not to like them because I was sure they were the turtles that did "Horse With No Name" which *Really* makes my skin crawl up an octave, they didn't perform it so it must've been another group. They did a song called "James Dean" that was pretty good. They did another called "Witchy Woman," nice vocal harmonies, and "Tequila Sunrise," which is the morning-after song for "Horse With No Name" came out very very pretty. I admit that I take a certain snobbish pride in remaining as totally ignorant as possible to all rock music that won't be considered valuable in the future; I am basically a clerk typist historian.

Meanwhile I was wandering around backstage, looking for Brian Wilson. I saw Mike Love and his girlfriend, who was very clean looking and nice, and she recognized ME which was really thrilling... one step away from the Boys themselves. I saw a group of trailers and went over to peer in when suddenly from the depths of Big Sur this long haired guy came out at me and said he, uhh, didn't, uhh think that uhh, the Beach Boys were into being uhh, bothered right then because they were uhh, practicing right now.

When they managed to amble onstage they showed up with their best foot forward. Really swell. The two drummers worked great together. I have to admit that I had never seen two drummers in one band before and I wondered if it would help at all, or be totally irrelevant. Well, they were so simple in what they played that it only intensified the beat, the entire band was one finely honed instrument.

Onstage with them was a massive force of instruments. Besides the double drum kits there were amps galore, a large organ, grand piano, electric piano, and something that looked like it could possibly be coaxed into having a synthesizer effect on sound. All this PLUS a gaggle of guitars, four lead vocalists including Mike Love who seemed to be the visual leader of the pack doing most of the introductions and carrying on a rapport with the audience while the Wilson brothers, Dennis and Carl remained pretty well hidden behind beards and downcast looks. Jim Guercio, the whiz kid who made the group Chicago into a national band of trend setters of double record notoriety (plus poster FREE), was up there playing bass and some keyboards.

Songwise they slipped in and out of eras with great ease. Mike announced that they were about to do one of the first protest songs and while I was holding my breath for "Eve of Destruction" to begin, "Little Deuce Coupe" roared out. They did a fantastic version of "Do It Again" which has to be one of the greatest rock songs ever, they did "Sloop John B." and it sounded just like the single. "Heroes and Villains" swung and "Bringing Me Down" was a true stair stepper.

The audience was ecstatic. They bounced, they gurgled, they yelped, like one huge baby; the Beach Boys bounced up and down on their knee crooning little dittys that charmed and amused it. The Boys played some material from their next album and promised the audience that they would be getting back to the *Pet Sounds* sound. They whipped into "Help Me Rhonda" with Ricki Fataar on piano. The kids did whatever dance they did and at the end of it Mike, who had been doing a surfers stomp himself, dedicated it to "... good old Brian Wilson, wonder of Rock and Roll."

They rushed off to get ready for an encore and I left. Those guys were terrific. For a moment, I was almost tempted to go back to California.

Jobriath
The Troubadour
Los Angeles

By RICHARD CROMELIN

Jerry Brandt isn't noted for doing things in a small way, but Jobriath, his latest project, might prove to be merely mildly successful. That's more than a lot of people expected, what with all that hype about a new superstar of international scope, lavish stage productions (the earth-shattering debut was first scheduled for the Paris Opera House; then Brandt toned it down to a run at Century City's Schubert Theatre; Jobriath ended up headlining the Troubadour, like Hoyt Axton or Jimmy Buffet)—veritably, we were to believe, a whole new mode of entertainment. Claims like that have a way of turning against their propagators, but Jobriath's show, while far from total vindication, suggested that he'll last longer than the Paradise Ballroom did.

Jobriath Boone (he introduced himself by his full name, perhaps in an attempt to downplay the dubious mystique factor) first appeared in an anti-spectacular manner, sneaking onstage in the dark while a tape of his "Deitrich/Fondyke (a brief history of the movie musical)" blasted its "Carmina Burana" way through the room. The lights showed him clad in a tight little green sweater and loose white pants, more like a slightly decadent Tab Hunter playing a Beverly Hills nitery than a rock 'n' roll phenomenon. At that point he was visually upstaged by his band, the Creatures, stylized epitome of the glittery/street-tough New York breed of group. Aside from the look, their impact was minimal, as they laid down adequate backing tracks but exhibited little flair or personality when they marked time while Jobriath changed his clothes behind a screen at stage right (coy? You expected to see a silk stocking flutter over the top, like in an Irene Dunne movie. No such luck).

There were two changes, and each escalated his character and charisma, taking him closer to the widespread androgynous image. The first hinted at the pseudo-ballet pose implied by the first album cover—white tights, bare torso (and a little pudgy at that), and a stiff white collar in which his head nestled like a piece of candy in its paper cup. The leather trip was next. Jobriath (or his designer) didn't give it an ultra-imaginative treatment, relying instead on the material's brute force and its power of suggestion. It was everything leather should be—superbly sensual, sexy, seductive, sinister, menacing, and at the same time inescapably amusing.

Jobriath appeared to feel best during these stretches of the show. He moved fluidly, certainly presented more vivid images, and even seemed to sing with more authority. Jobriath probably felt that it was necessary that he ease mildly into the theatrics, as if he had to deflate expectations and prove that he wasn't a gimmick-monger but an actual singer-songwriter before he could go on to something more interesting. Maybe someday the pressure will be less and he'll be able to experiment, to carry out some of the ideas that he only sketched at the Troubadour.

There was an incomplete feeling about his performance, and often it looked as if things were just a little, but crucially, out of sync. Bumps and twitches were off the beat, coming off as campy adornments rather than bolstering the force of the music. And that backing by the Creatures—mechanical, without dimension or any real life—flattened songs which on the new album (thanks to the help of Peter Frampton, John Paul Jones, et. al.) are full and fairly convincing.

Stylistically, Jobriath tries to tag a lot of bases—melodic hard rock, gradiose, eclectic opuses, show-tune rock, quiet club numbers. His invariably melodramatic tone seemed out of proportion to his surroundings, like a grand opera staged on a flatbed trailer. Lyrics were fairly inaudible, further undercutting effect, and the Bowie influence is a bit too blatant in musical style, singing and in certain aspects of the image: Jobriath is less space-age, more into traditional modes, and his personna is less brittle and mutable (and so less interesting). There's less imagination at work, as when his songs begin relying on repeated choruses to sustain themselves.

Jobriath's ascent to major star-level is highly questionable, though by no means impossible. He's definitely talented, but he's either going to have to stop being weird or generate an avid coterie of followers that appreciate his brand of weirdness. The most discouraging thing about that night at the Troubadour was a drab audience that didn't seem to have anything to do with the performer. Jobriath desperately needs a cohesive core of raving, adoring fanatics to set off the hysterical spark that is the Great White Light of rock 'n' roll. It's the thing that's ignited every star in history, and without it Jobriath seems to be only half there.

The Beach is Back!

California Consciousness & The Sounds of Summer '75

By GREG SHAW

Ecclesiastes might easily have been experiencing a vision of California in the summertime when he wrote that nothing is new under the sun. For indeed, it seems that whenever it gets to be around May in Los Angeles, time stands still as an eternal generation of tanned, surfboard-toting natives comes out of hibernation and heads for the beach; while kids suddenly appear underfoot on skateboards, surf music seems to be emanating from every frequency on the radio dial, and four or five new Beach Boys albums hit the racks.

One could almost say that the more the rest of the world changes, the more summers in California are the same. There is a timeless quality to it all that makes mockery of those who predicted the surfing trend would only last a few months, as they set about manufacturing ski music, assuring themselves it would be an even bigger fad. They were all wrong, of course. Summer music, California surf culture, and the entire aesthetic behind it, which has generated an unpredictably broad affirmation from every corner of the world, lives on with no sign of diminishing. And stranger yet, no one has come up with a more effective musical representation of this tenacious beach-and-sun mentality than the original surfing sound of 1963-65. Beach Boys records still sell in droves, reaching a new gener   each year just like *The Wizard of Oz*.

T   ost astonishing aspect of the whole phenomenon is the fact that this music, whose appeal has proven to be so universal, has always been the almost exclusive product of an amazingly small clique of writers, producers and singers. These people, less than ten of them really, appear each summer with new records, new projects, and new editions of their past triumphs, and these people alone have been able to do anything new in the genre they created, though others have certainly tried.

We've written about these people before, as previous summers brought out a growing following for their works. This year there's more to report than ever, and encouraging evidence of sitll more to come. Jan & Dean, separately and together, are finding a new audience for their music, while Brian Wilson is making records for the first time in years, the Beach Boys prepare to unleash their long-awaited new product, and Bruce & Terry (Johnston & Melcher) appear to be becoming one of the industry's most active production teams, with their Equinox label as well as outside productions with everyone from Barry Mann to David Cassidy, whose album is full of Beach Boys gems.

If anything sets the 1975 surf revival apart from those of previous years, it's the extent to which artists outside the inner circle are adapting the music to their own careers. As we go to press, Johnny Rivers is tearing up the charts with "Help Me Rhonda," the Hudson Brothers are moving up with their Beach Boys-derived "Rendezvous," and the Captain and Tennille (former Beach Boys sidepersons) have the 'Number One song in the country.

No one is ever likely to explain, in logical terms, why a style of music that started out as a mere novelty trend in 1963, should have proven to be so eternally relevant or endlessly adaptable — least of all the few geniuses who have been its fountainhead. They have no need to analyze; they just keep on doing what comes naturally, as they have all along. Perhaps it's this very naturalness that accounts for their continuing presence in the industry and our awareness. And for the timeless attraction of California summer music itself.

PHONOGRAPH JULY 1975

THE BEACH BOYS!

*Top Left, Mike Love; Bottom Left, Carl Wilson; Top & Bottom Right, Al Jardine.

NEAL PRESTON

By MITCHELL S. COHEN

"This is a serious surfing song," Mike Love announces from the stage of Madison Square Garden and the Beach Boys launch into a lively rendition of "Catch a Wave." It's opening line, "*Catch a wave and you're sitting on top of the world,*" prompts an ocean of applause and cheers from close to twenty thousand people, most of whom have only seen surfboards in American-International movies.

You used to be able to mark the coming of summer to New York by the first commercial for Palisades Park on top forty radio. The closing of that gaudy recreation area left few other telltale signs: Coppertone jingles, solid gold weekends; but this year the Beach Boys made seasonal identification simple by coming to town on the 12th of June and officially ushering in the hot-weather months as the Summer of '75 coast-to-coast juggernaut with Chicago rolled in like a 20-footer cresting at Malibu.

It's different here in the urban east. For us, the summer experience is the temporary escape of "Up On the Roof," the drilling of "Summer in the City," the neon-lit nocturnal adventures of Bruce Springsteen, Nik Cohn's accurately expressed introduction to *Rock Dreams*. Our summer movie is not a technicolor beach-blanket-bingo, but Paul Williams' *Out of It*, a low-budget black and white film with Jon Voight, Barry Gordon and Lada Edmunds about the sexual frustrations of vacation in boring Long Island. Two years ago, *Phonograph Record* ran a long feature, "A California Saga," on the surf music revival, an authoritative and convincing report from a west coast viewpoint on what the sound symbolized, its rise, decline and regeneration. Well, we love the Beach Boys here as well, but if their fantasy is an idyllic one—two girls for every boy; fun, fun, fun — from the opposite coast it is also a remote one, as we watch the meager waves on Jones Beach and flee indoors to get cool.

The Beach Boys are a national treasure, and one would have to be terribly cynical to think them anything but marvelous. The response at the Garden, from a crowd that ranged in age from barely pubescent youngsters born around the time of "Surfin' Safari" to middle-aged suburban types (many in attendance expressly to see Chicago), was nothing short of astounding. Upon hearing the opening notes of the likes of "I Get Around," "Surfer Girl" and "Barbara Ann" mass hysteria ensued: things thrown in the air, girls hugging in the aisles, grown men leaping out of their seats in unrestrained joy. Genuine, sustained Beatlemaniacal shrieks rose out of the audience. I think it's safe to say that the Beach Boys are the recipients of more warmth and all-around good feeling than any other existing group, and it's well deserved. They give the people what they want; the only question is whether that's enough.

Certainly they are exceptional live: Dennis slapping his snare with riveting force, Mike prancing in feather and glitter, Carl and Al harmonizing to perfection, Billy supporting on keyboards and additional vocals. They create a big, full sound on stage, their incomparable singing backed by a percussion-driven background. No real new territory is traveled—a trio of songs from *Holland* is their only acknowledgement of the '70s—but their enthusiastic performances of their past chart-busters, and the excitement they instigate ("Little Deuce Coupe" results in pandemoneum) makes a Beach Boy concert by far the most totally enjoyable show on the planet. When they returned to the stage after Chicago's (competent, overlong and overloud) set wearing N.Y. Ranger hockey shirts, to engage in a can-you-top-this give and take with the boys from Illinois, the playoff was simply no contest.

The Beach Boys are constantly in the air nowadays, in spirit if not in actuality. This season may shape up as an unusually splendid one for trivial pop, and it couldn't have happened at a better time, being the first summer of the past four that we can devote our full attention to matters cultural and frivolous, with no Presidential campaigning, Watergate or House Judiciary hearings to distract us. The atmosphere is clear, and the sounds are pouring in: Linda Lewis' disco remake of "It's In His Kiss," one of the most delightful, sprightly singles since Red Bird closed its doors; The Captain and Tennille's smash "Love Will Keep Us Together" (The Captain—Daryl Dragon—and his wife Toni are old Beach Boy co-horts, having participated on *Sunflower*. Their lp includes versions of "God Only Knows" and "Disney Girls"); 10 cc's Brian Wilson-influenced "I'm Not In Love"; the Carpenters; the posthumous Raspberries. The Troggs have a very weird single of "Good Vibrations," and Johnny Rivers' new single is "Help Me Rhonda," with back-up vocals by none other than Brian himself. Marilyn, Brian's spouse, just signed with Island and is currently cutting with Jackie DeShannon. Jan & Dean have their first new product out since Jan's accident, a single called "Fun City" and Dean has updated their hit "Sidewalk Surfing" for this summer's skateboard revival. *Shampoo* is still in local theatres, with "Wouldn't It Be Nice" terpointing the Beverly Hills amorality, and in many places one can still hear "All Summer Long" closing out *American Graffiti* and Mackenzie Phillips, in Dewey Webber Surf Board t-shirt, defending her new musical heroes.

As for the group itself, it is represented by two newly-issued repackages of older material: *Spirit of America*, a sequel to last year's blockbuster *Endless Summer* (perfect titles both), and *Good Vibrations*, a reprise of later period (*Pet Sounds* and forward) selections and not to be confused with a Pickwick lp of the same name. No musical organization is more worthy of having its history unearthed and re-analyzed than the Beach Boys, and all these compilations have a great deal of merit. It's great to see "Break Away," "The Little Girl I Once Knew" and obscure album tracks readily available, and the more recent songs have generally been overlooked in favor of the surfing-hot rod era, but there is something disconcerting about the level of nostalgia involved, especially in the light of no new product or substantial additions to the live act. The Beach Boys are stuck in a bind, and one can't help but sympathize. The cheers they've been hearing from one end of the country to the other have been for their past, which is enough to make anybody queasy about the future. They must be tremendously concerned about what to come up with next. Meanwhile, they act as Caribou back-drop singers for Elton John and Chicago and tour continuously. But where is Brian Wilson, or American Spring (dropped by Columbia after one first-rate single flopped)? What can the Beach Boys whip up to place them in the forefront of contemporary rock?

To dwell on what they might be doing is to undervalue what they are doing, and what they have done. To shout and stomp in a 1975 Beach Boys audience is to marvel at the fact that at the turn of the decade their credibility in the east was at a very low point indeed. Some date the change in direction from the night they shared the Fillmore East stage with the Grateful Dead, others from their entertaining the May Day troops in Washington, both events taking place in 1971. In four years, they've returned to the top. And yet I still have arguments with serious-minded politicos who consider the Beach Boys elitist, sexist, etc., and booed Mike Love for singing "California Girls" at a pro-Allende rally, but these types could never grasp the essence of the group. No doubt the accusations have some objective basis. There is something smug about the image of surf music; it conjures up pictures of a teenage master race of beautiful bodies (muscular or buxom, straight blond hair and materialist affluence in a whiter-than-white environment. The notions of masculinity ("They grit their teeth, they don't back down") and feminity ("The girls on the beach are all within reach if you know what to do") are strictly defined.

But Brian Wilson and the Beach Boys are the creators and troubadors of youth culture

---
"Brian is considering a return to performing."
---

mythology, of a western romantic vision that is beyond radical criticism. While Californians might see them as a reflection of what they are, the rest of us viewed them as a projection of what we

*Brian Wilson in the drivers seat once again with the next generation of Beach Boys and Girls.

might be. If they are, finally, greater than Chuck Berry (a debatable proposition), it is because their major influence wrote his pungent teenage tales as a wry observer and the Beach Boys were on the inside, and therefore could add first-hand experience and sentiment (Berry never wrote a love song as true as Brian's best ballads) to their adolescent narratives. They formulated the most identifiable and influential vocal sound in all of rock (Brian was the premier singer of tear-jerkers until Gram Parsons), but even more important, an American legend. They stand for something: a point of view, an attitude, a utopian ideal that nonetheless recognizes the painful (along with the joyous) realities of male-female relationships.

And like all major artists in the rock pantheon, but to a far greater degree than most, the Beach Boys kept an eye on summer as the time of year that summed up all the implicit and explicit theses of rock philosophy. "We've been having fun all summer long," "Summer means new love." Summer exploited commercially is a staple of rock: The Beatles, in particular, between the years 1964 and 1969 managed to pull a major rabbit out of their hat each time their fans were sprung from school (their Lester films, tours, *Sgt. Pepper*, "Hey Jude"). The Beach Boys made mythology out of economic expediency, making their subject, their *raison de etre*, coincident with the extended leisure time of the pop consumer. One feels in their music a heightened sense of the elements: sand and surf, country air; and a thematic release. Even if the period from Memorial Day to Labor Day in New York feels like the Drifters, in the summer of the mind the Beach Boys reign supreme and surfers rule.

It's 1975, and we look at ourselves more critically than before. The vital art of our time is melancholy, if not entirely pessimistic, and still there are positive signs on the horizon regarding the shallow pleasure of pop. There were skateboards in the hills of Los Angeles when I visited this past April, the Stones are barnstorming, the Brummels are back, Flo & Eddie are recording and we should hear the results of the David Cassidy sessions for RCA, on which Bruce Johnston and Carl Wilson played a prominent role. On an FM radio interview in New York, Mike and Carl were very encouraging about the immediate future. Specifically, Brian has slimmed down, is considering a return to performing, and is so anxious to get the boys back in the studio that he suggested a postponement of the joint tour.

"I think the Beach Boys will be the group to represent America during the Bicentennial celebration in 1976...We will be the group...when people want to know what is American music," Mike Love is quoted in *Downbeat* as saying, and a related rumor has the group recording "The Battle Hymn of the Republic" for their next album. Mike's statement is a simplification; their music hardly pretends to speak for the entire American spectrum, but it does represent a special part of our shared, or imagined, experience. They've captured unique scenes, 60-second snapshots from a Polaroid Swinger, action-shots frozen in motion: riding waves, dancing on the beach, sitting behind the wheel of a speeding machine. Even when the specificity of the subject matter was abandoned, the sound remained unmistakeably Beach Boys: the multi-layered texture of Brian's production, the complex, ethereal fusion of the voices. The masterworks of the "mature" Beach Boys, *Pet Sounds*, *Wild Honey*, *Sunflower*, are as rich in feelings and associations as their earlier successes, and no less wonderful for their relative sophistication.

PHONOGRAPH JULY 1975

*It's the same old photo, but it's the same old music come alive again this summer.

A new generation is learning about California dreaming from the Beach Boys as they make their way across the continent spreading the word about the delectable species of west coast female, the cool water, beautiful coastline, warm and out-of-sight nights, inviting us to "Do It Again" again and again. The million-and-a-quarter people who purchased *Endless Summer* have bought stock in a durable tradition. I love the Beach Boys' music totally and without reservation: their dopey sense of humor, their ability to turn their limited turf into a powerful metaphor, their capacity for making public fools of themselves, their unflinching romanticism. We need the Beach Boys because they sound so good, of course, but also because they fire our imagination and look eternally forward, capturing the core of our blind optimism with one promise: "One more summer and your dream comes true."

GOOD VIBRATIONS
Beach Boys
Reprise MS 2223

By BOBBY ABRAMS

It's eternally summer when the Beach Boys fill the airwaves, and to be listening to them when the sun is hot and the surf bitchin' is a double mitzvah, a bonus on top of a bonus. Growing up in the dreary bleakness of New York winters, the Beach Boys represented to me what the good life, California-style was all about: fast cars, with sleek bodies, and faster women, with sleeker bodies, golden and long, blonde, WASPY California hair. While such a fantasy may appear vapid, indeed substanceless, as Los Angeles often feels to a stranger, all the requisite pain that an Eastern intellectual requires in his listening pleasure is present, implied in the negative spaces of Brian's art.

But all this is past business, old hat; no longer is there a need to swap mythologies, to justify the Beach Boys as valid rock and roll. This collection is Warners attempt to cash in on the success of the group, and on Capitol's annual repackaging of Beach Boys hits for the summer doldrums. While in no way is it as well-packaged as the two recent Capitol albums, it too will probably go gold in a matter of days, for the demand for Beach Boys music seems nearly insatiable. In a similar vein, there is no quibble with the cuts Warners has chosen to include here: all are readily available on other re-issues and re-packagings, yet it is always interesting to see what someone else picks as their favorites. Listening to one of their greatest hits albums is very much like listening to the radio; sometimes it's a welcome relief to let someone else program one's entertainment.

Yet it is paradoxical that in the space of the greatest success the group has known, there has been no attempt to release new product. Nor has the world more eagerly waited on an acknowledged genius, not even after Dylan's accident, not even after the Beatles broke up. Periodic rumors of Brian's emergence from the sandbox notwithstanding, it seems unlikely that we will be hearing the 1975 version of the American dream. The group has settled into a comfortable groove, accepting the plaudits of past success in their live concerts (it could be reasonably argued that the Beach Boys are the most important touring group today), accepting gold and platinum records for these crassly commercial repackagings. To be fair, many of these records never went gold upon initial release. Yet having built an audience that spans two generations (many of those in attendance at the concerts could hardly remember these classic songs from their initial release date) the group refuses to come to grips with the trauma of debuting new work. It is indeed a shame, nay a sacrilege, and the continued re-issuing of greatest hits albums, instead of building confidence in their abilities as artists seems to have had just the opposite effect and I almost despair of ever hearing any new material. If for this reason alone, it is time to stop the re-packaging parade, or at least make an attempt to bring to the public unreleased or unknown material, cause there sure is no purpose in releasing material that's available on at least a dozen other albums. People in the culture business have a mandate to enrich the culture as well as their pockets, and while these albums may be filling the corporate coffers at Capitol and Warners respectively, they don't add a whit to our appreciation of the masters of a musical expressionism that accurately captured the feelings of America in the sixties as well as any poet has ever portrayed his society.

The Beach Boys' Girls

*Diane Rovell, Marilyn Wilson

*Toni Tennille (with husband Daryl Dragon).

By KEN BARNES

It's not exactly like that, of course. Girls aren't going out and rerecording "Our Surfer Boys" (by the Surf Bunnies, originally), "You Can't Take My Boyfriend's Woodie" (the Powder Puffs), or He's My Blond-Headed Blue-Eyed Whompie Stompie Surfer Boy, Number one in Australia in early '64 by the legendary Li'l Pattie. The beach bunny is not precisely a happening contemporary image for the present-day female performer.

But there's always been a place for women in California music, albeit usually a subsidiary one (ever heard of Carol Connors? Thought not, yet she wrote and sang on dozens of first-rate surf-styled records). That might be changing, though. For an obvious and else-where-noted example, Karen & Richard Carpenter have filtered harmony styles developed during the decade-ago surf boom into a bewitching formula that's engendered unlimited success.

Even more closely tied to the California coastal cliques are the Captain & Tennille. Daryl Dragon used to be Captain Keyboards for the Beach Boys live, wrote "Cuddle Up" and "Make it Good" with Dennis Wilson (*Carl & the Passions*), worked with Bruce Johnston and Terry Melcher and Dean Torrence and on and on. Toni Tennille used to sing background vocals with the Beach Boys (it wasn't *all* falsetto). The B-side of their first single (released first in late 1972 on two obscure labels before A&M picked it up) was Bruce's "Disney Girls." It's on their album, along with "Cuddle Up," "God Only Knows," and a new Bruce Johnston song called "I Write the Songs" which might be the next single. "Love Will Keep Us Together," that brilliantly-arranged, irresistible hit, certainly owes a little to "Heroes and Villains" as far as background vocals go. The whole album is suffused with that warm-California-sun feeling (not in the sense of the Rivieras/Joe Jones/Dictators but in an intangibly reassuring harmonic warmth) and is a delight — though hard-rockers may be put off by its decided MOR leanings.

And don't forget Marilyn Wilson and Diane Rovell, of Honeys/Spring/American Spring fame. Over three years later that long Spring album on UA sounds better than ever, a monument of exquisite arrangements, with some of the tracks quite conceivably ripe for reissue in a more receptive atmosphere ("Now that Everything's Been Said," "Forever," "This Whole World," and "Thinking About You Baby" seem to stand out in commercial terms). Not to mention the sublime Columbia single, "Shyin' Away/Fallin' in Love," now a collectors' item but undeserving of such an obscure fate.

Yeah, I know I said all that two years ago. But it didn't happen then (we like to say, "ahead of its time") and things really do seem different now as far as acceptance for female performers goes. Both Diane and Marilyn are once again active — they've reportedly submitted songs to the Captain & Tennille (another link in the chain). Marilyn has signed to Island with Jackie DeShannon to produce (another artist with countless great records to her credit). Meanwhile, Brian has supposedly lent background vocals to Jackie's Columbia sessions, and everything's looking up again.

I think it would all be great if the trend gets even hotter — I'm overpartial to lush, stacked harmonies, and what a great direction for contemporary female MOR to take, so much more substantative than Olivia's vacuous pseudo-country or Helen's equally washed-out pseudo-showbiz schlock. It's an odd ultimate mutation for the California surf legacy, but maybe women will give the music its greatest relevance in times to come.

single called "Fun City" and Dean has updated their hit "Sidewalk Surfing" for this summer's skateboard revival. *Shampoo* is still in local theatres, with "Wouldn't It Be Nice" terpointing the Beverly Hills amorality, and in many places one can still hear "All Summer Long" closing out *American Graffiti* and Mackenzie Phillips, in Dewey Webber Surf Board t-shirt, defending her new musical heroes.

As for the group itself, it is represented by two newly-issued repackages of older material: *Spirit of America*, a sequel to last year's blockbuster *Endless Summer* (perfect titles both), and *Good Vibrations*, a reprise of later period (*Pet Sounds* and forward) selections and not to be confused with a Pickwick lp of the same name. No musical organization is more worthy of having its history unearthed and re-analyzed than the Beach Boys, and all these compilations have a great deal of merit. It's great to see "Break Away," "The Little Girl I Once Knew" and obscure album tracks readily available, and the more recent songs have generally been overlooked in favor of the surfing-hot rod era, but there is something disconcerting about the level of nostalgia involved, especially in the light of no new product or substantial additions to the live act. The Beach Boys are stuck in a bind, and one can't help but sympathize. The cheers they've been hearing from one end of the country to the other have been for their past, which is enough to make anybody queasy about the future. They must be tremendously concerned about what to come up with next. Meanwhile, they act as Caribou back-drop singers for Elton John and Chicago and tour continuously. But where is Brian Wilson, or American Spring (dropped by Columbia after one first-rate single flopped)? What can the Beach Boys whip up to place them in the forefront of contemporary rock?

To dwell on what they might be doing is to undervalue what they are doing, and what they have done. To shout and stomp in a 1975 Beach Boys audience is to marvel at the fact that at the turn of the decade their credibility in the east was at a very low point indeed. Some date the change in direction from the night they shared the Fillmore East stage with the Grateful Dead, others from their entertaining the May Day troops in Washington, both events taking place in 1971. In four years, they've returned to the top. And yet I still have arguments with serious-minded politicos who consider the Beach Boys elitist, sexist, etc., and booed Mike Love for singing "California Girls" at a pro-Allende rally, but these types could never grasp the essence of the group. No doubt the accusations have some objective basis. There is something smug about the image of surf music; it conjures up pictures of a teenage master race of beautiful bodies (muscular or buxom, straight blond hair and materialist affluence in a whiter-than-white environment. The notions of masculinity ("They grit their teeth, they don't back down") and feminity ("The girls on the beach are all within reach if you know what to do") are strictly defined.

But Brian Wilson and the Beach Boys are the creators and troubadors of youth culture

---
"Brian is considering a return to performing."
---

mythology, of a western romantic vision that is beyond radical criticism. While Californians might see them as a reflection of what they are, the rest of us viewed them as a projection of what we might be. If they are, finally, greater than Chuck Berry (a debatable proposition), it is because their major influence wrote his pungent teenage tales as a wry observer and the Beach Boys were on the inside, and therefore could add first-hand experience and sentiment (Berry never wrote a love song as true as Brian's best ballads) to their adolescent narratives. They formulated the most identifiable and influential vocal sound in all of rock (Brian was the premier singer of tear-jerkers until Gram Parsons), but even more important, an American legend. They stand for something: a point of view, an attitude, a utopian ideal that

*Brian Wilson in the drivers seat once again with the next generation of Beach Boys and Girls.

nonetheless recognizes the painful (along with the joyous) realities of male-female relationships.

And like all major artists in the rock pantheon, but to a far greater degree than most, the Beach Boys kept an eye on summer as the time of year that summed up all the implicit and explicit theses of rock philosophy. "We've been having fun all summer long," "Summer means new love." Summer exploited commercially is a staple of rock: The Beatles, in particular, between the years 1964 and 1969 managed to pull a major rabbit out of their hat each time their fans were sprung from school (their Lester films, tours, *Sgt. Pepper*, "Hey Jude"). The Beach Boys made mythology out of economic expediency, making their subject, their *raison de etre*, coincident with the extended leisure time of the pop consumer. One feels in their music a heightened sense of the elements: sand and surf, country air; and a thematic release. Even if the period from Memorial Day to Labor Day in New York feels like the Drifters, in the summer of the mind the Beach Boys reign supreme and surfers rule.

It's 1975, and we look at ourselves more critically than before. The vital art of our time is melancholy, if not entirely pessimistic, and still there are positive signs on the horizon regarding the shallow pleasure of pop. There were skateboards in the hills of Los Angeles when I visited this past April, the Stones are barnstorming, the Brummels are back, Flo & Eddie are recording and we should hear the results of the David Cassidy sessions for RCA, on which Bruce Johnston and Carl Wilson played a prominent role. On an FM radio interview in New York, Mike and Carl were very encouraging about the immediate future. Specifically, Brian has slimmed down, is considering a return to performing, and is so anxious to get the boys back in the studio that he suggested a postponement of the joint tour.

"I think the Beach Boys will be the group to represent America during the Bicentennial celebration in 1976...We will be the group...when people want to know what is American music," Mike Love is quoted in *Downbeat* as saying, and a related rumor has the group recording "The Battle Hymn of the Republic" for their next album. Mike's statement is a simplification; their music hardly pretends to speak for the entire American spectrum, but it does represent a special part of our shared, or imagined, experience. They've captured unique scenes, 60-second snapshots from a Polaroid Swinger, action-shots frozen in motion: riding waves, dancing on the beach, sitting behind the wheel of a speeding machine. Even when the specificity of the subject matter was abandoned, the sound remained unmistakeably Beach Boys: the multi-layered texture of Brian's production, the complex, ethereal fusion of the voices. The masterworks of the "mature" Beach Boys, *Pet Sounds*, *Wild Honey*, *Sunflower*, are as rich in feelings and associations as their earlier successes, and no less wonderful for their relative sophistication.

*It's the same old photo, but it's the same old music come alive again this summer.

GOOD VIBRATIONS
Beach Boys
Reprise MS 2223

By BOBBY ABRAMS

It's eternally summer when the Beach Boys fill the airwaves, and to be listening to them when the sun is hot and the surf bitchin' is a double mitzvah, a bonus on top of a bonus. Growing up in the dreary bleakness of New York winters, the Beach Boys represented to me what the good life, California-style was all about: fast cars, with sleek bodies, and faster women, with sleeker bodies, golden and long, blonde, WASPY California hair. While such a fantasy may appear vapid, indeed substanceless, as Los Angeles often feels to a stranger, all the requisite pain that an Eastern intellectual requires in his listening pleasure is present, implied in the negative spaces of Brian's art.

A new generation is learning about California dreaming from the Beach Boys as they make their way across the continent spreading the word about the delectable species of west coast female, the cool water, beautiful coastline, warm and out-of-sight nights, inviting us to "Do It Again" again and again. The million-and-a-quarter people who purchased *Endless Summer* have bought stock in a durable tradition. I love the Beach Boys' music totally and without reservation: their dopey sense of humor, their ability to turn their limited turf into a powerful metaphor, their capacity for making public fools of themselves, their unflinching romanticism. We need the Beach Boys because they sound so good, of course, but also because they fire our imagination and look eternally forward, capturing the core of our blind optimism with one promise: "One more summer and your dream comes true."

But all this is past business, old hat; no longer is there a need to swap mythologies, to justify the Beach Boys as valid rock and roll. This collection is Warners attempt to cash in on the success of the group, and on Capitol's annual repackaging of Beach Boys hits for the summer doldrums. While in no way is it as well-packaged as the two recent Capitol albums, it too will probably go gold in a matter of days, for the demand for Beach Boys music seems nearly insatiable. In a similar vein, there is no quibble with the cuts Warners has chosen to include here: all are readily available on other re-issues and re-packagings, yet it is always interesting to see what someone else picks as their favorites. Listening to one of their greatest hits albums is very much like listening to the radio; sometimes it's a welcome relief to let someone else program one's entertainment.

Yet it is paradoxical that in the space of the greatest success the group has known, there has been no attempt to release new product. Nor has the world more eagerly waited on an acknowledged genius, not even after Dylan's accident, not even after the Beatles broke up. Periodic rumors of Brian's emergence from the sandbox notwithstanding, it seems unlikely that we will be hearing the 1975 version of the American dream. The group has settled into a comfortable groove, accepting the plaudits of past success in their live concerts (it could be reasonably argued that the Beach Boys are the most important touring group today), accepting gold and platinum records for these crassly commercial repackagings. To be fair, many of these records never went gold upon initial release. Yet having built an audience that spans two generations (many of those in attendance at the concerts could hardly remember these classic songs from their initial release date) the group refuses to come to grips with the trauma of debuting new work. It is indeed a shame, nay a sacrilege, and the continued re-issuing of greatest hits albums, instead of building confidence in their abilities as artists seems to have had just the opposite effect and I almost despair of ever hearing any new material. If for this reason alone, it is time to stop the re-packaging parade, or at least make an attempt to bring to the public unreleased or unknown material, cause there sure is no purpose in releasing material that's available on at least a dozen other albums. People in the culture business have a mandate to enrich the culture as well as their pockets, and while these albums may be filling the corporate coffers at Capitol and Warners respectively, they don't add a whit to our appreciation of the masters of a musical expressionism that accurately captured the feelings of America in the sixties as well as any poet has ever portrayed his society.

*Diane Rovell, Marilyn Wilson

By KEN BARNES

It's not exactly like that, of course. Girls aren't going out and rerecording "Our Surfer Boys" (by the Surf Bunnies, originally), "You Can't Take My Boyfriend's Woodie" (the Powder Puffs), or He's My Blond-Headed Blue-Eyed Whompie Stompie Surfer Boy, Number one in Australia in early '64 by the legendary Li'l Pattie. The beach bunny is not precisely a happening contemporary image for the present-day female performer.

But there's always been a place for women in California music, albeit usually a subsidiary one (ever heard of Carol Connors? Thought not, yet she wrote and sang on dozens of first-rate surf-styled records). That might be changing, though. For an obvious and else-where-noted example, Karen & Richard Carpenter have filtered harmony styles developed during the decade-ago surf boom into a bewitching formula that's

*Toni Tennille (with husband Daryl Dragon).

engendered unlimited success.

Even more closely tied to the California coastal cliques are the Captain & Tennille. Daryl Dragon used to be Captain Keyboards for the Beach Boys live, wrote "Cuddle Up" and "Make it Good" with Dennis Wilson (*Carl & the Passions*), worked with Bruce Johnston and Terry Melcher and Dean Torrence and on and on. Toni Tennille used to sing background vocals with the Beach Boys (it wasn't *all* falsetto). The B-side of their first single (released first in late 1972 on two obscure labels before A&M picked it up) was Bruce's "Disney Girls." It's on their album, along with "Cuddle Up," "God Only Knows," and a new Bruce Johnston song called "I Write the Songs" which might be the next single. "Love Will Keep Us Together," that brilliantly-arranged, irresistible hit, certainly owes a little to "Heroes and Villains" as far as background vocals go. The whole album is suffused with that warm-California-sun feeling (not in the sense of the Rivieras/Joe Jones/Dictators but in an intangibly reassuring harmonic warmth) and is a delight—though hard-rockers may be put off by its decided MOR leanings.

And don't forget Marilyn Wilson and Diane Rovell, of Honeys/Spring/American Spring fame. Over three years later that long Spring album on UA sounds better than ever, a monument of exquisite arrangements, with some of the tracks quite conceivably ripe for reissue in a more receptive atmosphere ("Now that Everything's Been Said," "Forever," "This Whole World," and "Thinking About You Baby" seem to stand out in commercial terms). Not to mention the sublime Columbia single, "Shyin' Away/Fallin' in Love," now a collectors' item but undeserving of such an obscure fate.

Yeah, I know I said all that two years ago. But it didn't happen then (we like to say, "ahead of its time") and things really do seem different now as far as acceptance for female performers goes. Both Diane and Marilyn are once again active—they've reportedly submitted songs to the Captain & Tennille (another link in the chain). Marilyn has signed to Island with Jackie DeShannon to produce (another artist with countless great records to her credit). Meanwhile, Brian has supposedly lent background vocals to Jackie's Columbia sessions, and everything's looking up again.

I think it would all be great if the trend gets even hotter—I'm overpartial to lush, stacked harmonies, and what a great direction for contemporary female MOR to take, so much more substantative than Olivia's vacuous pseudo-country or Helen's equally washed-out pseudo-showbiz schlock. It's an odd ultimate mutation for the California surf legacy, but maybe women will give the music its greatest relevance in times to come.

www.ingramcontent.com/pod-product-compliance
Lightning Source LLC
Chambersburg PA
CBHW081130170426
43197CB00017B/2810